Praise for *When the Band Played On*

"Randy Shilts's life story is so thoroughly enmeshed in the post-Stonewall decades. His indefatigable reporting was so important in breaking through to the outside world, with all the controversy that came with it—what we did (and reported) then made space for a very different role for queer communities. *When the Band Played On* left me wishing he were still here to help us make sense of the history in motion we are living through right now."

—**Carol Queen, PhD**, cofounder and director,
Center for Sex & Culture, San Francisco

"Randy Shilts was bigger than life as a journalist and author of some of the most important books about gay history. Michael Lee has captured Randy's voice through his meticulous research and interviews with those who knew him. . . . I am so appreciative to Lee for writing *When the Band Played On* so we could learn more about this quite extraordinary and kind man."

—**Colonel Margarethe Cammermeyer (Retired)**,
author of *Serving in Silence*

WHEN THE BAND PLAYED ON

The Life of **Randy Shilts,** America's Trailblazing Gay Journalist

MICHAEL G. LEE

CHICAGO REVIEW PRESS

Published by Chicago Review Press Incorporated

814 North Franklin Street

Chicago, Illinois 60610

ISBN 978-0-914090-30-4

Library of Congress Control Number: 2024939260

Typesetting: Jonathan Hahn

Every effort has been made to contact the copyright holders for the images that appear
in this book. The publisher would welcome information concerning any inadvertent
errors or omissions.

Printed in the United States of America

5 4 3 2 1

For my father, Gary—wishing you were still here to read this

CONTENTS

PROLOGUE

A CHARACTER IN
TWO SCENES

SAN FRANCISCO, FEBRUARY 1981. Folsom Street in late winter didn't feel much different from any other night of the year: overcast, foggy, and chilly enough for him to hug the well-worn bomber jacket tightly to his chest. A salty breeze mingled with fresh steam wafting out of the sewer grates as he strode purposefully past each darkened storefront. In Gay Mecca, there was always a scene to find, from chinos and polo shirts in Pacific Heights to leather, bondage, and nasty pigs in SoMa. Sometimes he'd wonder about starting over somewhere else, perhaps with a steady job instead of living from gig to gig, or settling down with a Mr. Right, instead of chasing Mr. Right Now. But at the moment, it was just another Saturday night in San Francisco. The clubs were throbbing with their hedonistic beat, and he didn't want to miss out.

At the corner of Dore and Folsom, he pushed past a heavy black curtain to reveal a lusty, smoke-filled den of disco and leather-clad bodies. The Brig was no bigger than the average apartment, a couple tiny rooms painted black to appear even smaller. An old pro by age twenty-nine, he quickly narrowed in on a likely prospect, sitting on a low bench toward the back: midtwenties, tall, not too skinny, with ash-blond hair and a freshly grown beard. The younger guy looked cute but approachable, sporting a pair of butt-hugging jeans and a flannel shirt.

"How're you doing tonight?"

"Just fine." He had a slightly understated demeanor, boyishly hinting that he was still learning the scene.

"Just fine, huh?"

"Yeah."

"Yeah?" The cocky half smirk was as irrepressible as his quick, sarcastic jabs. "Children starving, social unrest, and turmoil in the world, and you're just fine?"

"Yeah," the young man shot back. "I *was* going to say how much I enjoyed your last article in *Christopher Street*. But fuck you, you arrogant son of a bitch."

The comeback elicited an approving response. "I didn't think you knew who I was." The object of his attentions was named David, and of course he recognized the grinning, curly-maned figure. Love him or hate him, this was *the* Randy Shilts: television reporter, writer, and soon-to-be author. At the moment, he was also *the* Randy Shilts who'd accidentally spilled David's drink. Luckily, the kid had a handkerchief to clean it up, dark blue and tucked into his back right pocket. Recognizing its color and placement, Randy quickly got down to business: it seemed their interests were compatible.

"Know what I like?" he told David. "I like to tie boys up and spank them till they call me 'Daddy' and 'Sir.' I bet that turns you off."

No, David calmly replied, it didn't, but out of respect for his Master, he wasn't looking for anything on this particular night.

"You've got a Master?" Randy asked him, taking another sip of his beer. "How do you feel about having a Master?"

"It fulfills a need."

"I'm a Master sometimes."

They exchanged numbers and followed up a few days later. The next Friday, into David's Upper Market apartment walked *the* Randy Shilts, case of beer in hand. "I called him 'Daddy' and 'Sir,'" David later wrote in his diary, recounting the details of their sexual gymnastics. It was a memorable night, but David still felt it lacked a deeper intimacy. When someone was trying this hard to impress, the sex really became more one-sided, a validation of ego rather than genuine closeness.

Still, as they dressed, the two shared some friendly conversation. Despite a recent turn in national politics, the sexual revolution was showing no signs of slowing down here in San Francisco. On his way out the door, Randy paused, remembering to share one last important thing. "I'm one of the most interesting people you'll ever meet," he cheerfully told David before disappearing into the night.

———————

Montreal, June 1989. The Fifth International Conference on AIDS had erupted into full-blown revolution. Grassroots activists stormed the Palais de Congress during the opening ceremonies, demanding nothing less than full participation, along with a commitment from scientific and political elites to cooperate and coordinate with the HIV/AIDS community. For the first time, leaders of a global relief effort found themselves sitting alongside, listening, and responding to legions of patients with nothing left to lose. The protesters had done their homework and weren't afraid to boo whenever they detected a lack of urgency or sensitivity from the distinguished presenters.

As the fractious conference drew to a close, its final speaker sat onstage at the end of a table full of panelists, wearing what had become his signature look: white dress shirt and dark slacks with suspenders, accented with a flashy purple tie and green-and-white press credentials. The familiar mop of curly brown hair and rounded, square-framed glasses highlighted a bearded countenance that, like his always-cherubic torso, had gotten somewhat thicker lately. Randy looked healthy that day, maybe just a little overfed from the past two years of media tours. As he glanced down at his speech, a voice in the audience shouted, "There's no such thing as Patient Zero!"

After nearly an hour of detail-heavy presentations, *the* Randy Shilts took the stage, heralded as "the author of the book which, perhaps more than any other single written document, alerted the peoples of the world to this extraordinary pandemic." Since childhood, he'd practiced a studied, serious expression, which he was now trying to maintain before an audience that welcomed him with polite, but not especially adulatory, applause. Randy had shocked the world by vividly depicting the story of AIDS as a preventable crisis, abetted by political malfeasance, bureaucratic inertia, self-serving agendas, and old-fashioned bigotry. It had taken him a lifetime to reach this milestone, but the urgency of his message now mattered more than the recognition he received.

In the auditorium, his friend Cleve Jones stood among the assembled activists. They'd known each other for more than a decade—the Harvey Milk protégé dubbed the "media queen" and the journalist who'd helped make him famous. Both men understood the power and pitfalls of the spotlight. Many in attendance took a hostile view of Randy's brand of truth-telling, but love him or hate him, they needed his skills and influence with those who would otherwise ignore this global pandemic. As Randy stood before the angry, beleaguered assembly, he feared the time might come when he would desperately need them too.

And then, out came that half smirk. "I can officially announce that you have seen the last slide of the Fifth International AIDS Conference," he began. "Newspaper reporters don't have slides." It was a safe one-liner to open with, eliciting laughter and light applause. But then Randy continued to ad lib. "People ask, 'Can I get AIDS from a mosquito?'" he riffed. "Of course, you can get AIDS from a mosquito! If you have unprotected anal intercourse with an infected mosquito that's not wearing a condom, you'll probably get AIDS. Otherwise, you're probably fine."

The longer he joked, the quieter the laughter became, while his detractors' jeers grew louder. But Randy wasn't backing down, launching into a digression on the urban legend of gay San Francisco waiters ejaculating into salad dressing. In the dark lecture hall, Cleve grimaced—poor timing, wrong crowd. From somewhere in the hall, he heard someone shout, "Randy Shilts, you are such an asshole!" The usually unflappable Randy seemed momentarily rattled. "Gosh, you can get booed here and only say three paragraphs," he responded. "I've only started."

"Get the hook or the gong!" someone jeered.

"He's a whore," yelled another.

Squaring his shoulders, Randy gazed past the spotlight and continued. "As a journalist," he began, "my general mandate is to report the news and to try to define that nebulous commodity known as the truth. Sometimes getting at the truth means focusing on failures as well as success, because within the failures of any group of people are the clues to the mistakes of tomorrow, mistakes you want to avoid. And there are mistakes we want to avoid as we leave here today for the next year in the battle against AIDS."

The hecklers grew quiet. As Randy's tone became serious, so did his facial expression and body language. Leaning into the speech, he draped his arms over the wooden lectern, clasping it with both hands. The half smirk was replaced by a slight scowl as he gestured with clenched fists, describing how he imagined writing a headline someday that would be both his dream and his nightmare.

The dream, Randy noted, was of a day when he would report a momentous breakthrough in HIV/AIDS treatment. "I'll be at the press conference with a lot of you," he predicted. "And at that press conference, eminent scientists will unveil that armamentarium of treatments that will make HIV into a manageable chronic infection." But, Randy asked, will that day come too late? How many sufferers would needlessly die in the meantime? If the world had to wait until 1996, he warned, "one of the most momentous days in science will come and it will be utterly irrelevant." He spoke both as the world's most famous AIDS journalist and a helpless witness to the deaths of many friends and loved ones. At the same time, Randy avoided mentioning that his own life depended on the promise of that dream.

He hadn't finished sparring with the crowd, and they certainly weren't done with him. Randy earned loud cheers for crediting the activist coalition that had won substantial, long-awaited AIDS research funding. Again they applauded for his declaration that it wasn't good enough to say "science moves slowly" when the world urgently needed a solution. And then there was louder, longer applause when he told pharmaceutical and political leaders they needed to do more to hold themselves accountable. The friendly tides began to shift, however, when Randy addressed the activists in the hall.

In his estimation, there was plenty of criticism to go around, and he'd never been content to dish it out to just one side. With half the room applauding and the other half booing, he insisted that acts of anger, only for the sake of anger, wouldn't produce results: "This conference is not supposed to be a therapy session." Referring to a Barbados official who in her speech elicited boos and hisses for using the word "victims," he added, "Believe it or not, in the Third World there are greater concerns around AIDS than the semantic niceties imposed by the politically correct jargon of North American activists."

Randy's detractors and supporters now rivaled each other's volume, but just as the activists were reaching their crescendo, he pulled them back to his side with a series of emphatic statements. Scientists, he reminded them, owed their funding to the hard work of AIDS activists (applause). Even greater funding commitments were needed, he continued, for syringe exchange and other programs to prevent new HIV infections (applause). And, Randy insisted, world leaders must have a case of "severe dementia" for devoting less than a fraction of their budgets to saving lives, compared to the money spent on new armaments and perpetual warfare (loudest applause so far).

"Remember you are all part of history in this struggle," Randy added, "and historians will note how well you take up the challenge of urgency. How well you do, more than anything else, will measure our degree of civilization." Concluding with a quick thank-you and a flash of that irrepressible half smirk, he quickly retreated from the lectern, with many on their feet cheering while chants and catcalls rang out from the back.

Randy had again demonstrated his clairvoyance, as both his dream and his nightmare would eventually come true. With the turbulent 1980s drawing to a close, he left Montreal firmly established as *the* Randy Shilts, one of the most interesting people in the world, flush with wealth and fame and seemingly able to do whatever he wanted with his life.

True to form, Randy had managed to stoke both his critics and admirers. Still, as he traveled home to California, there remained another nagging, undeniable truth with which he'd need to reckon. Away from the public spotlight, Randy Shilts was well aware that, much like the emerging political movement he covered, he was now inescapably caught up in his own battle for survival.

1 | THE GRADUATE

THE RITUAL WOULD SELDOM vary. Every morning when he woke up, she was already waiting. There was no point in asking why; her anger never needed a reason, and he was too small to fight back. Still half-awake, he'd trudge to the bathroom and assume the position: underpants down, bent over the toilet, eyes clenched. The belt rarely missed its mark, and each time it connected, he'd squeeze his eyes tightly to hold back the tears. It was the only resistance he could offer; in teaching himself not to cry, he also learned to go numb. The only side effect was a persistent migraine, which would nag him for years. When she finally tired, he simply got dressed, covering the bruises as he readied himself for school.

While he would spend his life chasing big stories, the making of Randy Shilts began in a small house on Calumet Avenue in Aurora, Illinois. His father, Russell, known to everyone as Bud, served in World War II before coming home to raise a family. A Michigan native, Bud grew up in Galesburg, just outside Kalamazoo, marrying Norma Gertrude Brugh soon after she finished high school. When oldest son Gary arrived in 1943, Bud was completing basic training and preparing to ship out to Europe. Soon after Bud returned, Norma gave birth to Russell Dennis "Denny" in 1946. The family's third son, Randy Martin Shilts, was born on August 8, 1951, in Davenport, Iowa. After moving to Aurora, the family grew to include Reed (1958), Ronald (1963), and David (1968).

Even in the most prosperous of times, the Shiltses were always a working-class family. Necessities like school clothes had to last an entire year, and summer vacations meant long drives to visit relatives in Michigan. Those trips were among the few times the boys ever saw their extended family, and Gary remembered that Bud's mother, Lucille, was usually drinking heavily.

"Whenever I smell cheap perfume and whiskey," he recalled, "I think of my grandmother."

The Shilts residence resembled a boardinghouse more than a close-knit family home. But at least in a boardinghouse, Gary lamented, "friendships usually develop. There—none did." Some might charitably characterize the Shilts boys as "free-range children," suggesting a well-appreciated freedom and flexible boundaries. Instead, Gary's only childhood memory of any warmth or togetherness was huddling with Norma in the dark living room, eating popcorn as they waited for his father to come home. In postwar years, it wasn't unusual for veterans like Bud to retreat from family life. Gregarious and outgoing, he was known in high school for his "gift of gab," which served him well in lumber sales. But when he wasn't working, Bud preferred to be alone. An amateur architect, he'd retreat to his basement drafting table.

Managing the household fell entirely to a discontented Norma, wearing heavily on a woman Gary remembered as intelligent and artistic, an avid reader who never held a job outside the house. It's not that she didn't want to be married to Bud. One year his junior, Norma was known in high school for her ambition to "win Russ." In postwar years, she'd simply done what women were expected to do: stay at home, handle the housework, and raise children.

When Gary was young, Norma refused to touch alcohol, believing it unseemly for women to drink. But when she did start, she went straight to hard liquor. Whether it was boredom, exhaustion, or frustration with Bud's absence and suspected philandering, she developed a formidable drinking habit by the time her oldest son returned from the air force. Gary's younger brothers had learned how to mix a Bloody Mary each morning, exactly to Norma's liking, and she'd often be drunk by noon.

As Norma's drinking escalated, conditions at home only grew worse. The cleaning became more haphazard, with garbage piled in trash bags around the living room. In the kitchen, she struggled to make simple meals like pizza without burning the tomato sauce, and her bursts of anger—usually spankings and beatings with a belt—became more routine. As adults, Gary and Reed remembered her behavior not as abuse but simply as normal family life. After all, who really knew what was normal, compared to other families? Still, Gary acknowledged, "She would go crazy sometimes."

For the gifted and sensitive Randy, Norma's temper left a lasting impression. "My mother was given to horrible rages for as long as I can remember," he later confessed. By many accounts, Norma represented the definitive love-hate relationship of his life. "I felt my parents hated me. . . . As a child I didn't think anybody loved me." Moreover, because of their age differences, none of the boys were close enough to protect each other. With both Gary and Denny getting out as soon as they could, it never occurred to them to watch out for their younger brothers.

In adulthood, Gary came to regret those actions. "I was constantly at odds with [our] parents and I took a lot of my frustration out on my little brothers," he lamented. "I remember hating everyone there. Hate was the only way to keep from getting hurt. I can't remember ever doing anything nice for any of my brothers— even coming to their defense—or offering support with a problem they had."

Still stinging from Norma's belt, Randy would make the half-mile walk each morning to Freeman Elementary School. Tidily dressed and sporting a thick pair of glasses, he looked forward to spending time with the only grownups who seemed to like him. "School became my escape," he later wrote. "My teachers were substitute parents. I'd be very good in school and was always doing extra credit as a way of currying teachers' favor. In turn, I would get their approval." Survival through perfectionism would always earn him good grades. First, however, he had to make it safely from home to school.

The morning bell meant he could finally relax, but only for a few hours. Sometimes, the other children taunted him on the playground, describing what they'd do to him later. Sometimes they came after him with punches and shoves, pushing him into thorn-laden bushes. The moments that hurt most, however, were when the girls would join in the teasing. He thought they were his friends. Instead, they just laughed, calling him names like "sissy." To protect himself, Randy relied on the only defenses he had: an adultlike impassiveness, biting sarcasm, and, when needed, his legs. On days when he could make it home safely, he'd scramble through the front door to hear Norma complain. "She said that only sissies didn't hit back."

The term seemed to follow Randy everywhere. He read books all the time, had little interest in sports, and spoke in a serious, grown-up manner. Teasing easily hurt his feelings, and he absolutely hated fighting.

It was this seriousness that struck Stuart Jones when the two first met in sixth grade. In class, Stuart noticed what he described as a nervous tic whenever the teacher called on Randy. Before answering, he would sharply inhale, squint tightly, and push his glasses back, as if expecting to be slapped. Then, after pausing, "he would answer correctly, or brilliantly, or sarcastically."

Already, Stuart noticed, Randy seemed to have enemies. Although the two occasionally talked on the playground and walked home together, they neither visited each other's houses nor got to know their families. Still, Randy talked with Stuart more than anyone else in their class. He also seemed to be the only person Randy trusted. One day, Stuart remembered, Randy confided that some boys were planning to ambush him after school, but he'd come up with a plan. Stuart would unlock Randy's bike and bring it to a seldom-used door, so they could escape. Someone tipped off the bullies, however, forcing them to scramble.

Mounting their bikes, the two boys pedaled furiously, fending off a barrage of swipes and punches. Running alongside, the tormenters clutched and tore at Randy's arms. It took several blocks to shake the last boy, who kept pummeling until Randy could finally pull away. They escaped that day but said little else about it.

When the two reached middle school the following year, they simply never saw each other. "I don't know that he had any friend closer than me, which is kind of weird when you think about it," Stuart reflected, "because I didn't feel that we were that close."

———

He tried to look serious even when he smiled. Standing in his Eagle Scout uniform between Bud and Norma, Randy cast a wary eye toward the camera. The moment was ready-made for local news: the father, a scoutmaster for Wesleyan United Methodist Church, presenting his fourteen-year-old son with the God and Country medal. It's hardly surprising that Randy took to scouting. Alongside other boys, he was learning how to uphold a patriotic, morally responsible vision of American manhood. Out of sight from grownups, however, came other, more clandestine lessons.

Those first unspoken encounters were meaningless, after all—nothing more than curious adolescents fooling around after sacking in for the night. Easily dismissed as innocent play, Randy's first sexual experiences offered new sensations and fraternal comfort in the form of mutual touch and the intimacy of shared secrets. No one needed to know, and no one made trouble about it. It was difficult to even articulate those attractions, at least in any positive terms. "Nobody talked about that back then. There weren't words for it," he later recalled. "There wasn't a sense that gay people were a minority group that deserved civil rights. So there was no one I could talk to. It was my secret alone."

Pervert was one word for it. *Homosexual*, a term for sissies who never outgrew their embarrassing girlishness, was equally undesirable. The most accepting comment he'd heard, uttered by his favorite sociology teacher, was that maybe homosexuals were just sick, not criminals. More commonly, his brother Gary remembered, people just called them "fags."

Hearing these words only made Randy more determined to bury his truth. As he entered high school, he practiced hard to be as all-American as any other boy. In becoming the oldest son at home, he even formed a protective relationship with his younger brothers, taking Reed to downtown movie matinees and watching the Beatles together on *The Ed Sullivan Show*. To the casual observer, Randy's teenage life would seem normal in almost every facet. Only one person truly understood how hard he worked to get everything "just right."

Left to right: Randy, Reed, Russell (Bud), and Ronnie Shilts, 1964.
Photo by Norma Shilts, courtesy of Reed and Dawn Shilts

Randy barely knew Sally Eck when he asked her out to an Aurora West High football game in the fall of their tenth-grade year. The tiny, sweet-natured blonde from English class found him charming and smart, projecting confidence, and eager to try everything that high school sweethearts were supposed to do. Randy courted her with perfect manners, never raising his voice; even his cantankerous moments were gentle and mocking. "He didn't like my red lipstick, which was the only color I ever wore," Sally laughed. "And he would tease and call me 'Ruby.' He was kind of contentious, but very loving and very sweet."

Having no positive examples at home, Randy had to teach himself social graces; any little flub, Sally recalled, left him feeling terribly embarrassed. For their first homecoming dance, they went out for Italian beef sandwiches with fries and lots of ketchup—his favorite—not realizing that couples were supposed to go to fancy restaurants. He also didn't know that boys were supposed to buy their dates a corsage, until a girl pointed to a tiny floral detail on the waist of Sally's dress, asking, "Where's your flower? Is that it?" Mortified, Randy made sure that from then on, Sally had the best corsages and only ate at the finest restaurants.

The pair spent more time with her family than his, and Sally's relatives took to Randy easily. "We were meager people, but we had a sense of family," she recalled, "and he was accepted into the family very much." It didn't take long, however, for Sally to catch on to one of Randy's secrets: he was saving up to get away. In the evenings, he started working at a factory and took a weekend job selling shoes. With money, he was able to buy his own clothes, a suitably "Young Republican" blazer, dress shirts, and corduroys. Appraising the new wardrobe, his mother simply told him, "You look prancy. You're prancy."

"And that, of course, was an effeminate assault on him," Sally explained. Randy never told her about the beatings, but by then, Norma's tactics had changed. Once he grew big enough to fight back, she simply cut him down with words. For Christmas, Randy gave Sally a collection of Ayn Rand books. In turn, Sally asked her art teacher to make him a silver ring inscribed with a dollar sign, signifying the freedom that money represented. From his parents, he received a snow shovel.

In later years, Randy's teenage conservatism would become a source of embarrassed amusement, but at the time it made perfect sense. He belonged to a family of antiwar Republicans, whose father, a staunch Goldwater supporter, had joined the local John Birch Society, while Norma decorated the front lawn with anti-Vietnam protest signs. Moreover, Randy had cultivated a stubborn belief in success through individual achievement. He'd worked hard to get good grades while rising to the rank of Eagle Scout, holding two jobs, and courting a steady girlfriend.

A card-carrying member of Students for Reagan, Randy became Aurora West High's de facto conservative leader when he founded a chapter of Young Americans for Freedom (YAF). He was the movement's true believer, telling Sally that Lyndon Johnson hadn't really won in a landslide, as the ballot boxes had clearly been stuffed. After debating his history and civics teachers, he'd hand out leaflets made on a mimeograph machine that he kept in the backyard.

Outside school, those efforts began to attract attention. HE EATS, THINKS AND DRINKS IDEAS, the *Aurora Beacon-News* headline proclaimed in early 1968. Randy gave a studied, sober interview urging readers to "study the philosophies of our leaders [rather] than to just study what they do." He added, "The only way to understand issues is to study the 'why' behind them." In the interview, Randy championed a conservatism that claimed to welcome robust, principled debate from all sides. "Chances are he will continue to debate with his instructors, whether PhDs or teaching assistants," the story predicted. "And he doesn't expect to be out-talked."

By the end of his junior year, Randy's success seemed more a question of when than if, as classmates praised his principled conservatism and debating tenacity. "Always be so broad-minded as you now are," advised his history teacher. No one, not even Sally, knew that he was already questioning those beliefs. As 1968 brought one upheaval after another, Randy, a fervently antiwar conservative who loved debates but hated violence, felt conflicted as he tried to find a middle ground. Although he parted with the YAF, he quickly found that leftist activists had little use for his political philosophizing. When Randy spoke out against violent tactics at an antiwar activist gathering, a woman slapped him.

Retreating from his activism, Randy tried to refashion himself as an independent writer, poet, and cultural critic. Reviewing the Beatles' "Revolution" for West High's student newspaper, he took broad swipes at his own generation, characterizing them as ill-prepared masses unable to think for themselves. Critics who accused the Beatles of selling out were missing the point, Randy explained. The song was a commentary on today's self-styled, comfortably

Randy Shilts, West Aurora High School senior yearbook photo, 1969. *Courtesy of Aurora (IL) Public Library District*

middle-class revolutionary, the charismatic follower who repeats an empty slogan, "It's gonna be . . . all right."

With no movement to call his own, Randy seemed adrift. As his attentions to Sally seemed to wane, she turned to another, more persistent suitor: Randy's only friend from sixth grade, Stuart Jones. Throughout high school, Stuart had made no secret of his crush on Sally, and with Randy appearing to lose interest during their senior year, she decided to give his rival a chance. Randy protested that Sally must have lost her mind, but otherwise he did little to plead his case. Though they occasionally ran into each other around town, the two otherwise never spoke again.

After turning eighteen, the recent graduate faced more questions than his hometown could answer. Though he initially attended Aurora College, circumstances at home confronted him with one more painful truth. Two years earlier, his frustrations with "Mama Bitch and Papa Bitch," as he referred to Norma and Bud, had quietly reached a boiling point. At the time it seemed like a harmless prank, but Randy's scheme for getting back at them would haunt his conscience for the rest of his life. "I couldn't stand my parents in high school so . . . I poked a hole in my father's condoms and stole some pills from my mom," he later confessed.

"I don't know even if it was a prank as much as it was in anger," Sally reflected. Randy hated seeing people get hurt, and in the Shilts home, she emphasized, people had been hurt. To the best of his knowledge, the date seemed to coincide with Norma's sixth and final pregnancy. But in hindsight, older brother Gary took a skeptical view toward Randy's fear of being responsible. "A lot of sex with my dad involved alcohol," he explained, and Bud and Norma could be pretty careless with birth control. When Norma gave birth to her youngest son, David, she was approaching her midforties. Like many at the time, it never occurred to her to stop drinking. By the time Randy started college, it was clear that David was struggling; within a few years, he would be diagnosed autistic.

Among the Shilts boys, getting as far away as possible had become a rite of passage. Gary had left for college and the air force, while Denny fled the country to avoid Vietnam. Like his older brothers, Randy knew he needed to escape, but he didn't yet know how he'd do it. The idea came to him on Christmas Day 1969. Sitting stoned in a friend's bathtub, Randy's thoughts wandered as she told him about hitchhiking west. He'd love it, she insisted. People on the West Coast were so much more laid back. She'd even met people who went with both men and women—bisexuality! Randy made a mental note but said nothing. In his foggy, spaced-out mind, he was already making plans.

———————

January 15, 1970. Picking up the pace, he hurried toward the gate, clutching his ticket. Once aboard, he shuffled around the other passengers, finding his row and stowing his meager possessions. Sinking into the cushioned seat, he looked around. As the plane took off, this flat, unremarkable corner of the world began to fade away. Randy gazed out the window, finally able to relax. The indifferent hum of air travel made for easy daydreaming. In a few hours, he'd see mountaintops for the first time. Randy had saved enough money for a ticket to Denver; from there, he planned to thumb his way west. Reflecting on the day, his inner poet stirred:

He never again could find
The village
Below
(Even if he tried)
His peers could
Not see

The starlight showing
The way
Of course this was only
Upon a mountain-top
In a place (not far away)
In a time (not distant)

Taking only what he could carry, Randy set out the following day. Everyone he'd meet would see him only as he wanted to be seen; there were no secrets to protect and no shame to conceal. For the first time in his life, he was about to meet the world completely on his own terms. "Still," he recalled ten years later, "the big anniversary of my life."

2 | KILLING THE LION

IT DIDN'T TAKE LONG for Linda Alband to notice the new neighbor. A few years younger, the kid with unkempt curly hair had moved into the room next door. Tucked into the Portland hills around Goose Hollow, the ramshackle boardinghouse had a laid-back, communal atmosphere, with tenants roaming freely between each other's rooms. In the evenings, since no one owned a television, they frequently made dinner together and gossiped over bottles of wine. Soon after the newcomer's arrival, Linda and her floormates began finding daily reminders taped to their doors, counting down the number of shopping days until "Shiltsmas."

Eighteen-year-old Randy, a nonstop talker sporting a ridiculously tiny ponytail, had enrolled at Portland Community College (PCC), finding work there as a security guard and parking lot attendant. Money was tight, but among his neighbors he found interesting conversations, cheap alcohol, and communal weed. The second floor's cast of characters included Portland music legend Johnny Kuntz, producer Al Cooper, and a man everyone assumed was running from the draft who called himself "Scott Elvis." Everyone knew Randy was from the Midwest, as his accent was unmistakable. But he left them guessing how he'd ended up in Portland. A fellow boarder, a woman named Leslie, had helped him move in, and Linda knew the two sometimes had sex. All they managed to do, she remembered, was give each other yeast infections.

To Linda, Portland in 1970 was still a conservative city. She worked at the Federal Reserve in a steady but boring clerical job, where she could watch the antiwar protests outside. Even with the city's growing reputation as a leftist haven, she saw how the self-described counterculture could behave largely as a group of sexist, arrogant White men, including Randy. "He tried to act like the straight boy, which was oppressive," she remembered. "He'd come over and make messes in my apartment, and I'd say, 'Well, why don't you pick up after yourself?' He'd go, 'That's what women do!' And he'd come over and eat my food and never bring any food." Despite his bad manners, she found it hard to dislike her new neighbor.

"He talked a mile a minute, he was always opinionated and wanted to be the center of attention, and [he] succeeded many times. But he had a good sense of humor. That was the thing about Randy, he was really funny. He could be self-deprecating." On a Saturday in early June, Linda found Randy dressed up in his work clothes. It was time for Portland's Rose Festival, and next door to the boarding house sat a large, empty parking lot. "He put on his costume for PCC, had his little jacket and tied his hair back," she remembered. The lot was only used from Monday to Friday, but out-of-town visitors had no way of knowing it. Seizing the opportunity, Randy hustled enough money that day to buy wine for his floormates and still pocket most of the cash.

If Randy's midwestern conservatism seemed far behind him, he still lived by one important rule: make money whenever he could. Herself a former Goldwater supporter, Linda could appreciate his resourcefulness. For her first Shiltsmas, she presented Randy with a copy of *King Lear*, in honor of their shared love for Shakespeare.

Remembering dates wasn't Ann Neuenschwander's strong point, but she never forgot the first time she saw her best friend. Ann and her boyfriend Chris Schroeder had been saving up for a trip to Europe when a glitch with his draft physical scuttled their plans. Chris escaped Vietnam with a medical deferment, but not before their travel dates had passed. Instead, he used the money to buy a dilapidated house in Northeast Portland. In fall 1970 Ann and Chris were settling in and taking classes at PCC when Chris brought home one of their classmates, whose car had broken down.

When Ann met Randy, she felt an instant affection. "He had holes in his pants and his shirts, and he was scruffy," she remembered. "He was highly energized, and he couldn't go up the stairs without tripping, because he always had to go up the stairs at full bore." Together, they made a memorable trio: Chris, the lanky idealist, alongside Ann, a radiant blonde with kind eyes and a loving smile, and, well, Randy. "He had this curly, curly hair that kind of stuck out all over."

On a road trip, Ann began combing out Randy's hair, revealing, to his annoyance, the biggest, most ridiculous Afro she'd ever seen. Beneath that scruffy appearance, however, she only saw brilliance. Though young and poor, Randy stubbornly believed he'd someday be famous. Ann's new friend could barely afford clothes, but in all honesty, he barely paid attention to such trivialities. "He had to learn to care about clothes as time went on, but he only cared about writing and politics. He had to know everything."

Randy had a habit of compartmentalizing his social circles, so Linda barely knew Ann, Chris, or their other friends. But individually, they all remembered the same kinds of adventures: silly things like pooling their cash to buy booze, petty shoplifting, and all-night conversations fueled by weed, wine, cigarettes, and ketchup-covered french fries. To know and love Randy meant understanding that at least one meal per day had to include his favorite starch; sometimes, he'd even top his mashed potatoes with a pile of fries.

With Aurora fading into the past, Randy began journaling his impending transformation into—what? The possibilities seemed infinite. "I was overwhelmed by the knowledge that I will soon be going under a tremendous change and the account of both the physical and metaphysical implementations of this change will be fruitful," he wrote in mid-1971. "Now that my self-awareness [has] increased to some extent and I have a better perception of the workings of my relatively unusual mind it should be quite interesting."

That summer provoked a multitude of sensations to captivate Randy's attentions. On the Fourth of July, he found himself alone and tipsy with a male friend, who picked up and started playing his guitar. It didn't take long for Randy to begin singing along, uninhibited like the child he never was. The encounter unleashed a flood of sensual memories, causing him to feel torn between "Apollonian" wisdom and ecstatic, "Dionysian" impulses. The only words he could summon to describe his feelings were intellectual, drawing on the literature he'd read in classes.

In daydreams, Randy began to conjure exciting new planes of existence. He'd written so much in his first year of college: essays, poetry, even the beginning of a novel. From his English and philosophy classes, he began to identify with men like Hesse, Nietzsche, and Poe. Convinced that his moment of transformation had arrived, Randy was determined to fashion a grand philosophy for himself. Days of self-study turned into weeks of obsessing. Convinced that he was on the verge of a philosophical breakthrough, Randy imagined his warring urges as a contest for existence itself.

Captivated by a news story about a lion that was to be euthanized, he turned to writing about an untimely death, obsessing over images of loneliness and annihilation. Soon, Randy began to wonder if he was losing his mind. To his closest friends, he said nothing. But all of Randy's assumptions about who he was, how he viewed people, and what they thought of him were now in flux. His classes were growing tedious, filled with people he saw as "generally stupid" and teachers he considered incompetent. More alarmingly, Randy's idealism had begun to falter as he pressed for a creative breakthrough.

Over New Year's Day, Randy moved into a new apartment in Goose Hollow (the "Rat Castle") with help from Ann and Chris. Privately, he wondered how the two could even like him, because he didn't find himself that likable. As the winter term commenced, he confessed to harboring a deep fear of being alone, and, moreover, "sexual problems can no longer be ignored and shoved in a corner." Another "Dionysian upswing" soon demanded Randy's attention, taunting him with feelings that vacillated between boundless freedom and naked frailty. Smoking pot seemed to provide a sense of greater freedom, but lingering insecurities kept him feeling unsure of himself.

In the spring, Randy turned to sleeping with one of his professors, a woman who had a reputation for crashing college parties and hooking up with her male students. In what Randy characterized as his first "really heavy" sexual experiences, he savored the sensation of losing himself: "I began to get very drunk—not on any liquor but totally (stumbly, literally) intoxicated on [her]— when we balled my head was actually spinning and I was half in a daze—totally smashed—I could barely talk."

Although the professor frustrated him by sleeping with other men—a not-so-subtle refusal to be anything like a "steady" girlfriend—she mesmerized her young lover with hints of a more exotic sexuality. When she took him to another guy's place and sat between them, holding each of their hands, he wondered, was she hinting at a threesome? Taking Randy to a gay bar, she surprised him by hooking up with a woman. Soon after, she offered to introduce him to one of her gay friends. Now he was really intrigued.

Having the hint of permission, rather than judgment or belittlement, provided the opening Randy needed. For too long, he'd buried his desires in the safe routines of "normal" people, while suppressing the attractions he'd first explored in scouting. In March 1972, after months of struggling to find the words, Randy put his yearnings down on paper: "My deepest heterosexual and homosexual desires are coming into play."

By admitting his attractions, Randy was taking a substantial first step. Still, the pressure to act on those feelings was daunting, especially as he kept them hidden from his friends. Although he tried to clumsily coax other men into sexual play, Randy quickly learned that he'd have to navigate a completely different set of signals and behaviors. Encoded in suggestive glances and thinly disguised double meanings, the subtleties of sexual communication enabled men to court each other in public while avoiding any mention of what they really wanted.

Unless someone made a definitive declaration of gayness—not easy to find in 1972—Randy had to read each encounter with careful consideration. It wasn't easy to detect someone's interest, and sometimes the encounters left him more confused than before. A friend who'd reacted coolly to Randy the previous year now seemed to be flirting with him. Another friend, who'd recently married, was becoming unusually affectionate, touching Randy and tugging on his hair.

Even as he wrote about bisexuality, Randy's journals focused almost exclusively on men. He quickly tired of his professor lover, but worried that breaking up would keep him from seeing her gay friends. He drank more, thought constantly about sex, and then fretted over his obsession. Dreams of sex with men tumbled through his head, rousing him in the middle of the night and keeping him awake until dawn.

Those unfulfilled desires were eclipsing Randy's waking thoughts, leading him to grow bored and disappointed in the dead intellectuals who'd previously inspired him. The transformation he'd sought, the sudden upheaval that would thrust him into the annals of great literature, seemed to be slipping away. Of Nietzsche, he wrote, "I expected a mystical magic in a death and rebirth but it's slow, gradual—How do you will yourself to like yourself?"

"I've lost control of things so fast—I don't quite understand what's going on," Randy told himself. "I don't have any hold on it." Each passing week made the pretense more difficult to maintain. After a night spent in the company of a "latent homosexual" who sat around disparaging "faggots," he wrote, "I'm sick of having to hide that part of me—how can I overcome it if I won't even admit it?"

"I am terrified of people not understanding me and classifying me in a syllable—'weird,' 'strange,' or something of that nature." Every facial expression, passing comment, gesture, or touch left him feeling self-conscious and confused about other men's true feelings and intentions: "Sexual contacts have to be honest, since the physical body, hopefully cannot lie," he wrote. And since the physical body cannot lie, by Randy's own reasoning, then he had to reckon with a thundering, undeniable urge. He wasn't fighting back a momentary "Dionysian impulse." These desires were harnessed to a deeper truth: his hope that another man would show him the attention and affection he'd long desired.

On Easter weekend, Randy wrote of suddenly seeing the world with new eyes, pondering the ideas of death, resurrection, and reintegration. Staring at a reality he'd struggled mightily to grasp, he finally admitted what he wanted in the simplest words he knew. "I want to fall in love," he resolved. "I'm sick of trying to pretend I can make it with women when I want to fall in love—and be loved—by a man."

On May 19, 1972, Randy was scheduled to deliver a lecture to his morning anthropology class on the Yanomami tribe of the Amazonian rainforest. Instead, however, he hastily assembled a panel of guest speakers, who sat waiting at the front of the room as his classmates arrived. Over the spring term, his interests had begun to swing from abstract philosophy to the reality-based social sciences. However, now he was afraid of losing his creativity, and with it, any chance of becoming an author. "Maybe the lion is dead," he wondered. "I've lost control of things so fast—I don't quite understand what's going on. I don't have any hold on it."

The week had already been memorable with heavy partying, some discreet action with a friend of his professor lover's, and meeting author Ken Kesey. On top of that, a repulsive encounter with a male flasher had "alienate[d] me from penises all week (heavy)." When class began, Randy introduced the panelists: a friend of his professor lover's from the Gay Liberation Front, two women, and himself. In front of his entire class, Randy shared what had taken him a lifetime to understand and admit: he was a man who was attracted to other men.

In the leadup, he'd braced himself for blowback: words like *weird* or *strange*, or maybe just outright silence from the friends he wanted so badly to keep. Instead, almost everyone told him it was no big deal. They understood and accepted him, and nothing had changed. The relief was almost instanta-neous: "Sexually, the repressions and fears that governed the last 6 or 7 (and even more) years of my life have been virtually erased."

Over the next couple days, Randy broke the news to each of his friends individually. He'd already agreed to rent a room in Chris and Ann's house over the summer, but now worried that they wouldn't accept him. He started privately with Ann, saying, "I have something to tell you, and I don't know how to tell you."

"Well, just tell me."

"You know," Randy stammered, "I just don't know how you'll react. I'm not sure how you'll react, and I want to be friends with you."

"What are you talking about?" Ann began to wonder if he'd killed some-one. "Just. Tell. Me!"

Finally, he said, "I'm gay."

"I went, 'Oh, is that all?'" Ann laughed. "And he says, 'It doesn't bother you?' And I said, 'Well, no.'"

His talk with Chris followed the same script—prolonged fretting, repeating over and over how much he was afraid of losing a good friend. Like Ann, Chris also began to worry that Randy really harbored a deep, dark secret. News that his friend was a homosexual paled in comparison to what Chris was imagining.

Back at the Rat Castle, Randy invited Linda over to share the news. Her reaction matched those of most everyone else: So what? After Randy came out, Linda saw him become a happier, better person who stopped struggling to play straight and acted more collaboratively with the women in his life. "He stopped acting like women had to cater to him," she explained. "He stopped trying too hard to be what he wasn't and became more of a person in the process. And that allowed us to retain a friendship that lasted until his death."

Randy would remember the exact place and time of his coming out for the rest of his life. "Most of my friends know where my head's at and I have not been rejected," he wrote afterward. "In a period of about 48 hours . . . I told them all and was greeted with open arms." Like so many homespun tales, in later years the truth took on a few embellishments. In future depictions, he would boast of telling everyone he knew right away, but the letters, diaries, and memories of his loved ones offer a number of contradictions.

A letter from Bud just a few weeks later made no mention of any major news. He and Norma had moved the family from Illinois to his hometown of

Galesburg, Michigan. Their correspondences with Randy mainly talked about his younger brothers, especially Ronnie and David. Later that summer, in Randy's birthday card, Bud quipped, "Now you are a man so I will allow you to go out with girls!"

As Gary Shilts recalled, Randy waited to share the big news with his family for a few more years, when he began writing stories about the gay community in San Francisco. Adult bookstores were practically the only places to buy gay periodicals, he explained, and they also happened to be where Bud bought his pornography. When Randy became a prominent reporter, he was afraid that his father might see the family name headlining a page-one feature.

To test the waters, Randy called Gary's first wife, Barbara, and asked her to break the news. Soon after, Gary called Randy and delivered what would later become his most famous line: "Everyone has to have a gay relative to talk about." Years later, that quote would appear in *Rolling Stone* magazine, providing Gary with his one fleeting moment of pop culture fame: "My work is done on this planet."

On the eve of his twenty-first birthday, Randy moved south to Eugene and enrolled at the University of Oregon, where Chris and Ann would later join him. The summer of 1972 represented an extraordinary leap forward, but he knew there was still work to do. With self-awareness comes growing pains, which for Randy included moments of headlong romance, followed by crushing rejections. At times, he dreamed of liberating the sexually ambivalent men he chased, most of whom would never be so open with their feelings. If he could will them to embrace their true selves, maybe then they'd love him. At times, those highs and lows left him wanting to just sit down and cry. "I have to slow down, relax and allow myself to feel," Randy told himself. "I must allow myself love."

"I walk down the street looking at every male who walks by waiting," he fretted. After every rejection, he'd agonize over being seen as a "dirty old man," pursuing each new prospect beyond the point of reason. Having embraced his true self, Randy found that he yearned for more than instant gratification. He wanted to love and be loved in a deeper, longer-lasting way. Fulfilling that desire would require him to relax, see others for their true selves, and focus on "the people that make the sex, not the sex that makes people." To these marching orders, he added another simple, yet elusive self-commandment: "Love myself, more than anything."

3 | COME OUT FOR SHILTS!

IT BEGAN THROUGH WORD of mouth, leading to discreet meetings in a secret venue. Soon, enough people came to necessitate a larger space. Participants would enter through a side door, gathering in an open sitting room where they were welcomed and encouraged to speak freely. For some, it was their first time meeting others like themselves. Just blocks away from a bustling college campus, the Wesley United Methodist Center offered safety to the city's newest activist group, the Eugene Gay People's Alliance.

"It wasn't a large organization," cofounder Terry Bean recalled. The GPA's first meetings would draw a dozen or fewer people, but its proximity to the University of Oregon soon attracted much larger crowds, including students. Established soon after New York's Stonewall rebellion, the GPA began with a focus more on support than political activism. Terry remembered those meetings as providing safe space, where people could talk about their lives in a supportive environment. As a UO student in the late 1960s, Terry fit the profile of emerging gay leaders: young homosexuals, inspired by the antiwar movement, outraged by antigay discrimination, and bruised but undeterred by occasional fag bashings.

When Randy came to Eugene in the fall of 1972, he found a home in alliance meetings. "We had rap sessions," he later recalled. "And that was very crucial . . . in terms of integrating a positive self-image and understanding." At those meetings, Randy could unburden his insecurities and relate them to others' experiences. "It's sort of how our problems as individuals, being gay and accepting ourselves, how they related to a broader, political framework of us within a society in which we were brought up to dislike ourselves . . . and to not have faith and confidence in ourselves."

At the time, he recalled, lesbians seemed to prefer women-only meetings, leaving men to sometimes dominate the GPA. It wasn't unusual, then, to detect a hint of cruising among members. GPA discussions began to take on a political flavor as Terry and others talked of lobbying the city council for a gay rights bill. Randy, the one-time conservative turned hippie leftist, couldn't resist the temptation to reenter politics. After the weekly meetings, a small group would sometimes stay behind or go out for coffee, where Randy and Terry discovered a mutual love for debating. It didn't matter what position either of them took; both appreciated the intellectual exercise of staking out and defending their stance.

"We were both willing to play devil's advocate on any issue," Terry remembered. "I learned that way, and I think he did too, and enjoyed it." The GPA's growing political interest helped to stoke Randy's own ambitions. Attending rap sessions helped build his confidence, but simply gaining self-acceptance wasn't enough. "When I went to Eugene I think I resented the fact that to some of the people I slept with I seemed to be 'just another queer,'" he wrote. "I think I was really worried about this definition by orientation when there were so many other great things to my personality that I knew I just had to show people."

Heading into 1973, Randy moved quickly into Oregon's budding gay political scene. In a movement where many still shied from public spotlights, he had some natural advantages with no family nearby, no past in local politics, and few reservations about holding back. Despite a full class load and an on-campus job, activism provided opportunities for Randy to "gain the respect of all the gay people" by showing off his reasoning and wit, all while cruising other politically active men. The spirited English major quickly rose to leadership in the GPA, becoming a cochair when the organization established an "official" student arm. He didn't wait long to make his next move.

In early 1973, UO students were getting fed up with seeing their student government fees benefit only a privileged few. Amid calls for reform, Randy found himself drawn into the fray by the most irresistible of opportunities: sex. "One day in my [Expository Writing] class," he wrote, "I was cruising—rubbing legs with—this guy who after class said he was a [Student] Senator and I was shocked at listening to his few stories of corruption."

Seeing an opportunity, Randy entered the upcoming Student Senate elections, using his sexuality as a rallying point with women, minority, and progressive students. In a letter to the *Oregon Daily Emerald*, he proclaimed, "My exposure as a gay Senator will offer those assuming they have to hide with a visible alternative. My openness will also give these gay people the opportunity to reexamine themselves so that they can become more healthy and free in dealing with their sexuality."

Randy managed to win an open humanities seat, but a majority of students also backed an initiative abolishing the Senate in favor of a five-person Incidental Fee Committee (IFC), which would distribute nearly $1 million in student fees. Randy placed his name on the ballot again, winning an at-large seat and maneuvering to become the committee's first chair. Barely five months after arriving in Eugene, he was now the second most-powerful person in student government.

In this reform-minded era, Randy quickly aligned himself with a progressive, multicultural alliance to form a governing majority. "I was very powerful in the student government, so they really couldn't fuck with us," he later recalled. "And I was chairman. What we did was just put together a coalition of the gay and the minority end of things."

With Randy as chair, the IFC conducted a review of campus groups' funding, putting well-financed programs, including the Athletic Department, on notice. Instead, committee members set their sights on progressive priorities like subsidized on-campus daycare, women's studies programs, and support for minority student groups and the Eugene GPA. "With all this money," he told the *Daily Emerald*, "There's incredible programs we could do."

Even then, he wasn't satisfied, entering the race for student body president as an unabashed gay leftist, with Chicana activist and fellow IFC member Gloria Gonzalez as his running mate. No COMPROMISE, their fliers proclaimed, promising to run a "low-cost and issue-oriented campaign." Under the slogan "Come Out for Shilts," their platform promised to cut student fee allocations to the Athletic Department, distance student government from the office of the UO president, and cut bureaucratic waste while promoting tuition stability, daycare, tenant unions for dorms and co-ed housing, and supports for Vietnam veterans returning to campus.

In early May, their ticket came in a distant third, but the eventual winner, Greg Leo, soon realized that Randy, his committee, and its reformist agenda weren't going away. In its proposed budget, the IFC prioritized the GPA's student arm, childcare, migrant labor support, and monthly stipends for the committee members while reducing allocations to longstanding beneficiaries, especially the Athletic Department. The move drew a veto from Leo, prompting a vote to override the veto and strong words from Randy and the committee.

The two leaders battled for weeks in the *Daily Emerald*, with Leo charging that the IFC and its chair were acting outside of their established guidelines, and Randy countering that his committee was acting well within its constitutional responsibilities. Ultimately, UO President Robert Clark sided with Leo, overruling the IFC and maintaining the Athletic Department's funding levels, but the GPA's allocation remained mostly intact. With its first real funding, the gay student group had gained the stamp of legitimacy as an organization serving the needs of the campus community.

Harriet Merrick first came to Eugene in early 1972, before running out of money and transferring home to Portland State. In the fall of 1973, however, she followed her college sweetheart back to the University of Oregon, finding that quite a bit had changed while she was away. The Eugene GPA was clearly on the rise, and Harriet became a leader in planning its first Gay Coming Out Week activities. "It was just so crazy, and it was just so organic," she laughed. "We were all aswirl at that time."

"What I remember about Randy was this big Afro hair," she added, "and this swish and a swagger, a sashay ability." Heading down University Street, he always walked about ten paces ahead of everyone else, Harriet remembered. "It was just—there was a swing to it," she said. "I couldn't mimic it if my life depended on it. It was kind of like a . . . swagger and confidence and plenty of just *so gay*."

Harriet soon fell in love with the community, making herself at home among the boys who dominated GPA meetings and developing a deep fondness for her GPA comrades, especially Randy. "Being with Randy at any point in time, on any conversation, was like trying to stay up with a tornado. He was just . . . energy, a ball of energy."

Thanks to Randy's budgeting efforts, the GPA could use its new funding to raise awareness on campus, with speakers like Del Martin, Phyllis Lyon, and Morris Kight. While Harriet and others worked on educational programs and events, Randy looked out for gay political interests via the IFC. Although his unbridled approach may have irritated adversaries, among activists, he was considered a valuable partner and ally.

"The rest of us had our own mission, and that's okay, because it really takes many people, many layers to get stuff done," Harriet reflected. "And Randy was able to do what the rest of us didn't. We had a goal, we had an agenda. Randy had a different mission, which wasn't in conflict—never in conflict."

"Diplomacy wasn't necessarily his forte," Harriet allowed. But she never saw Randy act out of spite or meanness. "I perceived that as, that was Randy's energy, and his energy could be so overwhelming that . . . I'm sure some people considered him uppity!" To cap off the campus's first Gay Coming Out Week, Randy and the GPA sponsored a "gay-straight sock hop" on October 5, 1973. To the sound of '60s and Motown music, the mixed crowd intermingled and danced at the Erb Memorial Union, where Randy welcomed the crowd by proclaiming, "If you're gay, remember you are not immoral. You are not perverted. You are not sick. Most of all, you are not alone."

That evening, he picked up another lesson in gay culture. "There were three guys—one tall skinny black guy and two friends of his got long wigs on and pantomimed 'Stop In The Name Of Love,'" he later recalled. The impromptu mini-drag performance caught Randy by surprise; up to now, his gay experiences had mainly been through rap sessions, politics, and cruising. "I just thought it was hilarious."

In scarcely a year, Randy had made a profound impression on the campus, the results of which did not go unnoticed. Following the dance, the *Daily Emerald* observed, "The importance of the gay-straight hop lies not in its success but rather in what it represents. The hop was a place where gay people came together to just be people. Another portion of the University community may be able to learn to deal openly and honestly with other groups on campus. And, in the process, we all might learn something about ourselves."

At the end of his term as IFC chair, Randy opted not to run again. Despite his ascendance, he later reflected on what he considered the corrupting influence of politics. "You have to be sort of an asshole," he commented. "You can't live a pure idealistic life. You have to be practical. So, I realized I didn't want to be in politics. And also, nobody trusts politicians. Nobody trusts anybody in politics. So, I realized that that just wasn't going to work for what I wanted to do."

Randy Shilts, Christmas 1973.
Photo by Linda Alband, courtesy of the photographer

His skirmishes with Greg Leo had lasted well into the fall, with Leo and his allies challenging the committee's legitimacy (which a constitutional committee upheld) and Randy's progressive partners launching an unsuccessful recall attempt against the president. In early 1974, when students went to the polls to elect his replacement, Randy quietly stole away to San Francisco.

For those who worked alongside him, the era evoked memories of exuberance, joy, and good-humored teasing. "He was so good; he was so bad," Harriet beamed. "He was so complex and had so many different layers. Randy was a colleague . . . who was annoyingly crazy at times, and wonderfully so. I loved Randy." To love him, of course, meant dealing with that ever-expanding ego. "Sometimes I would feel a need to bad-time, like a brother-sister, slap him down a few, just to kind of keep him right angled."

Harriet later taught a university course called "Gays in a Non-Gay Society," which included future author and sexologist Carol Queen. Randy, at that point nearing graduation, enrolled but hardly ever attended, earning a C because Harriet's teaching assistants wouldn't let her flunk him. After the term, he approached Carol at a party, asking how she did in class. When Carol replied she'd gotten an A, Randy blew up, apparently insulted that she'd somehow earned a higher grade. "We just gave him shit," Harriet laughed. "It was friendly, it was, I would still say, joyful."

Randy took the abuse with good humor but didn't forget. Years later, when the bestselling author returned for a book signing, he teasingly wrote in Harriet's copy that she should've given him an A.

———————————

"While I try to be as arrogant as possible with my ideas, I try to be the opposite when confronting my writing, as a style. I want a lot of criticism." That invitation for scrutiny, offered early in Randy's college years, might surprise those who came to know him as confident, doggedly defensive of his work and, yes, arrogant. In the words of one longtime friend, "We used to have to take Randy's ego out and beat it once a week."

Few would deny his natural talents, but even fewer got a glimpse of his own self-criticism, and with it a determination to improve. In his fourth year of college, although still an English major with literary ambitions, Randy was beginning to realize that his writing needed help. "I couldn't write a simple declarative sentence because I was an English major," he later recalled. "They don't teach you how to write. They teach you how to read."

With an eye toward refining his grammar, Randy took his first journalism course in the fall of 1973. If he truly wanted tough feedback, he met his match in Dr. Willis Winter, who emphasized that in journalism, form mattered almost as much as substance. Though Winter praised Randy's attempt at an unbiased political essay, he soundly rapped the sloppy, meandering style: "Your presentation must be neater. Others are managing. Get with it. You're too good a student to let the form damage the substance."

Old habits, it seemed, took time to shake off. In a similarly verbose essay, Randy signed off with just a single, lyrical word, reminiscent of his adolescent poetry: "Floating." Winter responded dryly with his red pen: "I sure am. B–. Back to the style and thought of yesteryear. Seriously, Randy. The style interferes horribly with the message. Save it for the English Department."

Winter pushed Randy throughout the term, praising the strength of his ideas while hammering him on fundamentals like grammar, proper sourcing and citations, and conclusions that were relevant to course readings. In turn, Randy found ways to test his professor's boundaries by writing extensively on gay-related topics, including a case study on homophobia ("That's different," Winter commented) and a lengthy analysis of mass media's depictions of gay liberation.

Like others who would teach Randy, Willis Winter found the topics fresh, interesting, and worthy of encouragement. At the same time, his drumbeat message was perfectly clear: original thinking was no excuse for carelessness or lack of rigor. "Some fascinating ideas, some disappointing gaps," he commented on the gay liberation essay, taking aim at Randy's off-the-cuff style of intellectual discourse: "At times this read more like a happy hour discussion than a quasi-scholarly paper. That makes for interesting reading but it wasn't the effort I'd hoped you would produce at this crucial point in the quarter. A– – –."

Winter's firm but fair criticism seemed to sink in. With time, attention, and practice, Randy learned how to write cleaner copy and ground his stories in the everyday world. Gone were his attempts at high-minded philosophy, making anything that happened around him fair game for a story. By early 1974, all Randy needed for his English degree was to finish his senior honors thesis, which he focused on *King Lear*. But his trip to San Francisco during student elections had coincided with one of the decade's defining news stories, the kidnapping of Patty Hearst. After getting an up-close view of the ensuing media spectacle, Randy came back to school convinced that he wanted to be an investigative journalist.

Up to that point, his reporting experiences had been fairly shallow, occasionally writing stories for the *Daily Emerald* about his job with the campus Outdoor Program or the Eugene GPA. By May, however, Randy had joined the paper as managing editor. Instead of graduating, he would return in the fall with his most ambitious agenda yet, vowing to complete both his honors thesis and a second degree in journalism, all within a year. In the meantime, Randy was looking forward to a rare summer off from classes. It would be a summer like none he'd experienced before.

4 | PRETTY BOY

AROUND A HOT JULY bonfire, heads were slowly turning. At first, some men didn't recognize him. But even in the darkness, they couldn't help noticing: there was something . . . *different* about Randy.

"Who's that number?"

"It's Shilts, stupid."

"We got a new boy in town!" cracked Terry Bean.

"So Randy goes to the big city and comes back a queer."

It was a new experience, being the sexiest thing in town. Everyone, it seemed, had something to say. Instead, his attentions were drawn to a shadowy figure, probably in his late thirties, who wasn't especially attractive. "Black leather jacket, beer belly, far receding hair-line, an unattractive and even eyeless James Dean."

The stranger made the first move, provoking feelings of disgust and smug superiority. Following the man to his tent, Randy believed he had the upper hand until, fumbling in the dark, he grasped something unfamiliar: "A leather band with chrome studs tying his cock and balls together in one tight little clump . . . I was shocked, revolted." The cock ring–bound stranger wanted to be masturbated. Randy grabbed hold, gripping tightly. "I wanted to give him pain because I thought he would enjoy it," he later wrote. "I wanted to give him pain because he disgusted me."

Aroused by his own revulsion, Randy squeezed roughly, abusing the knotted flesh until the man cried out. Ignoring his objections, Randy kept jerking himself and the stranger off until they exploded in each other's hands, exiting soon after in breathless silence. Leaving the campsite, he could still feel the sensation of those tightly bound genitals. "I think if I [came] to know him, I would have hated him. But I will never come to know him, and hope never to know him again."

———————————

With summer creeping past its midpoint, a startling revelation had come to pass. "Of all the things I was told this summer, one achieves dominance, one was most important: suddenly Randy Shilts was pretty." To be sure, he was no stranger to playing the game. Even as he wrote about wanting one true love, Randy relished a good chase. It's just that his out-of-control hair, lack of fashion sense, and excitable demeanor made him an unorthodox player in an ever more image-conscious and selective scene.

The changes first dawned on him in mid-June, as he was packing for a cross-country road trip in a friend's Volkswagen bus. With graduation on the horizon, Randy wanted to give Chicago a fresh look and visit his family for the first time in years. Those preparations were interrupted by his neighbor, however, a "slight, weak, blond man" who resembled a young D. H. Lawrence. Together they sat awkwardly as the blond talked obsessively about a mutual acquaintance. "Whether he knew it or not, he was thinking sex," Randy recalled. "It took me minutes to seduce him." He fucked the D. H. Lawrence lookalike twice, saw him out, and then resumed packing. "For me," he wrote, "the sex was not at all meaningful; it was sex and only that. I have no doubt that I have had more sex in the past two months than the blond will have in his entire life."

With that lackluster fanfare, Randy's Sexual Summer of '74 had begun. A dramatic physical transformation soon followed when he visited his brother Gary in Aurora. When Randy decided to get a haircut, the change wasn't supposed to be dramatic, but the barber had other ideas. "Within 40 minutes, I was pretty boy." Complete with contact lenses, Randy's face burst forth, no longer hidden behind the overgrown Afro and thick glasses.

People seemed to notice. While visiting his parents in Michigan, he scored with a Kalamazoo couple in their thirties, then again with a PhD student from Ann Arbor. Soon, however, he was back on the VW bus, retreating to Oregon and the familiar comforts of his "West Coast Chic" lifestyle.

Frankly, he'd expected more from this adventure. He found his parents to be exactly who they already were, but his anger had softened after seeing how much he'd missed as Ronny and David were getting older. His youngest brothers were both difficult to handle, and his parents had grown weary and mellow with age. "They are people who carry no airs."

Returning to Oregon, he made a snap decision to follow his friends Chris and Ann back to Portland, renting a cheap room in a shabby old apartment building. After venturing down to Eugene for that memorable July 4th bonfire, he came back to find that, indeed, "pretty boy" seemed to be turning heads. Instead of spending hours alone and ignored at the bars, he was being cruised and groped by all kinds of strangers. For the most part, it was sex of convenience, with men who were barely worth remembering.

On the rare occasion when a handsome Daniel, John, or Gary swept him off his feet, reality would come crashing down once the initial euphoria faded. Inevitably, their enthusiasm would dwindle, they'd stop taking his calls, and he'd see them back at the bars, searching for another one-night stand. Randy understood; after all, he was playing the same game. But even as he bedded and discarded others in the same fickle fashion, playing the role of disposable sex object left him with a lingering distaste for it all. The game promised new adventures nearly every night, but how would he know when he'd finally won?

It didn't take long for Randy to fall into a nightly routine, heading first to the Family Zoo, followed by Embers. On one of those typical nights, he sat drinking with the other regulars, complaining about needing a job, when one of his new drinking buddies suddenly jumped up, crossed the room, and asked someone a few questions. Moments later, he came back with an offer. The Majestic Hotel, a well-worn bathhouse in downtown Portland, needed a clerk. Within minutes, Randy met his new boss, Ron—"a pompous, conceited, disgusting, little Capricorn." The Majestic's live-in manager let his hand wander over Randy's butt while they were talking. The job was his, Ron promised, as long as Randy showed up for the interview.

The Sexual Summer of '74 had taken an unexpected turn. The next day, Ron kept making unsubtle passes while explaining the responsibilities, until Randy obliged by giving him a discreet blowjob. "I'll never forget the look on the face of that disgusting man," he wrote. "He, lying on the floor, looking up at me. One testicle. He had the look of a humble, begging dog as he looked up at me. He utterly revolted me, and a bitter taste ran in my mouth." Randy's distaste was rivaled only by the surprise of his new boss, who told him that no employee had ever said yes to his advances before.

Randy would later recall his bathhouse misadventures in an unpublished essay written for *Blueboy*. His new coworkers weren't impressed by his college background, until he used his investigative skills to get Ron drunk, who let slip that he'd bugged the office. Knowing this information made it easier for them to slip outside to smoke weed or make a pass at a hot customer. Soon, even Ron couldn't help noticing how much better the place was running. As Randy typed out note cards explaining his job duties, Ron encouraged him to consider managing a bathhouse someday. After all, he advised, "This is a growth industry."

Ron wasn't wrong. The popularity of gay bathhouses was exploding as male homosexuality gained visibility. They were also, Randy noted, potentially lucrative. The Majestic had a seedy reputation, but it was honest about its function. The space boasted no extravagances like a dance floor, cocktail lounge, or cabaret, but it did have a group shower room and a television room for watching porn. On multiple floors, the hallways were populated with tiny rooms barely wide enough to hold a single bed.

For $2.50 an hour, Randy worked long days in the "clerk's cage," a desk behind bulletproof glass where he took customers' money and assigned them rooms according to the "toad chart," Ron's intricate system for assigning differently priced rooms based on appearance. "Cute" customers were assigned red-marked keys for $4 cubicles, located near the front entrance. "Semi-cute" men paid the same price but received black-tagged keys for rooms in the darker, less visible hallways.

"Toads," which the chart illustrated with photos of Leonid Brezhnev, Lawrence Welk, and Richard Nixon, were tersely informed that only rooms of $7–$10 were available. "Worst cases" were told that nothing was available, and they should try the Workout Baths up the street. Some poor souls would shuffle back and forth between establishments, with each claiming to be completely full.

Randy found the coding system heartless and cringeworthy, but his manager's suffocating personality left him little room to maneuver. With an apartment window overlooking the entrance, his crudely wired bugging system, and no life of his own, Ron spent hours monitoring the business. After making his own judgment on a customer's appearance, he'd eavesdrop to make sure the staff was charging the right amount.

During slow stretches, Randy passed the time laundering soiled linens and watching the Watergate hearings, as Nixon's drooping features scowled at him from the toad chart. On busy nights, the action would spill from private cubicles into the steam chamber and orgy rooms, whose mattress-lined floors made it necessary for staff to check every twenty minutes, to make sure no one was smoking. For their efforts at keeping the ancient building from going up in flames, employees were ridiculed as shameless voyeurs, who enjoyed spying on customers "happily engaged in every conceivable permutation of sodomy."

The Majestic's staff included "Skip," a rough "he-man" with a weakness for Republican-looking men in suits; "Sandy," who spent most days strung out on drugs; and "Cheryl," a pre-op trans woman who handled the swing shift. Cheryl had an almost motherly aura, Randy recalled, with looks that were considered "passable"; outside of work, she frequently tricked downtown with unsuspecting straight men. Cheryl also had no qualms about showing her breasts to curious gay friends and usually hid her Adam's apple by wearing floppy bows.

Everyone had reasons for hating Ron, but his particular brand of chauvinism helped bring Randy and Cheryl closer together. For work, she had to dress in plain sweatshirts, jeans, and sneakers. Furthermore, Ron let it be known that he rated her trans woman friends lower than even the toads. "Remember," he growled, "we're an institution for *men*. No girls or guys who look like girls."

Randy found his loyalties tested when one of Cheryl's friends tried to rent a room from him. Trapped by his boss's watchful eye, Randy had limited options. First, he tried the "full up" excuse, hardly convincing on a Tuesday afternoon. Then, he tried to pass the buck. "Well, you see my boss has this hang-up about this being a men's institution," he confided sheepishly.

The woman wasn't having it. "I think I can prove I've got all the necessary equipment," she answered, reaching to unzip.

Backed into a corner, Randy blurted out, "I'm sorry, we're full!" She'd have to try one of the baths down the street, which had already sent her to the Majestic. Exasperated, the woman smashed her purse against the glass before stalking out. Ron was quick to tell him he'd done well, but Randy instead recounted his actions and apologized to Cheryl, who nodded quietly.

Caught between his conscience and his job, Randy had chosen the latter, with remorse. His coworker Skip, on the other hand, always greeted trans women with a simple, gruff "Fuck off." Skip's hostility to trans women and effeminate men seemed especially curious, as he aspired to become the Emperor of Portland's Imperial Court. Since the 1950s, local drag queens had annually chosen an Empress and had recently begun crowning a consort to their queen.

Over the summer months, the Majestic's workers settled into a pattern so comfortable, it might've worked well as a sitcom. Obsessed with Watergate, Randy insisted that Shakespeare had foretold Nixon's demise in *King Lear*. Skip lusted after a buttoned-up Majestic regular with a hidden wedding ring, Cheryl recounted her latest tricks, and Sandy described the medical benefits of whatever drugs he was taking. Even Ron seemed to soften around the edges, owing to the sixteen-year-old lover who'd moved into his apartment. On August 8, 1974, Randy received two memorable birthday gifts: Nixon's resignation, and a Hostess chocolate cupcake with a single lit candle, presented by his coworkers singing "Happy Birthday" in a dark Majestic hallway.

On a cool Portland evening, Randy prepared for his autumn move back to Eugene. He'd left his bathhouse job, but the stories kept replaying in his mind. "I wanted this summer to be a trial run for what I would do when I joined the great oversoul which is now defined as real life," he reflected. "I'm beginning to appreciate that there is life after college, and realities after the dreams of earlier years." Fearing that he'd develop a reputation as a sex maniac, Randy told only a few friends about his Sexual Summer of '74. In the years to come, however, he'd remember his time among "a small society of outcasts" with fond amusement.

Randy's relationship with bathhouses was complicated from the very beginning. Although a patron himself, from the outset he found their business practices cynical at best, exploitative at worst. Thinking back on hookups that left him feeling disgusted and embarrassed, he discovered a compassion for the "toads" and "worst cases" who sought human contact in the Majestic's seedy confines. Everyone who walked through its doors, either as a customer or employee, had at least something in common: "lust . . . defined by a common sexual orientation."

By summer's end, the "pretty boy" had started growing out his Afro again. The year ahead would be busy, but as Randy readied himself to enter the world of journalism, he tucked away some interesting stories, the likes of which were mostly unknown to anyone outside of gay culture.

5 | THEY'D RATHER HAVE AN ALCOHOLIC

STANDING IN HIS ALLEN Hall classroom, Duncan McDonald could see he was in for a challenge. "In walks this fairly diminutive kid with sort of reddish brown . . . very undisciplined Afro, [who] had a purple boa around his neck and clogs," McDonald recalled. "He strutted in with what I called—I think about this all the time—a wary bravado. And [he] exuded probably a lot more confidence than he should've. But you know what? Probably not a day went by where he didn't feel the need to defend himself."

Randy's forwardness reminded McDonald of a yeoman named Kilpatrick he'd known in the navy who'd been surprisingly open about his homosexuality. "I remember how Kilpatrick had to constantly make himself bigger or stronger than he really was, just to kind of get through the fucking navy," he added. "We needed to understand what he went through even to do his job. And I felt the same way about Randy."

In McDonald's newspaper reporting class, Randy thrived by staying busy. Talkative but never disruptive, he took the work seriously but still had a habit of breezing past the finer details once he had a big idea. McDonald tried to apply a dose of humility. "I thought to myself, this is the last guy in the world who needs to be patted on the back," he explained. "He, in many ways, needs to be kicked in the butt a little more, because he is very, very good."

It was in the Erb Memorial Union men's room that John Mitchell first learned about his new classmate. "I was introduced to the subject of Randy Shilts on the side of the [stall]," John remembered. Among the usual witticisms,

33

someone had scrawled, "Randy Shilts is a fag!" Mitchell worked at the *Daily Emerald*, a magnet for the journalism school's best students, including editor-in-chief Drex Heikes and broadcast journalist Ann Curry. Even among these standouts, Randy seemed to excel. "And the rest of us," Mitchell allowed, "were pretty damn good."

Heikes hired Randy as managing editor, a job made easier, he thought, by Randy's openness. "It's kind of like he's had to develop a gregarious approach to life because he's gay," he explained. "What better person for the job than someone who treats everyone the same—as equals. He accepts everyone."

The *Emerald*'s staff typically worked long hours before trudging each morning to their early classes. Study parties were the norm, with booze, pot,

Randy Shilts at the *Oregon Daily Emerald*, 1975. *Courtesy of University of Oregon Special Collections and University Archives*

homework, and plenty of conversation about current events. On weekends, they'd all pile onto a sofa to watch NBC's new comedy show, *Saturday Night Live*.

In the aftermath of Watergate, journalism students were especially eager to find good stories. Randy's first investigative piece came during his class with Mike Thoele, another new adjunct professor filling in for Ken Metzler, who'd written the definitive book on creative interviewing. "I wasn't sure I belonged there at all," Thoele allowed, "and Randy made me less certain. He had skills that you wouldn't necessarily find in every journeyman journalist of that era."

Creative interviewing emphasizes preparation and rapport-building, drawing on psychology and the social sciences to establish trust. It requires authenticity, curiosity, patience, and a willingness to listen before probing for more sensitive information. At first, Randy's quick thinking and enthusiasm could be a little too quick, asking rapid-fire questions and jumping in before people finished speaking. Still, he took feedback well and made nearly flawless adjustments, causing Thoele to realize that Randy was outpacing his coursework. "I was constantly bugged by this idea of, what do I have to teach this kid?"

As an alternative assignment, Randy approached Thoele with an idea. For his first investigative feature, he wanted to write about drag queens. During the previous year's gay-straight sock hop, they'd delighted him; over the summer, he learned more about them while working at the Majestic. "It just bristled with such good interview possibilities," Mike remembered. "It was no problem saying yes to it."

The Portland Imperial Court's coronation ceremony drew revelers in everything from tuxedos to over-the-top camp. Randy landed interviews with reigning imperial majesty Donnie LaMay XVI, former empress Darcelle XV, and a state representative who was recognized for sponsoring a gay rights bill. The opening lines of his story sparkled with intrigue, transporting readers to the moment when Donnie LaMay crowned the new empress, Elsa XVII, before pivoting from the ballroom's pageantry to explain this colorful aspect of gay life to straight readers.

Drag, Randy clarified, should not be confused with transvestitism. Donnie LaMay and Darcelle compared it to fraternal orders and elk lodges, where heterosexuals gathered for drinks and cheap entertainment. "The whole thing is a show, a way to have fun," Darcelle explained. "It doesn't matter whether you're straight or gay, you have to learn how to laugh."

With a tale so unique and well-written, Randy scored his first big hit. The journalism faculty submitted his piece to the Hearst Foundations' monthly writing competition, resulting in Randy's first national award, fourth place, with a $300 cash prize.

———————

Heading into 1975, all signs pointed toward a rapid rise for the twenty-three-year-old Randy. His activism days appeared to be over, as he explained to the *Northwest Gay Review* how journalism gave him opportunities to change hearts and minds. Randy's aim was to work full-time at a daily, where he could hold a regular beat and offer his expertise on gay issues. However, he admitted, mainstream journalism could still lean conservative. "No matter how qualified I am, I might get the shaft. They'd rather have an alcoholic than a gay."

His *Emerald* coworkers had no such reservations. "I think this is worth mentioning," John Mitchell added. "He won that award as a reporter while he was managing editor . . . [which] is kind of like the HR manager for this entity." Outside of those responsibilities, Randy was assembling an impressive portfolio showing his versatility and range, from front-page features to campus theater reviews, student government reports, and the *Emerald*'s back-page filler, "Not So Long Ago at the U of O."

For his depictions of gay life, however, Randy started aiming for wider audiences. "I figured . . . all you have to do is get the facts out about gay people," he later recalled. "That's all you have to do is get the facts out and the facts speak for themselves. Basically I just feel you can put both sides out there and the truth will win out in the end." In February a reworked version of the Imperial Court story headlined the *Eugene Register-Guard*'s Sunday magazine, *Emerald Empire*. He soon followed it up with an investigative piece in the *Willamette Valley Observer*, illuminating how lesbians and gay men felt pressured to conceal their identities.

Again, the faculty submitted Randy's work to the monthly Hearst competition, where he fared even better the second time. The award letter, signed by Randolph A. Hearst, congratulated him on placing second, earning a $450 award. On the merits of his two prize-winning submissions, a coveted invitation soon arrived for the Hearst National Writing Championship, including round-trip flight to San Francisco and accommodations at the Clift Hotel.

The events that followed would remain disputed for the rest of Randy's life. On May 11, 1975, Randy arrived in San Francisco and made his way to the Hearst competition's first event: a cocktail party in the suite of the director of Hearst's college journalism scholarship program, Ira Walsh. "Did you see some of the bizarre stories entered in the contests?" someone asked. "One was even about transvestites!"

Randy eyed his drink nervously. "No, it wasn't about transvestites at all!" he interjected. *Drag queens weren't the same thing. They'd know that if they'd read the article,* he thought.

The party, comprised of judges, contestants, and foundation staff, fell into an embarrassed silence. As events proceeded, Randy detected an increasingly chilly response from the staff, even as he befriended his fellow finalists. One of his new friends mentioned hearing a Hearst staffer call Randy "too flamboyant" behind his back.

The contest included two speed writing challenges, the first involving a hard news article, followed by a personality sketch. He did well on the news piece, but the second was a little dry and had a minor typo. At the awards banquet, Randy won second place, a fair decision, he thought, as he agreed with the judges' critiques. But when collecting his medal, Randy couldn't help noticing how the foundation staff ignored him. Later, first place winner Kevin McCarthy told him that the staff admitted dreading the possibility of Randy winning.

With the competition finished, most of the finalists wanted to go dancing, and Randy, eager to play tour guide, took them to took them to the Cabaret, a popular gay disco that later reopened as the City. Although everyone seemed to enjoy themselves, Randy felt a chill when he ran into two Hearst staffers the next morning. "We heard about where you went last night," one of them said. He later learned that they'd questioned some of the other finalists, two of whom were allegedly told, "I don't see how you could go to a place where people were dancing with the wrong people."

Randy left San Francisco believing that he and his gayness were never really wanted there, packing up his second-place medal with assurances that a $1,000 check would be disbursed through his university. The first sign of trouble came when the foundation asked for his medal back to be engraved. The second warning sign came when it sent copies of every contestant's entries from the speed writing challenges.

Randy noticed that his articles were credited to another finalist, while someone else's writing was given his name. It had to be a photocopying error, he reasoned. The next day, the foundation called to say that the entries had been miscoded. Randy had not won second place but was merely a finalist. Instead of $1,000, he would only receive $250. The medal, he was reminded, would need to be returned.

Overcome with shock, Randy feebly agreed. As he thought it over, however, his mind began to spin. He knew that his work had been misattributed, but the difference in quality just screamed out to him. He could pinpoint the exact typo that had cost him first place. The judges had commented that the second-place entry had incorrectly written "that" instead of "who," he recounted. "And the lead of one of my stories was 'Dianne Feinstein is a woman that has learned her lessons.'"

"It was so devastating, because it was so unfair," he later reflected. "I just knew I was so good and that I'd do so well in this field, because I liked it so much and found it so exciting." The awards had boosted his confidence, while placing second nationally added a stamp of legitimacy. The university's president had already written to congratulate him.

"I remember it being a very dark day for him," John Mitchell recalled. "And it might actually have been longer than a day. It led to a rough period for him."

In the aftermath, Randy tried to find anyone who could help him. Professor Roy Halvorsen, the journalism school's point of contact with Hearst, had never actually met the star pupil, but he shared his colleagues' admiration. Randy called him right away. "I was outraged as anybody whose students had been so abused," Halvorsen recalled. Plainspoken and possessed with a stubborn sense of fairness, he contacted the foundation himself. "No less than a tie. If he won, he won," Halvorsen insisted. Their response didn't satisfy him at all. "I said simply that I am no longer your contact with the University of Oregon."

The School of Journalism's dean, John Crawford, echoed Halvorsen in a chastising letter to Ira Walsh: just call it a tie and let Randy keep his place. Walsh responded politely but firmly. The codes assigned to the finalists were transposed, thus both contestants had been credited with writing the incorrect entries. The foundation had considered awarding two second place prizes, but in the interest of fairness, decided against it. "If we upgraded the score on the piece written by Randy Shilts, would we not, in fairness, be required to do the same on others as well?" Hearst's decision was final, and in Walsh's opinion, it was fair. "Randy Shilts is a bright young man. He is an able student. We believe we would ill serve him by giving him an award he did not merit or win."

Although Randy only had circumstantial evidence, he was sure he'd written the better entry. Only the foundation staff knew which students' names were matched to which entries, and Walsh had insisted that the matter was closed. "It is conceivable that an office error was made," Randy acknowledged. "As a journalist . . . I cannot say it was due to prejudice unless I have black and white proof."

The evidence to support his suspicions would never materialize, but over time, Randy settled on his version of the facts, which he repeated with unflinching certainty: "They said they made a judging error. . . . Yeah. Right."

A mid-July twilight descended gently over the horizon as Randy steered through Portland's outskirts. These blue-collar neighborhoods offered him a sense of solace and familiarity as the sun began to sink in his rearview mirror. "I like these streets because they don't have curbs," he observed. "Instead, the lawns blend softly into the gravel and only a few run-over weeds ever complain about the lack of civilized curbs."

These solitary excursions in Randy's newly purchased used car helped distract him from his worries. Rent was due next week, he still hadn't bought car insurance, and his bank account showed only $37 to his name. "The pattern is distinct," he told himself. "They graduate, can't find a newspaper job and then unsuccessfully try to free-lance two or three articles."

Randy saw what was likely coming next. "Once their cars break down, however, they get their bar jobs and then slowly stop writing. Before long, they even stop talking about writing." He'd assumed freelancing would be easy. "After graduating from college with more honors and journalism awards than you can shake a Smith-Corona at, I figured the magazines would come begging at my feet for a few priceless paragraphs from my typewriter."

If not success, then at least some stability would be helpful. "Here's the scoop," he wrote to Ann and Chris. "For the past two months of my yet-young freelance career, Randy plays a monthly game called 'Go for Broke.'" In better times, he'd hide away $500 for emergencies. Now, it felt like a good month when he had even five dollars. From his freelancing income, he'd carefully budget his expenses, including $70 rent for a room in Southeast Portland. "And then," he recounted, "Usually in the last week of the month, something happens where I have to blow all my money." At the moment, one of his car wheels was about to fall off.

At least the San Francisco trip hadn't been a total waste. At the national gay newspaper the *Advocate*, news editor Sasha Gregory-Lewis had invited Randy to stop by during his visit, speak with their writers, and take some pictures for a potential feature. It seemed like good publicity, and as rejections from prospective employers were piling up, he also needed a job.

At the *Advocate*, Randy found a sympathetic ear. "Sorry to hear about your disenchantment with the straight media," Sasha wrote, offering to send him as much work as she could. "Freelancing is not generally the most lucrative thing to do in the world," she added, "unless you have a couple of books under your belt, or have established a name some other way."

Randy's *Advocate* debut as "Northwest Correspondent" came in June 1975, in an article on colleges' gay studies courses. It was an unremarkable story, made more interesting by the fanfare he received as the paper's newest addition. The feature included Randy's photo in a tan sport jacket, leaning back and smiling. "Randy Shilts is an up and coming member of a new breed of gay people in America," the *Advocate* proclaimed. "The open young gay person trying to break into a profession." In a separate issue, the editors cast shade at his writing contest fiasco: "We'll overlook the fact that the Hearst newspaper empire originated 'yellow journalism.'"

While freelancing wouldn't pay much, Randy was actually getting paid to write, and the *Advocate* offered him wider exposure. The paper would pay him up to $150 for longer features and up to $20 for smaller briefs, and Sasha would entertain reprinting his earlier work for $50. For years, he'd scraped by with any job he could find, but now he vowed to work only as a writer. If he was to avoid being sucked into an everyday job, some other freelance gig would have to come along.

Though his byline began to appear more frequently in the *Advocate*, Randy's attempts to break into a daily didn't fare so well. He did manage to get published a couple times in *Willamette Week*, but for the most part, he was stuck. At every opportunity, Randy pressed Gregory-Lewis with new ideas, detailing his expanding network of northwest sources. When she encouraged him to focus on national stories, he pitched features on gay Jewish groups, gay parents, and rural gays, as well as a profile on a Seattle professional networking association known as the Dorian Group, a "gay chamber of commerce" comprised of older, more conservative members of the community.

In Washington State, Randy caught word of probate proceedings involving a middle-aged gay couple fostering a troubled gay teen, whose custody had been revoked by a judge who refused to even hold a hearing. The monthslong dispute ended with the teenager remanded to juvenile detention until another placement could be found; in his coverage, Randy closed by quoting the motto inscribed above the judge's bench: "The impartial administration of justice is the foundation of liberty."

Simultaneously, Randy kept coming back to his deeply hurt feelings around the Hearst awards. Desperate for cash, he tried again to recover his rescinded prize money and rally support from the U of O's faculty, led by Roy Halvorsen. To Halvorsen, the underlying injustice of the matter concerned how indecently a student had been treated. "I wish merely to communicate to you my feeling of utter disenchantment with your organization as the result of its shoddy treatment of our contestant," he wrote to Ira Walsh. "Such treatment, it seems to me, is unworthy of an organization with the lofty goals, values and motivations that the Hearst Foundation claims."

In the end, everyone stuck to their own version of the facts, and for many years after, the U of O journalism school simply declined to nominate their top students for the Hearst awards, out of disgust for how Randy had been treated.

"Sooner or later I better sit down and ask myself what it is I want out of my body, out of my mind." Glass of wine in hand, Randy settled in for a round of what he considered typewriter therapy. With the end of 1975 approaching, he sat staring at a life that seemed stuck in neutral. "I seem to be nobody, nowhere," he wrote. "Despite the fact that I have some talent, no one seems ready to make use of it and I have ever-familiar feelings of rejection—loneliness. Unappreciation."

Thinking back on the past five years, Randy wondered, *Was it all beginner's luck?* The Hearst disappointment, followed by this monthslong slide, left him questioning whether he truly belonged in journalism, or if all he really wanted was to become famous. "To be sure, I never will surrender my desire to be an important person," he admitted before quickly recanting. "I should clarify that: I don't need to be important." But, he added, "I need to be loved and/or liked. I use my career as a way of getting that affection and attention which I feel (perhaps erroneously) that I cannot get through myself."

At the moment, he was living out of a suitcase, having packed up and headed north on a six-week search for stories. Until he found a new city to call home, he told Sasha Gregory-Lewis, he'd write up and phone in his stories from the road. It wasn't his first option. After an October fling with a cinematographer from Wisconsin, he'd tried to convince the editors to send him to Chicago as a permanent correspondent. Gregory-Lewis sent back her regrets, saying there just wasn't enough money to pay him a staff salary for doing essentially the same work in a different city. What about moving to San Francisco, she suggested? He'd certainly have more work with the *Advocate*, and the freelance market was much larger.

Romantically, Randy's efforts had fallen into the same, predictable pattern, spending upwards of twenty hours a week at the bars. Even on those occasions when romance struck, he'd soon lapse back into crushing self-doubt, followed by an overeager desire to please. "How inadequate I feel next to him," Randy wrote of his Wisconsin fling. "Utterly inadequate. Here I am, working for a second-rate paper which doesn't seem to give a shit about me, writing second-rate stories by formula."

By process of elimination, San Francisco was his most logical destination. Yet, he dreaded the prospect of starting over. "A major thing which has me hesitating . . . is the fact that I'll be at the bottom again," he fretted. "In a crummy apartment, sparsely decorated, living a poor man's lifestyle. The kind of lifestyle I've lived all my adult life."

In Moscow, Idaho, he'd profiled gay activist Gib Preston, a former conservative who'd stayed in his hometown rather than flee to a larger city. Next, the open road took him to Vancouver, followed by a visit to Seattle's Stonewall Therapeutic Center, a groundbreaking facility where openly gay counselors worked with gay patients and ex-offenders, focusing on disrupting the homophobic messages they'd absorbed and confronting their harmful thoughts and behaviors. Each person's homosexuality, instead of being treated as the cause of their condition, was accepted and affirmed.

"I could relate to them all," Randy observed. In case after case—the lesbian who wanted to leave treatment and find a relationship, the pedophile who disclosed feelings of inadequacy around other adults, the compulsive "tearoom" cruiser—Randy connected with aspects of himself. He ached for a meaningful relationship, struggled to behave maturely in grownup situations, and cruised for sex just as compulsively.

"A key focus of the center was not stuffing feelings and I became intensely aware of all the feeling-stuffing I do. All the men I've liked without telling them . . . what I wanted to say, but never did. All the people there had lessons for me." On one hand, Randy realized that he wasn't alone and that plenty of gays shared his struggles. On the other hand, after coming so far and learning so much, he still had no idea where he was headed. "A part of me says that I'm learning a lot from these feelings, but another part says that I'm learning only loneliness."

The only story he had left to cover was a Seattle appearance by Sergeant Leonard Matlovich, the gay serviceman featured on a *Time* magazine cover that fall. Touring the country with national gay leaders Bruce Voeller and Charlotte Bunch, Matlovich himself was hardly a new story, but he and Randy struck up a lasting friendship from their encounter. More intriguingly, Randy had attracted the attentions of Voeller, a founder of the National Gay and Lesbian Task Force. A dashing figure in his early forties, the scholar-turned-activist commanded attention with both his handsomeness and his advocacy. When Voeller met the starry-eyed freelancer, the seduction didn't take long.

"We had terrific sex together," Randy gushed over his typewriter. "He accepted me and repeatedly told of how he was 'taken in' by me." They carried on throughout the weekend, with Randy confessing his anxieties to Voeller, who soothed him with compliments and encouragement. He'd fantasized about sleeping with Bruce for months after reading about him in the gay press. Likewise, Voeller confessed wanting to meet Randy for a long time as well. "He said I was a good writer."

"How could anybody not like you?" Voeller teased, why would he spend the entire weekend with someone he didn't admire? When the weekend ended, however, Randy once more sat alone, puzzling over his feelings. "I think it's a rejection I feel when I leave these weekend lovers," he pondered. Still, the usual loneliness felt different this time. In the arms of someone who was clearly a big deal, it felt like maybe Randy could be important too. Thinking back on their lovemaking, he resolved, "If I want to do something of which to be proud, it's up to me and I better get to work."

One lesson was already becoming clear: Randy needed to embrace some humility and accept that he had yet to become the big deal that he wanted to be, and he was going to have to work for it. "Don't try to opt for a big position unless you're willing to get your ass in gear and earn it."

Heading into the holidays, he began planning his next steps. Sasha Gregory-Lewis had invited him to stay at her home in Half Moon Bay so he could check out San Francisco. With a new year and a fresh start barely two weeks away, he accepted the invitation. "I'm brimming with ideas of stories to do in S.F.," Randy wrote, "and sincerely hope we can work something out so that I can move down there and start doing some of the writing of which I think I'm capable. (I yet have to operate up to my potential.)" Signing off, he added a breezy afterthought that practically winked from the page: "Bruce Voeller told me to send you his love."

6 | THE MISFIT OF CASTRO STREET

THE FAMILIAR FEELINGS WERE hard to miss: trying to catch a break in a new city, desperately needing validation, and dreading the prospect of defeat. Randy arrived in the Bay Area determined to work his ass off but knowing he needed some breaks. At the *Advocate*, only Sasha Gregory-Lewis had been helpful. New editor-in-chief Robert McQueen, his attentions fixed on another young freelancer, had only offered to show Randy how to get to the nearest street corner. It was a not-so-subtle message.

"Does he know what it is to stand like a slut?" Randy seethed. "Like a whore on a street corner, somehow hoping that one of the Castro Street tramps will pick you up?" To the crowds roaming San Francisco's rapidly growing gay ghetto, he could've easily been mistaken for just another transient on the sidewalk, tricking for a place to stay. His self-respect flattened, Randy could barely hold back the tears. His ambitions, only recently revived, seemed on the verge of collapse before he'd even settled in. "Here I am—the nobody whore. Alone again."

With nowhere else to turn, Randy steered his car through the run-down streets of the Mission District, arriving at an unremarkable apartment building where his only friend in the city was waiting to take him in. After Linda Alband moved to San Francisco in 1973, Randy became her first and most frequent visitor. Now she, her roommate Annie, and Annie's young son, Adam, made room for him in their tiny flat near Dolores Park. For now, he had a place to stay and, most important, friends to cheer him up. "We were in a rough neighborhood," Linda recalled. Adam was the only blonde child on a diverse, working-class block, where most parents held two jobs and spoke little English.

The living arrangement exemplified the squalor and opportunity of San Francisco's changing demographics. Linda's apartment was conveniently situated between the night life in South of Market and the Castro District, leading to all kinds of outrageous encounters. On one memorable occasion, Linda introduced Randy to a workmate whose gay friend had once sung backup for Janis Joplin. Nicknamed "Pearl" by Janis herself, he effected a flawless imitation, Linda remembered. "He'd channel Janis Joplin," she whispered reverently. "It was really strange."

Randy and Pearl took the women on a rollicking tour of the city's gay bars, elbowing past the Toad Hall bouncers who tried to keep women out so that Linda and her friend could enter. For their efforts, the women rewarded them by insisting they go to the lesbian hangouts, Peg's Place and Maud's. The women inside were more amused than offended by the two fearful young gays, causing Linda to laugh. "Boy, were they scared. They were just really scared to

Randy Shilts in Linda Alband's San Francisco apartment, mid-1970s.
Photo by Linda Alband, courtesy of the photographer

go into the lesbian bars. And the women were just fine with them! They just thought it was all so funny."

The evening wasn't over. "We were so drunk, we ended up at the 99-cent pornos," Linda continued. Seated in a shabby old theater in the middle of the Tenderloin, surrounded by old Chinese men who didn't want to pay for sex, the foursome giggled their way through a succession of terrible old black-and-white films, with titles like *A Rod for Revenge*. "You know, we were so drunk and laughing, I'm sure we ruined the show for these guys. We were so bad, but we had a big night out."

The more Randy explored, the more he came across facets of gay life that defied easy stereotyping. "I was a deejay in a couple of gay country bars," friend Howie Klein remembered. Already a well-traveled music journalist and promoter, Howie had worked with both Jefferson Starship and Blue Öyster Cult. The two hit it off because Howie liked to play younger "outlaw" country artists like Willie Nelson, as well as the occasional ballad for slow dancing. "Randy liked it, liked the atmosphere and what that place was all about," Howie recalled. "It was a free-spirited place that wasn't like the discos that were popular at the time, which neither he nor I liked very much."

Beyond music, the two also found they agreed on other issues concerning gay culture. The arrival of the "Castro Clone" reflected a new "post-camp" aesthetic, which demanded a certain conformity: "people who wore the same kind of clothes," Howie remembered, "or the same kind of pressed jeans and a kind of a look and a kind of a mustache."

"You know, at one time to be a gay man meant to be a rebel," he continued. "It literally was something that was attractive to people who had a rebellious personality and a rebellious nature. And then suddenly there's this whole clone mentality, which was the opposite of being rebellious, where people were just trying to be robots and just be like everybody else. And I know I found that to be kind of repulsive, and I think that Randy and I bonded around that."

If the clothing makes the man, then gay male culture by the mid-'70s was blowing up old stereotypes of how to be a man who made love to other men. Aside from the ever-popular stroke magazines, "serious" newspapers like the *Advocate* packed their pages with nightlife features and advertisements signaling how to dress, talk, and posture oneself, depending on the setting. Randy's explorations soon took on a more salacious aspect, from hardcore leather bars to self-discovery courses promising to expand one's sexual horizons.

At home, he spared Linda few details. "He'd tell me everything, like, he'd feel bad that he didn't like to take it up the ass, so he was taking classes on learning how to do it, and they were using carrots," she recalled. "But then he decided there were so many bottoms out there, that he didn't need to feel guilty anymore."

With a stable living situation and steady friends, Randy quickly found his focus, but he wasn't about to rest easy. "The *Advocate* is no place to spend a lifetime or even a long career span," he told himself. "At best, it is a place to develop my writing talents until I go to the next level." His vision for that next level hadn't wavered: a regular beat at a major newspaper, with a respectable readership and reputable content.

Being the new face in town, at a national gay paper with stiff local competition, Randy needed credible sources and fresh story ideas. Nobody in San Francisco had even noticed his arrival, but Randy was determined that people would soon know his name. The work began in earnest at Linda's kitchen table, where he'd sit typing for hours. *OK, Shilts*, he vowed as the pieces seemed to fall into place. *Go in there and give them hell.*

The idea came from several back-and-forth exchanges with Randy's news editor; the result would be longer and more intricate than any story he'd ever written, breaking the silence on an issue that hit decidedly close to home. Since its earliest issues, the *Advocate* had made brief mentions of the scattered community centers, social services, and Alcoholics Anonymous groups helping gays around the country. Tucked mostly into passing news briefs, the coverage was generally eclipsed by political news and an abundance of advertising for gay bars and bathhouses. Now, the paper's new investigative reporter was suggesting that addiction could be endemic to gay life itself.

"Out of sight, removed and at an uneasy distance from thought and conversation, the subject of alcoholism in the gay subculture has been ignored for far too long," Randy wrote, detailing in eight tight pages the complicated conditions driving what experts considered to be an unrecognized pandemic. In 1975, Los Angeles social worker Lillene Fifield released findings from a three-month study, suggesting as many as one-third of that city's gay men and lesbians were either in a crisis stage or rapidly approaching that level of drinking. Though Fifield's findings came from an admittedly limited sample, Randy did his homework, corroborating her data with anecdotes from gay addiction counselors in Chicago, San Francisco, Kansas City, and Seattle.

To say the least, Randy was tackling a risky subject, illuminating a darker side of gay life and questioning a community pillar, which also provided substantial ad revenue for the *Advocate* and other papers. Gay bars were big business, and Randy understood the culture all too well. The bar scene may serve a vital social purpose, he argued, but it also took advantage of customers' loneliness with cheap drink specials and free salty snacks to keep them thirsty. Among lesbians, who had fewer bars to choose from, he described how private house parties often functioned in the same way.

"There are no new alcoholism stories," a gay addiction worker in South Carolina told him. "Just 150 variations on the same theme." Among the men he interviewed, Randy found a pattern: drinking to cope with being gay or having to keep it a secret; as a response to loneliness or to stress caused by their job or family; or with a codependent friend or lover who would try to help by mixing cocktails after work, pouring some wine to calm the nerves, or keeping the liquor shelf at home fully stocked. It could take years to recognize the symptoms of addiction, and when gay alcoholics did seek treatment, Randy warned, "they often find that nothing is there."

Gay men and lesbians who went to mainstream treatment providers were often warned to conceal their identity, or that they'd have to deal with their homosexuality before tackling their addiction issues. Some were discharged simply for admitting they were gay. One solution, Randy suggested, would be to have more gay organizations, staffed by gay workers, who understood and could help other gay people with their problems. In a few short years, providers like Seattle Stonewall and L.A.'s Gay Community Services Center had already expanded from tiny volunteer efforts to secure significant public funding. Beyond simply fostering acceptance of lesbian and gay identities, these mostly unknown workers helped people work through problems like depression, loneliness, addiction, mental illness, and homelessness.

For those who completed treatment, Randy described a sense of optimism and renewal. "The recovered talk of a rediscovered *joie de vivre*, amazing new reserves of energy—and, they all add, a startling and new-found appreciation of their sex lives." Still, he noted, treatment alone wouldn't solve a problem that was part of gay culture itself. Just as lesbians and gay men were working to liberate themselves from an oppressive society, so too would they need to liberate themselves from addiction.

It was Randy's most extensive writing to date, longer than his *King Lear* thesis and harder-hitting than his award-winning college journalism features. His tone, blending hard numbers with personal stories, hinted at familiarity with the subject matter, but on that point, Randy revealed nothing. At his suggestion, the editors added a disclaimer reminding readers of his nationally recognized work. In the same issue, an accompanying commentary labeled alcoholism "an insidious disease," which the gay community needed to address by supporting its own community services.

Beyond simply writing newsworthy gay stories, Randy had demonstrated a willingness to illuminate the complications and pitfalls of life among the liberated. From here, his writing accelerated to where it seemed that Shilts-authored content filled at least half of each new issue. Since he was rarely assigned to cover any A-list luminaries, he instead set about finding what was newsworthy in everyday life, among ordinary people. Even the latest fashion trend, "the year of the curl," earned a Randy Shilts byline, as the hottest men suddenly seemed to be modeling his ever-present Afro. After years of trying to reconcile his scruffy, unconventional looks with an increasingly chiseled, hypermasculine gay aesthetic, he drily observed, "Permanents are the biggest thing to hit gaydom since Crisco."

His career seemed to finally be regaining momentum. In the same Tax Day issue where he detailed how little the government gave back to gay taxpayers in benefits and services, Randy also seized on the issue of sexual ambiguity in rock 'n' roll. Profiling the likes of Mick Jagger, the Kinks, and Elton John, he chided the music industry for tiptoeing around homosexuality with subtle, innuendo-laden lyrics. The songs made much more sense, he argued, if Elton would just admit he was singing about other men.

For an insider's perspective, he turned to San Francisco legend Sylvester, whose anthems seemed to succeed because listeners could interpret them however they wanted. As one of pop music's only openly gay celebrities, Sylvester knew how full the industry's closet was. But, he told Randy, commercial viability mattered more within the industry than being openly gay. The kind of honesty Randy imagined just didn't connect with the general public. With a touch of exasperation, he conceded, "Homosexuality doesn't sell records."

The voice Randy had been refining since college was beginning to assert itself. In story after story, supported by his growing web of sources, he laid the foundation for a simple premise: the experiences of everyday gay folks were newsworthy, and gay people would be better served by putting everything, no matter how uncomfortable or unsavory, out in the open.

Next, he turned his sights toward another underattended crisis reaching epic proportions. "Gay V.D. workers have stopped using the term 'epidemic' lately," Randy announced in April. "The diseases have made inroads into the gay community that health experts call 'pandemic.'" Again, he had the sources and figures at his command. According to the Centers for Disease Control, roughly half of the nation's male syphilis cases could be attributed to gay men, along with 40 percent of male gonorrhea infections. Other infections, like herpes, genital warts, and hepatitis, were also on the rise.

Much of the problem, he argued, lay at the feet of America's public health establishment. Though government officials "bellyached" at the number of sexually transmitted diseases passed among gay men, the response was largely more of the same: dumping money into public programs that remained insensitive to gays, while providing next to nothing for education programs or clinics run by and for the gay community.

As with his alcoholism story, the heroes of Randy's reporting were the unknown, overworked workers at gay clinics and chronically underfunded community services. With private physicians, gay patients were likely to fare worse. Randy cited patients who had been treated with outright hostility at clinics and hospitals, where instead of proper treatment they found themselves harassed, intimidated, and lectured about their lifestyles. Doctors often neglected to collect rectal or throat cultures for gonorrhea, despite a growing number of cases attributed to anal sex. Yet again, it seemed, the gay community was having to fight a pandemic on its own.

Randy's investigative approach was clearly making an impression on readers, as nearly every issue included mostly favorable letters. "Mr. Shilts obviously did his homework quite well," one reader wrote of the alcoholism feature. "A million dollars of government funds could not do as much good for the cause as the article you have published." Another added, "Mr. Shilts, God Bless!" Although fewer, his critics also put in a word, taking issue with supposedly sweeping conclusions about the "gay community—whatever that overgeneralized term may mean," that used "scare language" in the manner of infamous reparative therapy advocate Charles Socarides.

For better or for worse, Randy was getting recognition, and with it came a sense of security. In midspring, when the *Advocate* made him a full-time staff writer, he paid for hypnosis to quit smoking and moved into his own place. "I was just glad when he moved out and wasn't living with me anymore," Linda remembered, "because then I didn't sit up and wait for him to come home." Even in the gayest parts of San Francisco, men were known to turn up dead or brutally beaten. With Randy's nose for finding stories, Linda couldn't help worrying. "When he first was living was us . . . he'd also drop little bombs like, he was thinking about infiltrating the gay Nazis. That made me really nervous."

After a year of upheaval leading to what finally felt like an arrival, Randy packed his old Toyota with camping gear and headed down to Big Sur. "I've got quite a bit to figure out," he wrote to Ann and Chris. "Well, honey, here I am in my first full-time job, having achieved a career . . . and what do you do now?" Randy's head was filled with recent anniversaries. "I've realized how much I've gone through," he wrote. "Now I want to sort of purge all that from me and get going on something new."

Yet, at every turn, Randy was confronted by familiar feelings. His retreat into the redwoods evoked memories of scouting, sleeping under the stars, and being startled at every sudden noise. On the second night, he met an aspiring young actor, irresistibly wholesome, who was hiking the trails with an equally adorable Irish Setter. It only took some brief flirting and a bottle of wine for them to snuggle in for the evening, but not much would happen beyond that. "We're to see each other again," he recounted, "but by the time I read this again he will be forgotten."

By the next evening, Randy had fully regained his Eagle Scout form, coaxing a humble fire out of leaves, twigs, and chunks of fallen redwood. With aching muscles, he sat waiting for his cocoa to cool, whittling stir sticks with the knife he'd bought for the trip. He'd overshot his destination by a good four miles. Across the creek, he noticed a pair of handsome guys settling down together. The feelings he'd tried so hard to set aside were again stirring up. Why couldn't that be him?

"Would if my love was at the 8-mile campsite and I missed him," he wrote, then caught himself. "Jesus, I can't let myself do anything without a would if behind it. That has been a problem." Every chance encounter left him longing for a more permanent intimacy. Unable to shake the loneliness, Randy felt his frustrations boiling over. "So I've chased that big honey for four years now, four long lonely years," he lamented. "Through the 80° hallways of baths, through hundreds of crowds in hundreds of bars to catch only a silent glimpse of what could be."

By morning, the couple had already vanished, and in their absence, Randy felt a longing to return to his new home in the city. Packing up the campsite, he made a final climb, ascending to the top of a rocky scenic outgrowth. Gazing upon the densely packed treetops below, he reflected on how crowded his life was becoming: "My head is filled so with the voices of those around me that I often lose touch with that voice of my own."

With that, Randy hiked back through the forest and found his way to the open road. Life wasn't perfect, he acknowledged, but it was the only path he could follow. In these reflective moments, it seemed that a retreat into solitude only reminded him of how lonely he really felt.

———————

It was during an unmistakably gay fundraiser for state assembly candidate Art Agnos that David Goodstein, the *Advocate*'s publisher, spotted a bearded young newcomer in the crowd. Working his way across the room, Goodstein tapped the young man's shoulder, only to abruptly pull back when attorney Walter Caplan swung around, revealing his HARVEY MILK FOR STATE ASSEMBLY button. "Oh, son, you've made a big mistake!" Goodstein thundered, poking his finger in Walter's face. The larger-than-life kingmaker then launched into a tirade about Milk and his followers, calling them "street people" who were chasing dreams of revolution, who had no common sense or patience.

The shabbily dressed camera shop owner was viewed mainly as a nuisance by self-appointed leaders like Goodstein. A recent law school graduate, Walter wasn't particularly interested in taking the bait, but he attracted the amused attention of one of Goodstein's reporters. Covering the event for the *Advocate*, Randy waited to chat with Walter until Goodstein stalked away. Then, in full view of his boss, Randy invited Walter home. "I don't remember exactly what we did that night," Walter laughed. "But knowing me, I have a pretty good idea."

The era's laid-back energy made it easy for young Turks like Walter and Randy to strike up a conversation, sleep together, and then stay friends. As they sat up all night talking, Randy told Walter his entire life story. The next morning, Walter remembered, Randy gloried in the noisy traffic and construction work. This, he beamed, was the sound of the city. "All of these noises and sounds just had him"—Walter paused to reflect—"effervescent."

As much as Randy could project confidence, Walter observed, "He was very much alone. It was all Randy. I mean, he didn't have a benefactor, he didn't have a penny, he didn't have anything. He had nothing but Randy." That determination to blaze his own trail reminded Walter of the man whose state assembly campaign had so angered David Goodstein. "He was a force in a way not dissimilar from Harvey. I mean, they were both really dynamic forces that were gonna do whatever they could."

From the beginning of Milk's political career, Walter had been a loyal foot soldier. Going against San Francisco's gay political establishment, the self-proclaimed Mayor of Castro Street projected an air of certainty about his, and the movement's, eventual victory. In Randy, Walter recognized that same determination. "He was very optimistic about who he was and what his future had in store. And it was exciting!"

Randy's career was about to gain even more momentum when the *Advocate* decided to send him to the Democratic National Convention in New York. In mid-July, press credentials in hand, he arrived in Manhattan dreaming big. The city had just hosted the official bicentennial celebration, with tall ships depositing an impressive collection of sailors from around the world in Manhattan's gay bars and bathhouses.

Randy arrived with two main objectives: find the definitive gay story at the DNC and showcase his abilities to major news organizations. From national movement leaders to closeted party delegates and protestors in the street, he canvassed the proceedings for any evidence of gay and lesbian inroads into the mainstream. That search, however, led him to conclude that there wasn't much to say.

For their part, Democratic Party leaders weren't feeling much urgency around an issue that was considered well outside the norm with heartland voters. Facing an incumbent president of middling popularity, the Democrats were playing it safe on social issues under the Carter-Mondale banner. At the same time, national gay leaders seemed satisfied with modest, low-profile victories. Randy noted an impressive flurry of press releases from the National Gay Task Force, but the accomplishments they trumpeted were undeniably pale:

establishment of a Gay Rights Support Caucus by four openly gay delegates, a petition signed by over 650 delegates supporting the repeal of laws prohibiting consensual sex, and on-the-record support of gay rights by the Democratic Women's and Democratic Youth Caucuses.

The moderate gays' approach was doing little to spark a groundswell for changing Americans' attitudes, customs, or laws concerning homosexuality, Randy observed. Gays working within the party had little in common with the street activists, and a gay rights rally in Washington Square, for which organizers predicted as many as 10,000 demonstrators, drew a crowd of around 650. Even as establishment leaders tried to put a positive spin on their accomplishments, Randy offered a cloudier summation: "Gay rights have yet to emerge as an issue which either the politicians or the voters take seriously as a national concern."

It made for a bleak assessment, but that unenthusiastic tone was nothing compared to the blackening moods and fatigue that had begun to preoccupy his days. Something felt off, but words, for once, escaped him. Randy returned to San Francisco with plenty of reason for optimism, but instead, he was struggling to even get out of bed. "The dark moods didn't make any sense," he later recounted. "The blackness persisted—each day a little darker than before."

As July rolled into August, he turned to others for support. "People at work are getting worried about me because I've been acting strange," he wrote to Ann on the eve of his twenty-fifth birthday. "I mean I've been quiet, subdued, uncheerful—seriously. I don't know what's happening." A week later, the situation wasn't looking any better. "I've been so god damn miserably catatonic that I haven't had the energy to do anything much less write a letter," he complained to Ann. "This is getting serious. I don't know myself."

As the listlessness and dark moods reached five weeks without any sign of improvement, Randy could only come up with one explanation: "I think it's because I've been so miserably lonely." It had to be the surest cause. "I don't think I have any reason to get better so I'm not." The truth finally dawned on him when, looking closely in the mirror, Randy realized his eyes and skin were yellow. A visit to the clinic confirmed the culprit was hepatitis B.

"My doctor thinks I'll be getting better in a week or so," he told Ann. "I'm so relieved. Hopefully I'll be returning to my old cheerful and energetic self." The diagnosis raised Randy's spirits, but his optimism proved premature as, instead of getting better, he started feeling worse. Signs of improvement were followed by sudden, severe relapses, a pattern that repeated over days, weeks, and eventually three and a half more months. As Linda and other friends came by to check in and bring him chicken soup, Randy watched from the sidelines as the '76 election rumbled toward Carter's narrow victory over incumbent Gerald Ford.

After such a wildly productive start, Randy's reporting shrank from nearly filling entire issues to a feeble trickle. He fully returned to work just before Christmas, weak but on the mend, sorely missing his Oregon friends, and hopeful that life would finally return to normal. Before taking on the year ahead, however, Randy had a score to settle with the disease that almost killed him. The experience had been a wake-up call, and he returned in full force to the *Advocate*, determined to sound the alarm.

Echoing his earlier work, Randy assembled an impressive array of experts from around the country, weaving together transmission facts with epidemiology and casting a familiar scowl at public health's flimsy efforts to address another deadly gay health crisis. But unlike those previous features, this one adopted an unusually personal tone.

In vivid detail, Randy recounted his nightmarish illness and infuriatingly slow recovery. Setting aside his usual quasi hypotheticals, he centered the story around his own frightful experiences, making it clear that he'd contracted the disease sexually. In making an example of himself as a hep B survivor, he assumed the uncomfortable position of signaling exactly what he'd done to become infected.

"There is a greater possibility of picking this up in the gay community because of sexual techniques," Dr. Selma Dritz, of San Francisco Department of Public Health's Bureau of Disease Control, told him. "Even if it's penis to rectum—the penis will eventually get to someone's mouth, or when it's touched, it will carry the germs." Coming from someone just a little older than his mother, her frankness around the mechanics of anal intercourse immediately commanded Randy's attention and respect.

Over her career in public health, Selma had amassed an impressive number of admirers. She was direct, considerate, respectful, and, above all else, a really good quote. His affection for the venerable doctor, it turned out, was mutual. In the future, the two would rely closely on each other whenever sexual health issues arose. Just a few months later, Randy would cite her again in a report on gastrointestinal infections, bluntly headlined, "A New Plague on Our House."

For the moment, however, Randy was looking forward to putting the year behind him. While out at a restaurant on New Year's Eve, he picked up a familiar, and not unwelcome, signal in the men's room: "Cute little devil." Maybe he could ring out the year on a high note, after all. Randy coaxed the sexy stranger home, navigating the hopelessly chaotic bedroom where he always kept a pathway to the bed. The visitor suddenly paused. "He said he had to get something from his car—and then he disappeared."

Waiting for the sound of returning footsteps, Randy realized his trick had left him. Naked and alone, he had only his thoughts to keep him company as midnight arrived. It was a near-perfect letdown, symbolizing the highs and lows of the past year. Was there anything to look forward to in the new year, other than more dashed hopes and unfulfilled desires? From the vantage point of his cold, half-empty bed, it was difficult to tell.

7 | THE FOREST FOR THE TREES

HE HAD TO WAIT the entire trip to tell someone, dashing off a quick, giddy note to Ann once he'd come home. "This probably will be a letter you never expected to read," Randy wrote. "I know I never expected to write it." In January, he'd gone to Oklahoma to cover a proposed gay rights ordinance that was polling surprisingly well in Tulsa, but it was his visit to the Queen of Hearts, a local gay bar, that truly captured his attentions. "I saw him standing in a disco there and I knew I had to have him."

Diminutive and soft-spoken, Daniel Yoder sported wavy dark hair and a thick mustache adorning "the greatest smile I've ever seen in my whole life." After a couple weeks of love letters and long-distance calls, Dan decided to leave conservative, small-town Oklahoma for life in the Bay Area with Randy. It was difficult to tell who felt luckier. "The main reason he's coming here is because he said he 'was afraid of losing' me by staying in Oklahoma," Randy wrote to Ann. "I just can't believe that anybody could possibly be afraid of losing me."

Quiet, shy, and with a lifelong hearing impairment, Dan rarely spoke up in crowds, Randy believed, to avoid teasing. In many ways, they were perfectly matched: the soft-spoken Dan, with no desire for fame, and Randy, perpetually craving attention. But with the excitement of his first live-in lover came a new set of worries. "Danny isn't like me," Randy fretted. "He's normal and I'm not sure that he knows me well enough to know that I'm . . . well . . . a little different from your run-of-the-mill 25-year-old." They marked Dan's arrival with a honeymoon trip to Oregon, and by late spring, they'd moved into a quaint Victorian duplex at Liberty and Valencia.

Meanwhile, Randy found out that public television station KQED was seeking a gay reporter for its popular program *KQED Newsroom*. "I thought that might be a feather in our cap," recalled George Osterkamp, who offered Randy his first freelance television gig, "something that would fill out our news coverage in an area that we just weren't doing anything." Presented with a skilled journalist who understood the complexities of gay issues, the veteran news director didn't hesitate.

"Nobody was doing anything," Osterkamp explained. "So, I thought this was a chance to make our mark. I feel like I took a chance on Randy, and Randy took a chance on us. And I think it worked out pretty well." For a nightly news show known for brash, innovative reporting, hiring an equally brash young journalist made sense. Randy threw a multitude of ideas into his pitch, including many he'd already published in the *Advocate*. At the same time, television offered tempting ideas for broadening his portfolio.

"While I was very interested in coverage of the gay community," George recalled, "Randy wanted to be able to cover other things, and he would pitch a lot of other stories that had nothing to do with gay life. Sometimes there was competition among reporters who were designated as the health reporter, or the environmental reporter, or the political reporter."

Beyond newsroom politics, Randy also had to learn brevity in a medium where images were more powerful than words. In the beginning, his scripts still resembled newspaper stories. "We had a lot of print reporters who were trying to learn television," George remembered. "Randy learned faster than most, but he still had that big learning curve of what to strip away and what to keep."

The year was quickly becoming the most captivating in gay liberation's young history, presenting both Randy and the movement with surprising opportunities. "My whole world is trembling," he wrote to Ann. The timing couldn't have been better, as gay advocates and their opponents alike were looking to Gay Mecca to better understand the emerging phenomenon of gay politics and visibility. "When you're looking at the late '70s, early '80s in the Bay Area, there is no way you could be a relatively cognizant human being and not overlap into gay politics," explained journalist Laurie Garrett, who got to know Randy as a reporter for KPFA radio.

"We'd joke around whenever we saw each other," Laurie remembered. "And of course, you couldn't escape his charm and wit. He always had wisecracks. He had these witty little monikers he would assign to certain political figures. And you'd go, 'Oh, yeah. That's exactly spot on.'" Microphone and clipboard in hand, Randy began appearing on Bay Area airwaves in late February with a flurry of topics, including a lesbian mother at risk of losing her children in a custody fight, a profile of gay teacher and activist Tom Ammiano, and an interview with the biggest gay celebrity he knew, *Tales of the City* author Armistead Maupin.

Osterkamp felt vindicated by his decision. "I remember reaction coming in saying, 'My god, I didn't know about this,' or 'This is pretty interesting,' or, 'What about that cute new reporter?'" Positive responses generally outweighed the negatives, he added, although Randy's voice did sound a little weird. Randy remained sensitive about his appearance, but the more he saw himself onscreen, the harder he worked on presentation.

"The thing that pissed him off most about writing was that nobody recognized him," friend Ken Maley recalled. Well-connected in local media, Ken at the time was acting as publicist for Armistead, his Telegraph Hill neighbor. "Randy had this really major physical hang-up about his appearance, and in terms of sex and scoring and being recognized." As a TV newsman, however, he could finally walk into gay bars and turn heads. "He wanted to be star fucked," Ken added. "Definitely."

After only a few months of domestic bliss with Dan, Randy found himself needing exactly that kind of validation. "Their sex life wasn't satisfying for Randy," Linda explained, "because Dan was just kind of emerging as being a self-accepting gay man at that point. He was pretty vanilla, in terms of sex, and Randy was less so." Though they officially broke up in June, the two kept their apartment and remained emotionally intimate. "Their relationship was one of the stronger relationships of Randy's life with a man," Linda acknowledged. "One of the more lasting ones."

Meanwhile, Randy was noticing a chillier reception from the *Advocate*. In addition to spending work time arranging TV interviews and camera crews, his use of content from one job to write stories for the other wasn't sitting well with the editors. For his part, it was a period he viewed with ever-growing frustration. With David Goodstein in charge, the publisher promoted his preferred office-seekers while minimizing coverage of dissent. For months, Randy was responsible for compiling news briefs from "the national desk," allowing him to monitor both the ever-growing list of gay rights proposals and conservative counterinitiatives. When he flew to Miami to cover Anita Bryant's Save the Children campaign for *New West* magazine, his *Advocate* bosses initially agreed to pay his travel expenses. However, by the time he touched down in Florida, they'd reneged on their promise. Consequently, none of his coverage of Dade County's defeated gay rights law appeared in its pages.

Effectively blocked from covering the contentiousness within movement politics, Randy sharpened his sights on another sore spot: the plight of gay and lesbian youth. From San Antonio to Eugene, he assembled another array of sources detailing the hazards faced by gay teens. For every youth who fell into homelessness, hustling, or drug culture, Randy noted, there were even more who suffered quietly because of invisibility, isolation, and ostracism. Gay services that wanted to help were often rebuffed by funders who wouldn't touch the issue. The few places that stood out, it seemed, were those where youth had organized themselves. For those in suburbia and beyond, however, such supports remained well out of reach.

Although Randy's stories frequently evoked reader responses, the gay youth feature stood out for prompting the most vitriolic comment toward any early Shilts piece. "Ours is a culture that worships youth and heaps rejection and abuse on those no longer young," wrote one San Francisco reader. "It delights and pleases me to reflect that somewhere some arrogant, ageist young faggot is having problems because of his youth. You only have to be 'over-30' to appreciate the poetic justice of it."

In the aftermath of Bryant's Miami victory, tensions were climbing as an antigay backlash was gaining momentum. That summer, gays laid the blame for San Francisco gardener Robert Hillsborough's brutal murder squarely on Bryant, as Randy authored a heartbreaking account of the victim's final moments. Local gays responded forcefully, taking to the streets to voice outrage against Bryant's crusade and the vigilantism it inspired.

"People were very, very angry," friend and fellow journalist Randy Alfred told him in a KQED interview. "They were angry, they were frightened, and they just wanted to express it." A member of Bay Area Gay Liberation (BAGL), Alfred helped organize patrols around the Castro neighborhood, distributing whistles and training volunteers to fill the void left by a largely indifferent police force. Although he and Randy had briefly overlapped as *Advocate* freelancers, the former maintained an affinity for grassroots activism, while the latter worked to establish a foothold in mainstream news.

That chaotic summer marked the beginning of the end for Randy's tenure at the *Advocate*. Writing mainly for the gay press offered little room for

Randy Shilts in Palm Springs, California, September 1977. *Photo by Ken Maley, courtesy of Ken Maley Papers, James C. Hormel LGBTQIA Center, San Francisco Public Library, San Francisco*

advancement, and his overseers showed little interest in letting him critique movement politics. With Ken Maley acting as his informal agent, Randy made another risky move, dropping back to part-time at the paper and shopping himself again as a freelancer. Thanks to Ken's connections and growing recognition of his television work, so much more now seemed possible.

Over Labor Day weekend, Randy basked contentedly in Palm Springs, a guest of Ken and Armistead as they worked on novelizing *Tales of the City* at the home of Hollywood legend Rock Hudson. "The house had some of Rock's '70s caftans, and we would go and do drugs and drinking and wear these caftans," Ken remembered. High out of their minds, the partygoers would drive around in a big Buick convertible, blasting the radio and pranking Liberace by driving up to the front door, disturbing his poodles, and roaring off into the desert. In the poppers-laden heat of this Palm Springs getaway, Randy lounged contentedly in one of Hudson's caftans as Ken appreciatively snapped his picture. Fortunes, it seemed, were turning in his favor.

Somehow, the Harvey Milk–owned Castro Camera shop always managed to keep its doors open, even though its owner preferred campaigning over actually running his business. Around Harvey, a growing cadre of young militants and new arrivals would come to argue, strategize, organize, or just shoot the bull. Some, including shop assistant Dan Nicoletta and Harvey's ex-lover Scott Smith, did what they could to keep the place from falling apart. If anything noteworthy transpired when Randy first met Harvey, the moment has been lost to history.

"Randy Shilts was a camera store customer, first and foremost," Dan remembered. An aspiring photographer, Nicoletta came to work at the shop in 1975 after Harvey registered him to vote, finding himself caught up in numerous campaigns at age twenty. "[Randy] would come into the camera store both to drop off film to be processed and to visit with Harvey and Scott."

Cleve Jones, the street kid turned organizer, enjoyed holding his own with Randy in that setting. "There was a whole cadre of us who were mostly White, middle-class-background guys with good educations," he added. "We were all quite cocky. We were all extremely aware that what we were doing was brand new and had never been seen before." In many ways, the spirited conversations echoed Randy's college experiences. "There was definitely a competitive thing with him among our ranks," Cleve added. "Generally speaking, we were very supportive of each other's efforts, and Randy had a lot of us who were really rooting for him. I don't think he was always in touch with that reality, but people did want him to succeed."

"Randy was like a young punk kid. We all were," recalled Anne Kronenberg, the leather-clad, motorcycle-riding young lesbian Harvey hired to manage his campaign for San Francisco Board of Supervisors. "You met him, and you knew he was incredibly ambitious. He had a mouth on him too, and he got pretty caught up in how cool it was doing what he was doing, and it made him not part of the group after a while." Naturally, the perpetual candidate and the up-and-coming journalist had plenty to gain from each other. "[Randy] was someone who hung out in the campaign headquarters because he loved Harvey," Anne affirmed. "He would just come and talk to Harvey. So, Harvey cultivated that, because he did work for the *Advocate* at that point and [Harvey] was trying to get the *Advocate*'s endorsement, which was pretty far-fetched."

To Randy's thinking, the story of gays' rise to power was occurring right under the *Advocate*'s nose, but while many young gays were rallying to Harvey,

David Goodstein threw his personal support behind Rick Stokes, the establishment's preferred candidate. "[Stokes supporters] were more the activist type that wanted to go to tea with the mayor," Ken Maley observed. "They didn't want to be out front, they didn't want to be identified, but they also had a very internal motivation, in that they were self-appointed advocates of gay issues. They did not necessarily want to push any buttons or boundaries. They would be polite." Like his youthful followers, Milk was tired of being polite. "Too radical, unpredictable, and you know, Harvey could make Randy look very mannered," Ken noted.

In the same issue with the *Advocate*'s endorsement of Stokes, Randy offered an even-handed profile of all the major gay candidates in the Fifth District. On the crowded ballot, clearly the strongest contenders were Stokes, who'd amassed an impressive largest fundraising haul, and Harvey, running once again on retail politics and a drumbeat message of hope, above all else. Harvey repeated his familiar story of a lonely gay kid in a faraway town, embodying the life so many had come to San Francisco to escape: "The parents throw them around. School-mates taunt them. They may end up being alcoholic closet cases—but one day, they're going to open up a paper and see that an openly gay person was elected to the San Francisco board. That's going to give them hope." Stokes, on the other hand, offered a decidedly patrician pitch: "It would do a lot for the cause of gay equality nationally to have a responsible gay person on the board."

On Election Day, Harvey Milk made history, crushing the opposition as he swept into office with a reform agenda ranging from antidiscrimination to dog-shit cleanup. And two months later, Randy and camera crew joined the supervisor-elect and his supporters on a brisk, three mile walk to his swearing-in. At City Hall, Harvey granted the young punk kid who'd hung around his shop an interview as they strode together across the building's ornate rotunda. In the flurry of activity to follow, however, Randy was largely absent. After this day of historic firsts, he hopped on a plane for a cross-country trek covering more than forty days, eleven states, and nine cities in search of new stories and new connections with media outlets in New York, Boston, Atlanta, and DC.

Although the trip offered great professional opportunities, Randy was traveling with familiar personal baggage. A quick stopover in Michigan brought him face-to-face with another piece of unfinished business. He'd laid down some pretty big hints to his parents, mailing them news clippings carefully glued to construction paper to conceal the sexually charged ads on the back. Randy first brought up the subject alone with his father, finding that Bud had figured it out a long time ago. "It's fine with me because I don't have any problems with myself," he told his son, allowing that he'd known men he'd wanted to kiss, so maybe everyone was a little bit gay.

Bud was finally talking to Randy like another adult, but the frankness of their conversation was jarring. Youngest son David's condition meant Bud might never be able to retire, and Ronny was fast becoming "the baddest kid in Galesburg, Michigan." Already using pot and speed at fourteen, Ronny had a penchant for sneaking off and hitchhiking his way to Chicago, Florida, even San Francisco—wherever he knew a family member he could call. Regarding Randy's sexuality, Bud cautioned, don't push it on Norma, whose battles with high blood pressure weren't going well.

The next day, Randy sat alone beside his mother, reading the newspaper while she watched TV. Setting down the paper, Randy glanced at Norma, swallowed a deep breath, and caught himself. "I just couldn't think of the right way to bring it up," he lamented. "So I didn't."

After wandering for forty days, Randy returned home to a city bursting with opportunities. At the same time, he privately felt more responsible than ever for his aging, exhausted parents. Returning to his Liberty Street apartment, he confessed to Daniel the fear of how his teenage pranks may have caused his youngest brother's birth, unburdening his conscience to the person he trusted more than anyone else to love him unconditionally.

Whenever Belva Davis heard "So how did I do?" she knew Randy was asking for a pep talk. Widely admired among Bay Area broadcasters, Belva had quietly made history as the nation's first Black woman in television news in the mid-1960s. By 1978 she was no stranger to the business, and in her newest venture, she became both a mentor and a second mom to the kid member of her news team. "[Belva] is a person who reaches out and likes to take people under her wing," George Osterkamp observed. "I'm not surprised she liked Randy."

Just as Randy was finding his footing on TV, KQED did a major restructuring, rechristening its news program as *A Closer Look* and bringing Belva aboard as anchor. Each night, reporters narrated their stories over footage from the field, then joined her for a conversation. The new format, playing to Randy's strengths as a talker, quite literally gave him a seat at the table. From her vantage point, he was going up against the same fraternity that had been slow to embrace her a decade earlier. To gain their respect, she counseled, Randy needed to ignore their cutesy side comments.

"They're picking on you because that's what they do," Belva told him. "And you know, you wouldn't have been the guy they would've chosen to build into a star, so you have to be a star to prove it." Furthermore, she added, "You've got to get a voice that you can hear in your head that says, *I can do it, I can do it.*" It was sound advice, and Randy had made strides in his brief time on television. Once he got the hang of it, TV took far less work than print journalism. But writing left a longer impression: "In fact, it is those skills that can make me famous and successful like Armistead."

He'd long sought a byline in the *San Francisco Chronicle*, but to get picked up by a national daily, he had to do more than simply report on the same mundane topics any staff writer could cover. After years of trying, Randy finally earned that chance by offering a truly closer look, illuminating an aspect of gay life that the public likely hadn't imagined. On a Friday night he might normally spend cruising the bars or bathhouses, Randy surrendered himself at San Francisco's Hall of Justice, where only the watch commander knew the truth behind his weekend-long incarceration. "If these guys find out you're really a reporter," he warned, collecting the new inmate's thumbprint, "you could be in for big trouble."

After negotiating with the county sheriff, Randy arranged to spend three nights undercover in the "queens tank," a separate, protective wing of the county correctional facility where gays who were arrested on petty charges like theft, drug possession, or hustling did their time. Here, Black and Latina drag queens and transgender women, many of them charged with prostitution in the Tenderloin, comprised the gay tier's dominant group.

Handled by staff who used their preferred names and pronouns, as well as doctors who provided them with hormones, the jailhouse queens passed the time feminizing their denims, doing each other's hair, choreographing *Soul Train* dance routines, and courting the cell block's masculine men. Because of its reputation as the jail's most peaceful tier, some straights even tried faking gay at booking, to do their time in comparative comfort. "But," Randy concluded, "jail is jail—an unhappy alternative no matter how gay the tier."

Despite his efforts to be sensitive, Randy's account still included some mainstream misconceptions about transgender women, especially those from communities of color. Recalling an earlier era's assumptions about homosexuality, he noted, "Influenced by the more stringent sex roles of their own worlds, I found these prisoners adopting feminine roles rather than the newer masculine gay male roles of the educated white middle classes." Even with these cultural blind spots, however, he tried to humanize the complexities of gender, sexuality, poverty, and crime, writing a decidedly unique human-interest story that didn't fit the dominant narrative of gay life at the time.

Meanwhile, as Randy was preparing to leave the *Advocate*, its publisher handed him one unforgettable parting gift. Not content with throwing his money around the political world, David Goodstein had become a champion of est, the self-actualization seminars founded by human-potential guru Werner Erhard. Eager to capitalize on its growing popularity, Goodstein was launching "the Advocate Experience." Along with most of the *Advocate*'s staff, Randy and a handful of others, including Ken Maley and Dan Yoder, attended the inaugural session, with Goodstein promising the two-day event would harness the budding energies of gay liberation to the tenets of "I'm okay, you're okay, we're okay."

The agenda moved from Goodstein-led lectures on self-acceptance to exercises in trust-building and revival-style forums, where participants confessed their insecurities and pledged to vanquish their self-defeating thoughts and behaviors, to approving applause. Silently, Randy noted, the cutest boys' confessions always seemed to draw the most applause. Goodstein's pitch to the "graduates" on how *they* could transform gay culture by providing the names and addresses of their friends, who would each pay $150 a pop for this weekend of enlightenment, smelled an awful lot like a cash grab. Instead of just walking away from the *Advocate*, Randy cheerfully tossed a journalistic grenade right at its publisher, in a story for *New West*.

"It all comes out as beautiful fantasies that we can create," Randy observed. Dryly humorous but darkly serious, his account offered a warning about wealth, power, egotism, and vulnerability in a community still finding its legs. At a moment when the Reverend Jim Jones wielded significant influence over city politics and media, skepticism toward yet another personality cult was not unwarranted. Randy underscored his message by detailing an Advocate Experience exercise in which attendees were asked to signal their agreement by raising and keeping their hands extended as Goodstein read a series of statements. "Oh no," whispered one participant, who observed a certain familiarity in the salute. "I was afraid that it would come to this."

The story marked Randy's first direct challenge to gay liberation's self-appointed leaders. In burning his bridges with the *Advocate*, he was signaling to other publishers that gay life held an abundance of interesting personalities, power struggles, and newsworthy stories. Moreover, the piece put wealthy gay leaders, chief among them Citizen Goodstein, on notice about manipulating gays to serve their own interests. Randy may have been part of the community he covered, but he would not act as its unquestioning spokesperson or stenographer.

Not surprisingly, some segments of the community didn't take kindly to his reporting. "I can't stand when people dislike me," he fretted privately. "They make me feel like they're right and I'm wrong. At the same time . . . they were acting like a bunch of fools at that seminar. I shouldn't give a shit. It's not like they ever liked me or respected me before."

"I think there was a clash in Randy between his ambition and his devotion to gay rights," observed Ken Maley. "Randy's personality and his ambition, which was the heart of his personality, was destined to have conflict. I think sometimes Randy got so enamored with the next stage that he just dismissed the past like, 'So what, I don't care.' So, he would burn bridges, thinking that the next phase didn't matter." To find his voice, as Belva had counseled, Randy had to distinguish himself from the community he covered, a move that some would never forget, or forgive.

Like a kid on Christmas Eve, Randy could barely sleep. Standing in the mirror, he was admiring the latest addition to his wardrobe, a trendy new Lacoste shirt bearing the stitched alligator logo. "The adrenaline gets zooming on days like this," he told himself.

> *Tugging at the collar of my alligator shirt.*
> *Approvingly.*
> *Like I had just joined a club.*
> *Fascinating.*

A record-setting crowd of over three hundred thousand was descending on San Francisco, adding strength to an especially forceful 1978 Gay Freedom Day Parade. Accessorizing his alligator shirt with a black necktie, Randy canvassed the crowd with camera crew in tow, interviewing friends David Kopay and Armistead Maupin beneath a cloudless summer sky. Speaker after speaker took the stage at City Hall, rallying the crowd as defeats around the country seemed to be pointing toward a showdown between California gays and Anita Bryant's ascendant counterrevolution.

Armistead Maupin (left) and Randy Shilts, San Francisco Gay Freedom Day Parade, 1978. *Photo by Ken Maley, courtesy of Ken Maley Papers, James C. Hormel LGBTQIA Center, San Francisco Public Library, San Francisco*

The urgency was unmistakable. Only weeks earlier, State Senator John Briggs had used San Francisco as a backdrop to deliver the petition signatures to put Proposition 6 on the statewide ballot. The initiative, if enacted, would forbid homosexuals from working as schoolteachers and allow for the firing of any teachers who supported them. Amid the pessimism of a likely defeat, Harvey Milk was aiming to at least win his own city, with a focus on canvassing neighborhoods and face-to-face politicking. To the assembled throng that day, he delivered an emphatic call to action, exhorting gay people everywhere to come out as an act of political power.

Standing on the dais, his back to the massive crowd, Randy told the camera, "It might be easy to miss the forest for the trees," given the rally's many references to local disputes. "For the fascinating thing about this event may be not the specific news issues of the day. But rather, it's fascinating that just nine years after a small riot in an obscure gay bar, that these events should be happening at all."

Modern gay liberation had come of age in less than a decade, forcing Americans to reckon with uncomfortable ideas around self-expression, gender roles, and sex. Curiously, however, Randy seemed more interested in covering Prop 6 proponents, especially Briggs, than the gay activists trying to defeat it. The heart of the initiative beat strongest not in cities, but in the small towns where Randy followed Briggs to document the emergence of Christian fundamentalism as a political force.

The senator was supremely confident, having personally witnessed Anita Bryant's victory in Miami, where he'd gushed his excitement to a curious California reporter. By the time Briggs realized that the curly-haired San Francisco freelancer was, in fact, a homosexual, the two had already struck up a rapport. Randy had a knack for connecting with these kinds of conservatives, gaining Briggs's confidence in a manner that allowed for wisecracks and off-color asides.

Anita Bryant may have been a true believer, he reckoned, but the man campaigning to restore California's moral order was mainly focused on higher office. Leveraging his ambitions against the rights and dignity of an unpopular minority seemed like a safe wager, but privately, Randy noted, Briggs admitted having no real animosity toward the people his speeches and campaign literature coarsely equated with child abusers and murderers. "It's politics, just politics," he liked to say.

Writing for the *Village Voice*, Randy took the story of Prop 6 away from San Francisco to the town of Healdsburg, California, where Briggs came to rally voters at the expense of a well-respected local schoolteacher. "Under my initiative," Briggs proclaimed, "the mere fact of being homosexual is considered immoral and he would not be allowed to teach." The loud jeers of gay demonstrators only reinforced the determination of Briggs's supporters. At the same time, Randy noted, establishment Republicans had never warmed to the senator. The initiative's fundraising had stagnated, virtually no one in the party's mainstream had endorsed it, and the campaign still lacked a television ad strategy or physical headquarters.

Instead, the senator was staking his campaign on communities like Healdsburg, where equating homosexuality with drugs and prostitution—or child rape and murder, as Prop 6 campaign literature depicted it—was more likely to be accepted at face value. "The bottom choice when people go into the voting booth is whether they're going to vote *for* homosexuality or *against* it." With a few weeks to go and polls indicating a tightening race, the senator still believed he had the upper hand. "It's a monumental job to convince people to vote for homosexuality—it's a job that just can't be done."

Since their first encounter in Miami, Randy had wondered whether Briggs really believed his own rhetoric. Even after learning about his favorite reporter's sexuality, the senator never seemed personally bothered by it. And for Randy's part, he never heard the antigay vitriol as an attack on his person. "I never took his protestations against homosexuality seriously. I wasn't sure how Briggs took them himself."

When KQED hosted a debate, moderated by Belva Davis, Randy sat alongside Harvey and activist Sally Gearhart. Responding to a caller who asked if Briggs actually knew any homosexuals, the senator replied, "Sure. Randy and I have known each other for a long time and I think he's an interesting fellow, a fine reporter. . . . But I wouldn't want him teaching my children." Later, Belva recalled the fierce dressing down Randy gave Briggs off camera after the debate had concluded.

Randy's efforts to stay publicly neutral had irritated gay activists, and Briggs's casual mention of their rapport only added to their frustrations. However, Dan Nicoletta recalled, Harvey would scour the local papers every day for mentions of the gay community, believing that any attention was good for political theater. In mid-October, the Fifth District supervisor sent Randy a handwritten thank you note "on behalf of all of us for opening up the can of worms and helping us to raise funds."

In another freelance piece for the *Chronicle*, Randy detailed his behind-the-scenes friendship with the senator, just one week before the election. In his personal files, his notes offered hints as to what he wanted the piece to achieve: "Private V Public Briggs." The man who railed demonstratively against homosexuals, assailed them to go back in the closet, and exaggerated their purported threat to children, actually didn't give a damn about anything but his career.

Appearing on the same day Briggs tried unsuccessfully to disrupt San Francisco gays' Halloween festivities, the story might have landed a hit if not for some critical choices. In explicitly referring to his "friendship" with the senator, Randy drew attention away from *what* he knew—that Briggs was a cynical, manipulative opportunist—toward *how* he'd come to know it. In setting the tone around their casual chumminess, Randy effectively elevated his insider's perspective above his closing argument: "John Briggs, in the eyes of John Briggs, is just a politician, riding a popular cause."

The fact that Briggs thought gays were fortunate to have him as an opponent, instead of "some crazy" who wanted them thrown in jail, certainly made for interesting background. But the final product buried the senator's inconsistencies deep within the details of their relationship. The larger point would be lost on casual readers, leaving Randy to face the irritated activists he'd befriended and covered over the past two years.

"Gag me," Anne Kronenberg groaned. "It's like, 'Hey, wait a minute. You are one of us, what the fuck are you saying?' I just remember the feeling like, 'Oh my god, that goddamn Randy Shilts. Who does he think he is?' And are you doing this at the expense of the gay community that you are a part of?"

Election Night confirmed a history-making defeat for Prop 6, as just a few feet away from Harvey stood Randy, looking on and smiling as cameras flashed. Intramovement skirmishes aside, gay activists around the country were only facing the beginning of a decades-long battle, and, for now, Randy's transgression appeared to be forgotten, but not by all.

THE HUMAN SIDE OF HITLER, proclaimed the hand-scrawled headline to a mocking typewritten "interview" by "Randy Shits—the gay journalist friend of Adolph Hitler," whose reporting bore an "amazing similarity" to a recent story in the *Chronicle*. "Have you come to know Hitler personally?" the fictional interviewer inquired. "Oh, yes," Mr. Shits replied. "Al (we're on a first name basis) and I get along famously. As his favorite Gay reporter, I've gotten to know the private Al Hitler, a man who casts a far different profile than the public crusader."

The hit job came courtesy of activist Arthur Evans, known for crafting angry leaflets under his pen name the Red Queen. "He's actually quite charming when he's off stage," Evans's Mr. Shits enthused. "And when he's on stage, we smile pleasantly at each other whenever he calls for the annihilation of Gays and Jews. The truth is that he's not really a bigot at all; he doesn't actually believe in what he says publicly. You see, it's all just a matter of politics, and in politics, anything is fair."

It was neither the first nor last time someone would drop the *l* from Randy's surname. Puerile taunts aside, however, the leaflet revealed a sentiment that some Shilts detractors would hold until their dying days: "Gay opportunists in journalism are as dangerous as straight opportunists in politics."

8 | SHADOW OF A DREAM

"GOOD EVENING." IT HAD only been a week since she'd calmly guided viewers through details of the horrifying Jonestown massacre, but of all the tragedies she'd ever cover, Belva Davis would remember November 27, 1978, as the most difficult of her career. "Tonight, we expand our program to one hour to bring you the tragic story of the murders of San Francisco Mayor George Moscone and Supervisor Harvey Milk. Both were shot this morning, and tonight, ex-supervisor Dan White is being held at the Hall of Justice on two counts of murder."

The newscast cut to footage of Acting Mayor Dianne Feinstein, who stated, "As president of the Board of Supervisors, it's my duty to make this announcement. Both Mayor Moscone and Supervisor Harvey Milk have been shot and killed."

Among shouts of disbelief, a voice exclaimed, "Oh, Jesus Christ!"

Feinstein continued, "The suspect is Supervisor Dan White."

Over footage recorded by her husband, Bill Moore, Belva continued: "Shock, fear, dismay, disbelief, all jumbled together."

It had been a tumultuous several days for White, who'd resigned his seat, only to turn around and ask to be reappointed. After learning that Moscone would decline his request, White had bypassed City Hall security and visited the mayor's chambers, putting a series of bullets in Moscone's body before slipping out a back door. Belva continued, "Just down the hall, the discovery of another body had been made, that of Supervisor Harvey Milk."

The footage shifted to policemen racing through City Hall's chaotic corridors. Following an interview with Assemblyman Willie Brown came film of the two men's bodies, bagged and ready for removal to the coroner's office. *A Closer Look* continued with a mix of in-studio and voiceover segments for another twenty minutes until Belva turned to the kid member of the news team, waiting beside her. "Tonight, Randy Shilts takes a closer look at Harvey Milk and the gay community, which is now stunned at his murder."

Like everyone else, Randy was trying hard to remain professional. "Just eleven months ago," he began, "Harvey Milk led a march of one thousand to his inauguration at San Francisco's City Hall. For them, and many San Francisco gays, Milk's election was of immense significance. Milk was the first openly gay politician elected to any city post in the United States."

Randy's expression faltered only once, a quick furrow of the brow as he added, "[Milk] said he was trying to prove that you could be open about being gay and still make it." Over clips of the late supervisor, he continued, "Few thought that Harvey Milk would leave City Hall as he did today, on a stretcher, the victim of an assassin's bullets."

Recounting Milk's repeated runs for office and his instant star power as supervisor, Randy managed to provide the only lighthearted moment of the broadcast, describing the cat-loving Harvey's triumphant, well-publicized pooper scooper law. "That ordinance gave him a chance to show off his characteristic sense of humor," he noted. "Well, that humor, and Milk's ability to pull together a wide base of support, had left some gays hoping that Milk might someday be the first gay mayor of San Francisco. But today, that hope ended."

The broadcast cut to Randy on the street, the Castro Theater looming prominently over his shoulder. He'd arrived at City Hall just minutes after the shootings but ended up detailing ordinary people's reactions in Harvey's stunned and terrified neighborhood. Over footage of men and women wiping away tears, Randy offered, "Many in the gay community feel that antigay prejudice may have prompted White to allegedly shoot Milk."

While it was true that Harvey had opposed the former supervisor's reappointment, some viewed White's actions as proof of a deeper homophobia. "A significant amount of motivation was that Harvey Milk was gay, and that's why he was killed," an unnamed man remarked. "I don't believe that anybody in their right mind could say he was shot simply because he opposed the reappointment of Dan White."

Back in the studio, Randy shared that Milk was no stranger to assassination threats and had made a tape recording in case he was killed while holding office. He wanted nothing splashy for a memorial, Randy emphasized, and no demonstrations in the streets. "Instead, Milk said, 'I can only hope that they'll turn that anger and frustration into something positive. I hope that every professional gay will just say, 'Enough.' Come forward and tell everybody,' he said. 'Wear a sign. Let the world know. Maybe that will help.'"

Randy concluded with details of a march planned that evening from Castro Street to City Hall. His final comment spoke to what people seemed to need that night, as the streets radiated with the candlelight of thousands, stretching from the seat of city government to a neighborhood mourning for both the idealists, and the idealism, lost that day.

Within twenty-four hours, Randy's role in Harvey's legacy would come into focus, thanks to a phone call from the East Coast. On the other end was St. Martin's Press editor Michael Denneny and his close friend Charles Ortleb, cofounder of *Christopher Street* (and, in 1980, the *New York Native*). "I was having dinner with Chuck, which happened almost every night," Michael remembered. "And we decided at dinner that there ought to be a biography."

When news of the assassination hit, Michael, a former student of Hannah Arendt's, immediately recalled an earlier, forgotten era of gay activism. "We were having the first wave of reaction and being thoroughly aware of what happened to [Magnus] Hirschfeld and the gay movement in Germany," he explained. An early triumph of Hitler's Third Reich had been the eradication of a flourishing counterculture, which had promulgated a tolerance for open expressions of homosexuality and gender nonconformity. "They were far in advance of where we were in the mid-'70s, so we knew the whole movement could be wiped out again."

"So," Michael continued, "we thought at least we ought to get the story into a book, which is like putting a little boat on a stream and just hoping, if things get worse, at least we'll get the record there, and someday in the future, somebody will find it." The previous year, he'd visited San Francisco to meet some of the promising young gay writers on the West Coast. On the recommendation of his friend John Preston, he'd reached out to Randy, who'd taken him to a dinner party hosted by Armistead Maupin. Following Harvey's assassination, he and Ortleb quickly settled on their first choice for a Harvey Milk book. "Actually, we called Randy up from the restaurant and said, 'You've got to write this biography.'"

Randy didn't hesitate to name his terms. He'd need $15,000, he said, for the work time and research expenses. Over the payphone, the three men reached an agreement. Ortleb would pay $5,000 for a twenty-five-thousand-word essay in *Christopher Street*, from which would come the outline for a book proposal. It would be a stretch, Denneny said, but he thought he could get $10,000 for the advance. And with that, Randy stepped to the front of the line to chronicle Harvey's newly taken life.

It should have been a heady moment: his first book opportunity, pitched by well-respected members of the New York literary world. Still, it would take some time for Randy to wrap his mind around the enormity of what happened. The city seemed trapped in an apocalyptic shroud, yet his attempt to momentarily escape—a visit to his parents in Michigan for the holidays— offered no solace. Among the Shilts brothers, Christmas meant passing around a bottle of Wild Turkey and swapping dirty jokes. But Randy, still reeling from the assassination, could only muster one word for the festivities: "miserable."

At one point, the brothers set about hazing the newest family member, sister-in-law Dawn. A shy math nerd with big glasses who'd married Reed the previous summer, Dawn's conservative religious upbringing had left her ill-prepared for her new in-laws. That day, mother-in-law Norma had greeted her with a card that said, "Here's your fucking Christmas card," with a hand-drawn picture of herself inside. Seeing Dawn's discomfort with his brothers' sexually suggestive teasing, Randy interjected, "Don't do that." Though they'd only just met, his quiet act of chivalry cemented Dawn's affection for her West Coast brother-in-law. "I felt like he was my protector."

Back in San Francisco, Randy tried to shake off his melancholy by plunging into the *Christopher Street* story. The challenge, he realized, was to cast Harvey as a central figure in gay liberation's coming of age: a former Wall Street conservative turned liberal agitator, whose grasp of neighborhood politics and enthusiasm for everyday people made up for the absentmindedness, perpetual money woes, lack of manners, and shabby dress. The actors involved were abundant: loyalist Jim Rivaldo; union leaders Allen Baird and Howard Wallace; wealthy, self-appointed respectable gay leaders ("RGLs") David Goodstein, Rick

Stokes, and Jim Foster; and politicians Dianne Feinstein, George Moscone, Art Agnos, John Briggs, and Dan White.

With characters as varied as the threads in a tapestry, Randy had to fashion a coherent storyline around a straightforward premise: "'All the forces in the world are not so powerful as an idea whose time has come,' read the hand-lettered motto from Victor Hugo that Milk displayed on his wall—and Milk devoted his political career to the notion that acceptance of homosexuality was just such an idea."

To Harvey's thinking, if the gay movement would identify with the little guys, fighting in solidarity with other bullied and displaced groups, then it stood to gain more than by trying to blend in with the moneyed, "respectable" establishment. And, Randy noted, these kinds of alliances would not be forged at cocktail parties, fundraisers, or convention backrooms, but in the taverns, union halls, small businesses, and sidewalks that comprised what Harvey envisioned as "America's Gay Main Street." People who were beaten down in life could identify with the rough-around-the-edges Harvey, who may have made some off-color comments but was accessible and funny, and people knew he cared about them.

It was the enduring sense that he would stick up for them that swung people hard toward Harvey Milk, regardless of what movement leaders said about respectability. After defeating Prop 6, Randy observed, some activists were already talking up Harvey as Moscone's eventual successor. That his life was taken by ex-cop Dan White, the simmering, resentful embodiment of a clannish brand of masculinity, was indicative of just how threatening his message really was.

"Let the bullets that rip through my brain smash through every closet door in the nation," Randy quoted Harvey's tape-recorded will. "It was as if Milk knew . . . that he was indeed born to be a martyr." But eliminating Harvey wouldn't erase the ideas he had championed. "Gays had a martyr now," Randy proclaimed, "and with this they attained a respectability that would forever seal them into the mainstream of the city's political life."

Published in March 1979, Randy's essay would earn praise from many, including Harvey's successor. "It really was a great story," wrote Supervisor Harry Britt. "The community thinks you're wonderful!" Others, however, were quick to make their dissatisfaction known. "I feel some responsibility for Randy Shilts' acceptance as a writer since The ADVOCATE gave him his first real job as a reporter," David Goodstein wrote to Charles Ortleb. "And we are not unhappy that he no longer writes for us."

Never one to back down, Randy reminded his former boss of comments he'd made in his *Advocate* office, signaling that nothing said in his presence was ever truly off the record. "If Mr. Goodstein has difficulty remembering statements attributed to him about Harvey Milk, it is probably because he made so many statements against Harvey so frequently."

The narrative of Harvey Milk, the martyr, was just beginning to take shape. Meanwhile, San Franciscans waited with dread to see how justice would be served for his confessed, unapologetic killer. The news arrived on May 21, when a jury of Dan White's peers found him guilty on two counts of voluntary manslaughter, meaning he would walk free in just a few years. In the lead-up, some had suggested a peaceful candlelight vigil, but in light of this abdication of justice, there would be no peace that night.

"Out of the bars and into the streets," Cleve Jones declared, wielding Harvey's old bullhorn as an outraged crowd gathered at Castro and Market. At his urging, the demonstrators began marching to City Hall, moving fast and angry as the crowd swelled to an astonishing size. As pleas for calm were bitterly spurned, the evening rapidly devolved into hours of brutal conflict between gays and the police, while a nervous Board of Supervisors remained holed up inside with Mayor Dianne Feinstein.

The action eventually moved from City Hall to a retaliatory police assault on Castro Street's businesses and their patrons. Throughout the evening, Randy followed the unrest as closely as he could, scribbling observations in his reporter's notepad. At one point, he began adding simple annotations with times and locations, but the conflict was moving too fast to keep up. His notes for the evening ended with several unconnected statements: "Undirected anger . . . Shifting back and forth . . . No demands . . . No leaders . . . Nothing but anger . . . Focus shifted to street . . . Not sure."

The next day, Randy and his camera crew seemed to be everywhere. "More than glass got shattered in last night's riots," he proclaimed. "A lot of myths about San Francisco's gay community got shattered too." Charges and countercharges were already flying in the press, but nobody from the gay community would apologize for rioting. At Feinstein's press conference, Randy questioned why the city hadn't been prepared, complaining, "In the gay community, for weeks people have been saying that there'd be a riot if there was a manslaughter conviction. How could it be that nobody ever heard about it from your end?"

Inside the Elephant Walk bar, victims showed him their bandaged head wounds, cuts, and bruises. "In the past," one patron shared, "I was always willing to stand in the background, let somebody else do the activism, let somebody else do the pushing and the chanting and the shouting." When Randy asked how the experience had changed him, the young man answered, "Well, I'm not going to stand in the background anymore."

"I had two people inside me fighting," another White Night survivor commented. "One said, 'Let's be a monitor. Let's stop this violence. Let's stop the window breaking.'" But, he told Randy, "Then I'd turn around and I'd see police brutality. I'd see three or four policemen brutally beat innocent people that were trying to stop the violence. And another part of me says, 'I've got to stand up and fight.'"

In summarizing the riot and its aftermath, Randy tried to gauge its place in history. "Today, it looks like the gay movement is taking the path of many minority movements of the 1960s, but where that path goes next is anybody's guess." Behind him, a handwritten flier proclaimed, Pigs Start Violence. Lesbians/Fags Don't.

White Night had occurred on the eve of Harvey's forty-ninth birthday, with a massive party planned for Castro Street. Despite the previous night's violence, Cleve and a legion of hastily assembled volunteers made sure that no one in the Castro would be victimized that night. For Randy, being in the right place at the right time seemed to again bring an immediate payoff. At Oakland's independent station KTVU, the popular *10 O'Clock News* program wanted someone who understood the complexity of gay politics to report on gay issues. Once again, Randy was the best-known journalist to call.

Producer Randy Shandobil was responsible for crafting the program's in-depth feature for the bottom of the news hour, which meant keeping viewers from changing the channel. "The station was kind of dropping off at about 10:25," he recalled, "and the news director wanted to come up with something to carry past the half hour so we could sell at a higher rate the second half hour."

If Randy wanted to keep making inroads into television news, he had to work at distilling the intricacies of a raucous, multiheaded movement into stories the average viewer could understand. And as San Franciscans began to dust themselves off and move on from White Night, he found himself confronted by another vexing obstacle. The proposal for Harvey's biography still remained stubbornly unwritten, as if it were the shadow of a recurring dream, eluding his waking mind before it could be written down on paper.

———————

"Oh, I heard you got handcuffed to a parking meter on Polk Street at 3 AM?" Cleve always had a way with words, and the sight of Randy stammering and turning red brought a measure of perverse satisfaction. Whenever he felt Randy got the story wrong, Cleve had no qualms telling him directly, leading to sometimes ferocious debates over principles and politics. But, Cleve recalled, they always remained friends, and the arguments would inevitably devolve into good-natured rounds of gay cattiness.

"I created you!"

"No, I created you."

"Bitch! Nobody heard of you."

"Nobody heard of you."

"You wouldn't have gotten any of that shit published if it wasn't for me."

Cleve took pride in giving good copy, but his emergence as a go-to source came in no small part thanks to Randy. In the void left by Harvey's outsized personality, it would appear to some that he'd anointed the curly-haired "media queen" as the movement's heir apparent, leading them to wonder just how close the two had actually become. But even if there had been an attraction, Cleve emphasized, it would've been entirely one-sided.

"I don't think I would have ever gone to bed with him," he recalled. "I don't remember any kind of sexual tension." The sight of Randy's frumpy, crumb-covered clothing was bad enough, let alone the condition of his living space. "I mean, most of us would not go in his apartment. Everything about him was fucking messy."

Such was the lifestyle of a hardscrabble freelancer, living from gig to gig. In addition to television, he was writing for *Christopher Street*, *Village Voice*, and the gay stroke magazine *Blueboy* ("there has to be some redeeming social importance in these," teased Randy Alfred), as well as sometimes reporting for KSAN radio and filling in as a stringer for *Newsweek*. Meanwhile, Cleve received his own wake-up call about working with the national media when CBS News came to him and other leaders, promising to produce a balanced news feature, but instead releasing a sensationalized hit piece titled "Gay Power, Gay Politics."

Condemned by activists and journalists alike, the story seemed to conflate certain hardcore gay subcultures with gayness as a whole. "Buttfucking and blow jobs in Buena Vista Park, they were dirty-minded heterosexuals and that's all they cared talking about," Randy jeered after the story aired. "The gay phenomena in [San Francisco] represented hundreds of thousands of people throughout the U.S. who live decent and fulfilling lives, and they had one interpretation of what gay politics is."

Though painful, the entire affair provided a necessary lesson for those working to advance the cause by massaging the messenger, a point that Randy would underscore in his own feature on Cleve for *Christopher Street*. Although activists' revolutionary proclamations worked well against the backdrop of large rallies, they made for cringeworthy viewing when played over footage of seedy S&M clubs, sex toys, and shadowy figures cruising public parks.

Randy's toughest battles through this period were less with the community than with his own listlessness. Weeks and months were passing, yet he still hadn't started work on the book or found a literary agent. At times, he even found himself doubting his suitability to write Harvey's biography. To avoid meddlesome fact-checking and potential lawsuits, at one point Randy even considered fashioning the entire story as political fiction. His would-be editor wasn't having it. Creative impulses aside, Michael Denneny would always say that Randy was better off sticking with nonfiction.

As for gay politics, in late 1979 Randy drafted a retrospective for *Blueboy* on the decade gone by, with an eye toward what the movement was facing in the 1980s. In balancing its successes and setbacks, he noted that professional activists still had little to show in actual political victories. Sure, he acknowledged, civil rights laws had been passed in a smattering of progressive towns, and a handful of gay politicians now openly held elected office. Meanwhile, some prominent legislators, mindful of their liberal constituencies, were beginning to see the value of hiring the better-known gay activists as aides. But, Randy asked, shouldn't gay enclaves in major cities have more to show for their efforts than one elected supervisor, a handful of commissioner appointments, and a few activists-turned-consultants?

The legacy of the 1970s, he continued, lay more in the commonplace way that people now understood and spoke about sex and sexual expression. As evidence, he cited the increasing regularity of gay-themed plotlines on televi-sion. "Here is where the real American culture lies," he declared. "Here is where gays have found success—and a far more profound and lasting success than the [lesbian and gay movements] seem to imagine."

Social changes that once seemed like shockwaves, Randy noted, had opened a front for all sorts of lifestyles to be expressed openly and with growing confi-dence, leading to victories at the cultural level that easily surpassed gays' politi-cal gains. "The gay phenomenon represented the only social cause indigenous to the 1970s," he wrote. "Thus its ability to succeed in permeating American lifestyle—without significantly changing [the] political status of gays—suc-cinctly reflects the fizzling '70s."

If gays' acceptance was a matter of inevitability, as Randy seemed to believe, what was one to make of the gay community's future? On this point, he observed, "Unless pressured by a direct external threat, it appeared that even by 1979, gays clearly were more interested in manning the discos than the barricades." In the decade ahead, Randy predicted, the challenge would be less about organizing "nostalgic" marches on Washington and more about "the ability to tackle the significant lifestyle problems which exist in our own community." Here, Randy focused almost exclusively on the problems of urban gay men, like himself.

"The nation's gay neighborhoods offer little in the way of healthy support systems for the growing numbers of gays trying to do the unprecedented—create a bona fide sense of community in the so-called gay community." Enclaves like the Castro were swelling beyond the capabilities of the community services, shel-ters, and ministries that were trying to combat the problems that now seemed endemic to gay life. "During the '70's," he observed, "many gays have success-fully thrown off the old social morality which once held us down—the morality of shame, concealment, and embarrassment. Our big challenge is to find some kind of morality—some code of ethics—to replace what we've thrown off."

And therein lay the rub, as detractors would later take issue with Randy's characterization of gay men's "lifestyle problems." Even as he lamented the "gayttoization" of the Castro ("The major common denominators for gays today are the three D's—dope, dick, and dancing"), there he was: lonesome, drinking, and looking for sex alongside everyone else. "In essence, we've lost the shame," Randy continued, "but failed to gain any genuine sense of pride. Without our own morality, gays simply are left drifting in a nihilistic ozone of incredibly kinky sex, hoping the booze and disco music will deafen us to our own cries of alienation."

The paradox of Randy Shilts would always be that in critically covering his community, he became an unacknowledged actor in his own stories. By openly questioning the self-defeating patterns of gay life and assailing the motives of its leaders, he revealed, intentionally or not, a litany of his own dissatisfactions. But even when he questioned the community's direction or political tactics, he never entertained the notion that gayness itself wasn't normal.

Instead, even Randy's most pointed critiques of gay life contained an unmistakable desire for a kinder, more inclusive gay culture. "In the most basic anthropological sense," he lamented, "a community is supposed to offer support, a sense of belonging and purpose. So far, we've failed to provide these most basic needs."

The imperative for doing so, he argued, lay in a groundswell of young people, who'd encountered more public conversations around homosexuality than any prior generation. "Within a few years," Randy predicted, "they will be crowding into the streets of the gayttos in unprecedented numbers, looking for the 'gay community' the gay activists have somewhat speciously been discussing all those years. They will need more than a washboard stomach, a can of Crisco, a bottle of poppers and an after-hours bar."

Perhaps, Randy mused, gay liberation's greatest accomplishment was that, despite its growing pains, legions of people had taken real steps toward living open, honest, more fulfilling lives. "[It's] hard not to think that if the 1970s demonstrated that acceptance of homosexuality is an idea whose time has come," he speculated, "then the 1980s will show that gays are a people whose time has arrived." Gays would experience unprecedented visibility and acceptance in the next decade, he predicted, but if they were to become full-fledged communities, then more people needed to get serious about the work of helping each other stay healthy, safe, and sane.

Shilts sauntered into the office and slapped the 180 pages on Denneny's desk. "Here's the goddamn manuscript," he growled.

"I thought I was supposed to get this last week," Denneny snarled back. He wasn't about to take any shit from some West Coast prima donna.

Whenever Randy sent his editor new chapters, he liked to preface them with a little cinematic embellishment. The research and writing finally commenced in 1980, as he'd finished the proposal and secured representation with literary agent Elizabeth Pomada, resulting in a book contract with St. Martin's. Though short of what he'd asked for, the advance was enough for Randy to buy his first new car, which, like a proud son, he drove to Belva Davis's house, honking outside until she came out to have a look.

The euphoria was short-lived, however, as KQED announced the cancellation of *A Closer Look* in August 1980. Coming not long after KTVU had dropped him—for appearing in a local magazine's "10 Most Eligible Gay Bachelors" piece, he later claimed—Randy's time as an on-air regular came to a sudden end. "By then I had been on TV three and a half years," he recalled. "Nobody would hire me. I couldn't get a job."

Living off the advance and a trickle of freelance income, Randy began the research with a flurry of solicitations. From the outset, he imagined a political biography patterned on the stylings of "new journalism," which would read more like a novel than a straightforward cataloguing of the late supervisor's comings and goings. "I think if you tell people a good story that's professionally done, they'll get the politics because the politics will be appearing in it," he explained, "but I want it to be a good story too." At the same time, he reiterated, it would be entirely journalistic, "every fact in it a piece of journalism, every fact is going to be substantiated."

Fashioning his tone and pacing after the novels of James Michener, "where each of the characters represents different sociological forces," Randy approached as many of Harvey's associates, intimates, and rivals as he could, even offering to mend fences with those he'd alienated. Although he struck out with David Goodstein, whom he'd recently pilloried in *Blueboy*, the solicitation fared better with former Milk rivals Rick Stokes and Jim Foster, as well as many of Harvey's followers.

"From my perspective, Randy followed through," Dan Nicoletta recalled. Randy made sure to include some of Dan's photographs, including the famous image of Harvey as a circus clown. "He had made a personal mission about getting one or two of mine in there," Dan recounted. "It would be in support of my career ascent. . . . He's understanding I'm a kid, probably closer to midtwenties by this point, who needs that bump-up."

For Anne Kronenberg, the timing seemed dubious. "I was not a happy camper when he was writing it at the time," she recalled. "After Harvey's assassination, I was so pissed off he was writing it. It felt to me like Harvey had just been assassinated [for Randy] to become famous and get his name out. It was so soon." Anne agreed to be interviewed, mainly to make sure Randy stayed true to the facts as she remembered them.

Harvey's former lover Joe Campbell also had reservations, Dan recalled, but it didn't keep him and Randy from sleeping together after their interview. Campaign volunteer Michael Wong found his meeting with Randy to be a bit perfunctory, until Michael began reading him passages from his meticulously kept diaries. "As I described my vantage point on the day Dan White murdered George Moscone and Harvey," Wong recalled, "Randy was trying to not let me notice that he was crying. He did not look up to me as he did during the interview and was wiping tears."

The project's most important backer was Scott Smith, Harvey's former lover and executor of the estate, whose efforts had earned him the moniker "the Widow Milk." Randy "had already evolved a very tight friendship with Scott," Dan Nicoletta commented. "I got right off the bat that it was very on fire, in the sense that they had agreed to be in this together."

At the same time, Randy's research into Harvey's earliest days was stymied by the only biological family he could reach. Although he'd previously interviewed older brother Robert Milk, Robert was apparently unhappy with that coverage and communicated that he expected to be paid. "This book does not represent a great money maker by anybody's standards at this point," Randy wrote in response. "It was a difficult book to sell because few publishers believe Harvey's story has any interest beyond San Francisco or local gays."

Harvey's closest living relative remained unmoved, and with the 1980 election running its course, Randy headed to New York in search of those origins. After all, aside from some colorful anecdotes and unverified claims, Harvey's first forty years were largely a mystery in San Francisco. To save money, Randy stayed at Michael Denneny's Central Park West apartment, working long hours at the dining table and sleeping in the front sitting room. Bolstered by his library searches and interviews, the narrative was taking on a cinematic style, which Michael encouraged while pushing back on Randy's tendencies toward ornate, "purple" prose.

Michael would win his share of those battles, and generally he enjoyed their working relationship. "There was this boyish ebullience about him," he remembered. Their long workdays often ended with nights of spirited dancing, and in Randy, he saw shades of the late journalist Lincoln Steffens. "Originally I thought he was somewhat naive," Michael observed, "and I slowly came to the realization that I was totally wrong and that he was right about his belief in investigative journalism."

To Michael's recollection, the two would only have one real argument, at the end of a marathon session editing *Mayor*. "After we finished work at eleven o'clock one night, he wanted to go down to the Club Baths," he remembered. "And, because I was involved with *Christopher Street* and the *Native*, we had already realized there was a real problem with the bathhouses." It wasn't unusual to see men in the clinic waiting rooms trading phone numbers, Michael added, as many seemed to view the waiting period after VD treatment as a mere suggestion. He offered Randy strong words of warning that night, but those objections weren't enough. "We argued vehemently for about an hour," Michael remembered. "But he actually went."

Returning to San Francisco, Randy made the book his full-time job, developing a fascination with Harvey's transformation from apolitical "gay everyman" to unlikely martyr in the ascendance of gay liberation. In the opening chapters, he weaved the birth of the homophile movement, Stonewall, and Harvey's modest East Coast upbringing together into one cohesive story. Guided by the vivid source material, his central character took shape as a homosexual who was very much of his time: a gifted athlete, devoted to his mother, stubbornly opinionated but well-liked, moderately successful but perpetually restless, and determined to keep his sexuality separate from his work and family life.

The Harvey later known by West Coast comrades came through in both his love of opera and theater and his charming, paternalistic (some might say codependent) romancing of young lovers with troubled pasts. But in building toward the era that would define gay liberation and elevate Harvey to legendary status, Randy revealed a man approaching middle age who had yet to find purpose in his life and who unnervingly predicted he wouldn't live past fifty.

By 1969 Harvey's politics and his hair were both beginning to loosen up. His arrival on Castro Street converged with the story of the city's audacious gay activists, as Randy paid tribute to figures like drag performer and activist José Sarria, whose candidacy for the Board of Supervisors predated Harvey's first attempt by a dozen years. Stories shared by activist and historian Allan Bérubé established the role of dishonorably discharged gay veterans and pre-Stonewall activists, who used their strength in numbers to challenge police and pressure city politicians through new political coalitions.

For anyone wondering how Harvey came to symbolize one of the movement's most impactful turning points, the book's second act tried to make the minutiae of movement politics interesting to casual readers. Harvey had been quick to embrace the ethos of "politics as theater," bringing his passion for stagecraft to sidewalks and street corners and embracing whatever attention the press afforded him. Despite no money and a sparse local history, Harvey the born-again populist posted surprisingly high totals. And while gay leaders declared that there was *no* gay vote for a "nut" like Harvey Milk, Randy noted, the rising vote totals with each election showed that once a constituency swung for Harvey, it swung *hard*.

While most of Harvey's efforts seemed like harmless stunts, Randy cast a critical eye on the case of Oliver "Billy" Sipple, a disabled gay veteran who thwarted an assassination attempt against President Gerald Ford in 1975. Although he'd begged the press to keep his name out of the news, Sipple found himself essentially "outed" by *Chronicle* columnist Herb Caen in a story planted by Harvey. The news led Sipple to become estranged from his family for a time, and later he experienced prolonged bouts of depression and alcoholism before an untimely death. In the aftermath, Randy noted, Sipple had attempted to sue several media outlets for invasion of privacy, for which he was represented by Harvey's personal attorney.

With the advantage of hindsight, Randy could imbue Harvey's rise with an air of inevitability, reinforcing his vision of colliding historical forces. And just around the point when Harvey embarked on his third ill-fated campaign, another character arrived, almost imperceptibly, in the background. Though already sprinkled with juicy gossip and salacious trysts, the narrative began to work in an occasional behind-the-scenes aside, revealing the inner thoughts of established players like David Goodstein. The tidbits undeniably added color to an already pulsing storyline, but by indulging his own unvarnished viewpoint, without acknowledging his presence, Randy would leave an opening for those who would challenge the veracity of his account.

By the time Denneny received Randy's second installment in March 1981, the protagonist was just about to clinch his history-making victory. Yes, the manuscript was probably littered with typos and spelling errors, Randy admitted, but he'd come down with "one of those nasty bugs you can get from sticking your tongue in the wrong places." The next installment, he promised, would document Harvey's only year in elected office. The torrid pace continued right up to the improbable repudiation of John Briggs and a previously unstoppable Religious Right. All he had left to write was the "jumbled" events that had rendered Harvey a bullet-ridden martyr, when suddenly, to Randy's astonishment, the words dried up.

As Michael waited, the Shiltsian literary voice, which had carried the lofty narrative all the way up to the day Harvey's captivating personality met the steely rage of Dan White's .38 revolver, went silent. Instead of writing, he was flooded with anxieties, fretting over every real or imagined problem: "No long narration, just lots of short hits, building into the drama of the killings and their aftermath."

He couldn't finish the book without writing the death scene, but where would he find the words to kill off Harvey? Desperate to shake his writer's block, Randy roused himself out of the apartment on what seemed like another ordinary Sunday afternoon. He'd been invited to a bon voyage party for an eccentric older woman who, in San Francisco fashion, embodied the city's Bohemian soul as much as the adoring gay men who'd come to see her off. He'd barely gotten across the room, however, when those always-searching eyes spotted an especially attractive specimen, with wavy brown hair and a manly, made-for-TV chest.

Having recently joined NBC affiliate KRON, meteorologist Steve Newman was still a newcomer. But, Steve admitted, he was already familiar with the man who stood in front of him. "I, of course, had read Randy's work and was aware of his reputation as a journalist for the *Advocate*," he recalled. "I hoped to one day meet him." Never one for graceful introductions, Randy put his new suitor to the test. "He was kind of snobbish about TV weathermen," Steve remembered. "He didn't think they had any value whatsoever; it was frivolous and a waste of airtime."

Steve refused to take the bait. "I reminded him that the economy has a lot of people traveling around, selling goods and services that are affected by the weather. I considered it a valuable service." The measured, reasonable reply caught Randy off guard, making it apparent that Steve was more than just a pretty face. The two exchanged phone numbers and went their separate ways, but the next morning, the KRON newsroom exploded with the news that President Ronald Reagan had been shot. Knowing there was little need for a weatherman, Steve slipped out and retrieved the number from his wallet. "I called Randy and he invited me to come over," he recalled. "We were inseparable from that day forward."

While Steve played hooky, Randy confessed his recent struggles. "He had reached the point of Dan White killing Moscone and Milk, and he hadn't written in weeks," Steve recounted. "After we had sex that first day, he went home and hit the typewriter and wrote the assassination scene. Somehow, I had managed to free up his writer's block."

Miraculously unstuck, Randy churned through the remaining chapters and sent them to his editor. "What can I say?" Steve reflected. "I'm that good."

9 | THE BEST OF TIMES (THE WORST OF TIMES)

THE CREASE BETWEEN ROCK formations offered barely enough room for the two hikers to pass, allowing a moment to bask in the California sun before plunging back into the forest. Randy paused, unbuttoning his denims and letting loose a pent-up stream of piss. The sight was too perfect for Steve, who appreciatively snapped a photo of his lover gripping his half-hard cock, mugging broodingly for the camera in his stylish aviators.

Every new adventure came with a sense of playfulness and possibility; soon after their first date, the notes and flowers began arriving at Steve's home and workplace. "I thought I saw a beautiful man pass in and out of my dreams this afternoon as I laid on a soft bed of kisses and considered the divine illusion of love," the first missive began. Many of the notes that followed kept it simpler: "I love you. RS."

When Randy offered to let him read *Mayor* while finishing the final chapters, Steve declined, preferring to wait for the finished product. After receiving the final manuscript, Steve recalled, "I picked it up at 8:30 in the morning and I didn't set it down until evening. It was wonderful, really wonderful. I knew it was going to be great." To celebrate, Steve took his cash-strapped lover on a two-week vacation, whisking them away to the Virgin Islands, his hometown of Sarasota, New Orleans, and the Mayan ruins of Yucatán. Throughout their trip, the book remained a constant companion. As the soon-to-be book author sat editing in the window of their Mérida hotel room, Steve snapped a picture for posterity.

"I spent all my time with him, morning, noon, and night," he remembered. It wouldn't be long before Randy left his Liberty Street apartment for a new life, and lifestyle, with Steve. For all that the two former Eagle Scouts had in common, they couldn't have been more different when it came to personal habits. Steve refused to give ground, forcing Randy to fill enormous trash bags with unwanted stuff, fold and put away his laundry, and organize his closet. "He would not let me go at his office," Steve allowed. "And I can understand that. He knew where everything was."

The attention they garnered as a high-profile couple added extra motivation for Randy to measure up. Soon, his go-to favorites, cheeseburgers and fries, gave way to healthier choices like chicken breasts, brussels sprouts, and spinach salads. Aided by a newfound motivation to exercise, Randy's soft, cherubic tummy began to tighten, revealing a taut, almost muscular midsection. Anything, it seemed, was worth the effort. "I need you so much I cannot afford the luxury of taking you for granted," he confessed, "and I love you so much that I would be a fool if I ever permitted myself such luxury."

By late summer, the two had settled comfortably into Steve's Cathedral Hill apartment when Randy's grand prize of opportunities finally presented itself. Faced with staffing changes, and well-aware of the public relations implications, the *San Francisco Chronicle*'s editors decided it was time to hire a publicly gay general assignment reporter, and two candidates were brought in to interview: the itinerant Mr. Shilts and his contemporary in the local gay press, Randy Alfred.

"Randy and I both knew that we were the two candidates," Alfred recalled. While the Yale-educated Alfred had the backing of *Chronicle* television critic Terrence O'Flaherty, he'd come to journalism as an activist, with all of his work at that time appearing in the gay press. Randy Shilts actually had a degree in journalism, a forthcoming book, and plenty of mainstream clippings to his name. "Would hiring me have been a mistake? No," Alfred allowed. "But from their point of view, first of all, I looked to be too much of an activist. I mean, I think back to my interview there and what I brought as clips, and from my point of view now, no wonder."

Not long after, the two bumped into each other in the Castro. As it turned out, the gay paper the *Sentinel* had offered Alfred the editor's job, so both men were happy for each other. When Alfred asked about the book, Randy paused, choosing his words carefully: "It's your review that I fear." If it was bothering him, Alfred countered, hire him to fact-check it. Randy hesitated, knowing that Alfred had been attached to a Milk-related film project. Wary of sharing material with a competitor, he turned down the offer.

Until this point, Randy's two most elusive goals had been a storybook romance and a career-defining job. At thirty, he seemed to have found both. The day before starting work at the *San Francisco Chronicle*, Randy started another letter to his partner. "All along," he reflected, "you told me I [would] get that job and you were right. Now I can only hope I succeed. I've got my lover, my job, my future. I love you and always want you by my side."

On August 17, 1981, Randy walked into the newsroom at Fifth and Mission as a full-time reporter for a nationally respected newspaper, and the first openly gay journalist hired to cover a gay beat. He brought along a diary to document any hostile encounters, but instead, he recalled, "Everybody was great. Everybody went out of their way to be nice." Others, however, noticed a certain guardedness in the ranks. "There were a bunch of World War II veterans who sat in the back and smoked and played chess and balanced their checkbooks and sometimes did what they called shirt-sleevers," remembered Katy Butler. "Which is, you sort of sashay out the back door and go to the bar that was in the alley around the block."

"I would say they were sexually nervous—some of them," commented colleague Susan Sward. Together with Katy, she and Randy formed a cluster near the city desk. His confidence was immediately apparent, Susan noted, but "I just remember looking at him across the room and thinking, *Oh boy. Here comes the flowered tie and the big curly Afro* . . . I thought, *Ooh, I don't know if the Chronicle is ready for this!*"

Seeing Randy on the outside looking in, Susan took to him like a sympathetic older sister. Over tuna sandwiches at a nearby café, she asked why he'd settled in San Francisco, to which he mischievously answered, "It was a candy store!"

True to his general assignment mandate, Randy's initial reporting stuck to mundane city matters like public drunkenness. Gay-related features began to noticeably increase, however, from human-interest pieces to reports of gay bashings and muggings that weren't usually covered outside the gay press. At the Castro Street Fair that fall, Randy bumped into Anne Kronenberg during a break in the entertainment. As they stood talking, an activist took the stage and began warning of an unknown illness, but no one was listening. "People were there to party," Anne recalled. "He didn't get booed, but nobody paid any attention. Just, you know, 'Stop being a downer. We don't want to hear about this.'"

In early June the Centers for Disease Control and Prevention had first raised concerns in its *Morbidity and Mortality Weekly Report*, an announcement that garnered a few ripples in the press. In the *Chronicle*, David Perlman quickly followed up with his own brief account, while the *New York Times* entered the fray in early July, after the *MMWR* reported that Kaposi sarcoma, a rare skin cancer, had been diagnosed in twenty-six gay men in New York and California.

After hearing about it from a friend, Steve came home and asked Randy if he knew anything about a gay cancer. "He took a deep breath," Steve recalled. "Yeah," Randy told him, "I have been looking at it." But when the *Chronicle* revisited the strange outbreak in midfall, the byline went to one of its science correspondents.

In fact, Randy's first in-depth human-interest story did examine the complexities of a confounding, underresearched condition. His source material, however, came not from gay cancer, but another holiday visit to Michigan, where the toll of caring for David was wearing on his aging parents. Approaching sixty, Bud was convinced he could never retire, while Norma was still struggling with high blood pressure, compounded by David's need for round-the-clock attention. Meanwhile, Ronny Shilts had joined the navy, only to go missing. Eventually, Bud filed the paperwork declaring his second-youngest son, who would never be found, to be legally dead.

In depicting his family's plight, Randy focused on how an average, working-class family struggled to care for its own. Norma had devoted herself to collecting news clippings on autism and joining every local advisory board on children with disabilities. She'd written a detailed, pages-long report on autism by hand, giving Randy newfound respect for his mother. "Having an autistic child is a life sentence," Norma told him. With his own life going better than ever, it seemed that Randy had forgiven, or at least set aside his differences with, the parents he'd once called Mama Bitch and Papa Bitch. When *The Mayor of Castro Street* was released in early 1982, it included a dedication to his mom and dad.

"This is *The Gay Life*, KSAN's public affairs show for gentlemen who prefer gentlemen, for women who prefer women, and for people who prefer people." For anyone listening at eleven o'clock on a Sunday night, Randy Alfred welcomed them in his most practiced sotto voce. "Tonight, our guest is Randy Shilts, the author of *The Mayor of Castro Street: The Life and Times of Harvey Milk*." The two shared a lot of recent history, and after reading *Mayor*, Alfred had plenty he wanted to say about it, warts and all. But this was talk radio of a more genteel variety, a collegial conversation in the background of listeners' kitchens, garages, cars, and living rooms. Serious points of contention would be saved for print.

"It is a big book," Alfred began. "It's big in terms of its implications. It's big in terms of its length. It covers Harvey Milk's entire life and its immediate aftermath, in great and sweeping detail . . . and I enjoyed it very much."

His guest was alternately effusive and giggly, describing the crunch of writing a book while living off his "crummy" advance. After the ordeal of writing it, Randy added nervously, "you know there's always going to be a couple things that are wrong hanging around." Alfred admitted to marveling at how *Mayor* linked the trajectory of Harvey's life to the expanding visibility of gay life, which Randy credited to having read every book that James Michener had ever written. "That's what I wanted to do for gay people, not going back ten thousand years, but at least getting the last fifty years of gay history."

The two agreed that if *Mayor* were fiction, no one would believe it. But Alfred quickly brought up his major criticism, that the concept of charisma itself had been underdeveloped. Randy had used the adjective "charismatic" liberally throughout, he noted, to characterize not just Harvey but also figures like Dianne Feinstein and former Mayor Joe Alioto. Taken slightly off guard, Randy offered that Feinstein was "viewed" as charismatic when she was first elected in 1969. But Alfred pressed his point, mentioning Gandhi, Martin Luther King, and Joan of Arc as leaders whose actions had transcended personal gain. "Charisma," he added professorially, "is the sail that makes the winds of change visible."

"Yeah," Randy feebly replied, "I'll buy that."

Alfred admittedly had some background here, having started a dissertation on charismatic leaders before abandoning academia for journalism. "The charismatic leader is someone who changes the definition of reality," he pressed, "who, instead of accepting the definition of being deviant, changes the entire definition system around. And I think Harvey was part of a whole movement that did it."

A meditation on charisma was clearly not what Randy was expecting. "Oh yeah, well I just didn't choose to develop that theme," he answered. "There are lots of themes in there." But, Alfred countered, the raw ingredients were sprinkled throughout the entire narrative—they'd just been left undeveloped.

The conversation moved on, covering points where the two more or less agreed. When Alfred asked him to describe Milk's legacy, Randy answered much more confidently, declaring, "Without any doubt, I think gay people are part of the mainstream political system. Some of the mainstream politicians don't know it, but we are, and we will forever be sealed into the system because of Harvey Milk." As a result of Harvey's martyrdom, he added, more straight people would stand up for gays in the political process. "They will not let us be forgotten," he emphasized. "They will not let us get screwed over the way we were screwed over in the past."

Alfred ended the interview with seemingly high praise. "It's a book of—like its subject—immense theatricality and sweep and verve; [it is] very good reading and gives you a good sense of who Harvey Milk was." Before leaving, Randy autographed his host's copy: "To Randy—My colleague who catches all the glitches and embarrasses the hell out of me, but who lived through all the madness and still works to keep up the dream."

Although the two parted amicably, it would be the last time they would speak for quite some time. Following *Mayor*'s February release, reviews in the mainstream press were generally positive, as were the gay papers outside San Francisco. But, as Randy knew, the most critical response would come from those who'd covered Milk alongside him. Instead of reviewing the book, the *Bay Area Reporter* opted instead to cover the "selling" of Harvey's legend. Meanwhile, David Goodstein's the *Advocate* was happy to accept St. Martin's advertising dollars but stayed silent in terms of news coverage or a review. When journalist Larry Bush later mentioned *Mayor* in a year-end review, the editors removed it and told him, "We ran out of space."

The responsibility for giving *Mayor* its closest review would fall on the man who'd called it "very good reading" on his radio show. Randy Alfred embraced this task with utmost seriousness. "Randy Shilts has written an exciting, but also disappointing, biography of Harvey Milk," Alfred began. He added, "*The Mayor of Castro Street* is imaginative, controversial, and flawed." On the whole,

Randy Shilts, reading from
The Mayor of Castro Street,
February 18, 1982. *Photo by
Dan Nicoletta, courtesy of the
photographer; nested poster of
Harvey Milk by Tom Eure*

Clockwise from upper
left: Scott Smith,
Dan Nicoletta, Steve
Newman, and Randy
Shilts, at the reading
of *The Mayor of Castro
Street*, February 18,
1982. *Photo by Dan
Nicoletta, courtesy of the
photographer*

Alfred praised how the book "skillfully weaves the woof of history to the warp of biography," marrying the themes of Harvey as gay everyman to his Jewish heritage and love of theatricality. But after praising the "trenchant analysis" of *Mayor*'s epilogue, Alfred took his colleague to task for many flaws and missed opportunities.

In the book's concluding passages, Randy wrote, "Had it not been Harvey Milk in San Francisco, the legend would have settled on someone else, in another city, at another time. Harvey's sense of staging merely ensured that his legend would also prove good theater." *Merely*? To Alfred's thinking, Randy had left his central thesis unanswered: "Was Harvey charismatic or wasn't he?" The question couldn't be avoided if the intersection of Milk's life with gay liberation had the significance Randy had inferred. "Harvey was just discovering how to capture people's imagination," Alfred argued. "As a developing symbol of hope and focus for change, he was *pre*-charismatic, and only his martyrdom confirmed his charisma once and for all."

From there, he unleashed a litany of complaints about the oversimplification of certain actors and constituencies and giving "short shrift" to some of Milk's close advisors. "Shilts' style emphasizes razzle-dazzle at the expense of precision," Alfred continued, "and all too often his coloristic detail is inaccurate." Noting "half a hundred" errors that could have easily been corrected, he called out the finished product's many misspellings and punctuation errors. Setting aside the brisk pace at which Randy had cranked out the manuscript, Alfred noted, several editors had presumably handled the text before it went to print. In a snarky aside about the risks of trusting one's work to New York editors, he advised readers to "save your money, and wait for the paperback."

Alfred balanced his criticism with a final appraisal of the book's merits, presuming that the author would, as promised, fix all of the errors and inaccuracies in forthcoming editions: "The book would then be a significantly stronger work of history." *The Mayor of Castro Street* did work as "political portraiture," Alfred acknowledged, and given the liberties Harvey would sometimes take with the facts, perhaps it was fitting to play fast and loose with some of them. After all, he concluded, "Politics is theater, and the medium is the message."

Alfred's review would appear in the *Sentinel* in its entirety, save for one crucial detail. Whereas he had titled it "Milk Bio Evocative, But Flawed," the publisher shortened the page-one headline to "Milk Bio Flawed." Even though the byline noted it was a review and not a news story, the impression would be that an expert had debunked the book altogether. As editor, Alfred had some say in that decision, citing spacing issues and buzz within the community, but, he admitted, "People have to pick up the paper."

It wouldn't take long to hear Randy's reaction. "[Alfred] wanted to be my fact-checker, to check all the details, because he knew that I was doing this on an extremely tight schedule," he complained, "and I did not have the money to do it for him, to pay for him to be a fact-checker." Bringing up Alfred's attachment to a Milk-focused film project, he added, "And I feel like I have been the victim of a literary protection racket. If I would've paid him his protection money and hired that individual to do all the fact-checking, I would've gotten a good review from him."

Stunned by the accusations, Alfred countered, "If it hadn't been in Shilts's voice, I would've suspected it was some kind of put-on, because it's unlike him." Randy knew the book contained errors and inaccuracies, he answered, and of course his review would've been more positive if anybody had corrected them. "But as it is," Alfred argued, "I would've been derelict in my professional responsibility not to point out flaws that he knew were going to be in it when he published the book." Alfred tried phoning to discuss the matter, but Randy refused to take the call. In hindsight, Alfred understood the hesitance to pay him for a fact check, as Randy couldn't have known that the film project had already been nixed. Even though he stood by his review, Alfred did regret allowing the truncated headline, which he'd never intended to serve as a takedown of *Mayor*.

Privately, Randy fumed at what he considered petty nitpicking. "The jealous types who eagerly chronicled every last misspelling are saying I lied and that I never intended to make changes," he wrote to Michael Denneny, adding parenthetically, "They're unsophisticated about the nuances of publishing and are making my life miserable." It would help, he suggested, if Michael would make a public statement affirming that revisions would be made to the paperback.

What exactly were the mistakes? In the midst of all the commotion, San Francisco activist Jim Gordon wrote to Randy, noting thirty-eight errors, sixteen of them factual and twenty-two of the grammatical variety, that he hoped would be corrected in a second printing. Consistent with Alfred's review, many of the factual errors were fixable. "The fact that most of the errors are picayune is a tribute to your carefulness as a writer and historian," Gordon wrote. "I really hope the book is a best seller, because it's an outstanding biography!"

The Mayor of Castro Street performed relatively well, selling twenty-one thousand hardcovers and, the following year, seventeen thousand paperbacks. Away from the contentious epicenter of Milk's adopted home, its influence made ripples in ways that almost never happened for gay-themed stories. Yet, almost from its inception, *The Mayor of Castro Street* had been plagued by disagreements over who really owned the story: the community or the author?

"I ended up being on his team anyway," Dan Nicoletta commented, "because I'm one of those people that kept on turning students towards that material, just saying, 'If you want Harvey Milk 101, this is where you go.'" Even in the eyes of its most pointed critic, the book, with corrections, had the potential to be a significantly strong work of history. Yet, the very presence of those correctable errors, coupled with the sentiment that "Shilts was cashing in," had served to effectively discredit the author in the minds of certain detractors.

In the decade following *Mayor*'s publication, those unresolved disputes would come back to haunt Randy as he tried repeatedly to bring it to the big screen. Various attempts to jump-start a film project occurred over the next decade, the most prominent being an effort by Warner Bros., with Oliver Stone attached to direct. Objecting to the depiction of homosexuals in Stone's 1991 film *JFK*, gay activists demanded that any biopic of Harvey Milk should not only be helmed by an openly gay director but also star an openly gay actor playing the lead. What's more, Robin Williams was heavily rumored to be up for the central role, leading Cleve to complain, "Why do they keep wanting comedians to play Harvey?"

After Stone's withdrawal, the prospects for a Harvey Milk biopic would languish for another decade and a half before screenwriter Dustin Lance Black's meticulously researched screenplay triumphed against the long odds of history and political squabbling. With Cleve facilitating a number of introductions and with Milk's associates providing source material, Black teamed up with director Gus Van Sant to break through where previous efforts had failed. If not for the drawn-out disputes over *Mayor*, Cleve allowed, the makers of *Milk* could have at least acknowledged Randy in the credits. But the film's achievements came too late to be seen by many of Harvey's foot soldiers, including the journalist who'd first characterized him as a transformational figure in American history.

"Thank you for your interest in the on-going Lion Taming Quiz." For anyone needing to handle a fussy but lovable lion, all the answers could be found in a handwritten pamphlet Randy had helpfully created for his lover. What to do when mad at your lion? "Pat him on the head and softly try to explain what's bothering you." How to better understand your lion's point of view? "You should let your lion talk first since he often is more upset than you are." What to do to punish your lion? "Punishment is not necessary since lions are so nice they never make the same mistake again if it makes his tamer love him."

Charming as he could be, life with Randy could also be one hell of a handful. But at least for the time being, even the rough spots didn't seem that rough. As he and Steve pushed past the one-year mark, their relationship became the longest Randy had ever kept with any man. And although his love notes came less frequently, they still appeared after the occasional spat or while Steve was out of town. For once, Randy had a lover who didn't disappear at the first sign of trouble, and for the time being, the good times outweighed the bad. "He did have a wonderful inner child that I tried to nurture as much as possible," Steve remembered. "And he had a rebellious child too."

Randy Shilts and Steve Newman in Mendocino, California, 1982.
Courtesy of Steve Newman

What might now be called an open relationship was what they both just called a relationship. Sexual monogamy mattered less than emotional commitment, so that nights out allowed for playing separately or bringing home a third. From their earliest days, such arrangements had made sense because both men preferred topping. And although neither considered themselves part of the leather and BDSM scenes, Randy especially liked to dabble. On visits to the Catacombs in South of Market, Steve recalled, his lover would prominently position himself just inside the entrance, filing his nails with an emery board while silently eying the new arrivals.

"It was a freewheeling party in San Francisco," Steve recalled, "and if you didn't go out on a Friday or Saturday night, you thought you were missing out on something."

While many facts were still being established about gay-related immune deficiency (or GRID, as some were then calling it), crucial details like the underlying cause, how it was transmitted, and how widely it had spread remained unclear. Mainstream news organizations still produced the occasional medical story, but most of the coverage came from a handful of gay journalists who, often against the wishes of their publishers and advertisers, insisted on keeping it there.

Both on the radio and in his role with the *Sentinel*, Randy Alfred had been generating more than his fair share of that coverage, inviting Kaposi sarcoma (KS) poster boy Bobbi Campbell to speak on *The Gay Life* and write about his experiences as a columnist for the *Sentinel*. For that same broadcast, Alfred also managed to secure a lengthy interview with dermatologist Marcus Conant and oncologist Paul Volberding, who were quickly becoming the leading local experts on gay cancer.

Randy Shilts's arrival on the GRID beat came nearly a full year after the first *MMWR* report, in May 1982. By this point, an astonishing two-thirds of KS patients diagnosed in 1980 had already passed away, while the overall death rate among those with pneumocystis carinii pneumonia was climbing to 30 percent. And with an average of one new case per day reported, scientists were facing the unnerving prospect of widespread contagion before they even knew for sure what was causing the disease.

"In San Francisco, it's an epidemic beyond anything that's acceptable," Selma Dritz told him. "It's like nothing we've ever had." Randy's story stuck closely to the available facts. The strongest predictors of GRID infection included high numbers of sex partners, frequent visits to bathhouses, and heavy drug use, but there were enough puzzling cases to complicate the search for a cause. At the same time, he noted, the politics around GRID were already taking shape, as California Congressman Henry Waxman was demanding to know why more federal resources hadn't been committed.

As medical stories go, the subject matter had little new to offer. But by highlighting how GRID patients reckoned with rejection, shame, and almost-certain death, Randy became one of the first mainstream journalists to cover the disease as not simply a medical curiosity but a full-fledged human-interest story. Wednesdays, he noted, had become the GRID support group meeting night, sponsored by the Berkeley-based Shanti Project, where members detailed their struggles with disclosing their illness to religious family members and, in one case, being banned from visiting a comatose lover by his relatives. Equally disheartening, Bobbi Campbell told him, was the impulse by many gays to focus on certain drugs used or "exotic" sexual practices, relegating GRID sufferers to the category of sexual extremes. "There is this need to focus on these aspects of the disease," Campbell remarked, "so people can put the victims at arm's length from themselves so it doesn't hit close to home."

With his initial foray into what would soon be named acquired immune deficiency syndrome (AIDS), Randy touched on several themes that would become hallmarks of his later work, including unheeded warnings, political machinations, and struggles with loss, rejection, and shame.

And then, not long after the story's publication, he took the summer off. For the moment, Randy's top priorities remained unchanged: his blossoming career and near-perfect relationship. For a blissful few months he was able to focus almost exclusively on both, renting a cabin with Steve in Tahoe City while writing his screenplay for *Mayor*.

The rustic confines provided enough distance from city life to enjoy rugged hikes, horseback rides, and easygoing lovemaking. "I must admit the weather-man and I are undergoing severe culture shock," Randy wrote to his newsroom colleagues in late July. "After seven years in San Francisco, I had forgotten that there actually were people who breed. Don't get me wrong—some of my best friends are heterosexuals—but that's all they've got up here. What I'd give to see one alligator shirt. Most of the people up here think camping is something you do in the woods."

Randy's byline remained inconspicuous in the *Chronicle* through the waning months of 1982. In October, a prominent feature on AIDS, gay men, and declining promiscuity went to another science correspondent, and when Dianne Feinstein vetoed Harry Britt's bill recognizing the same-sex partners of city workers, writers on the City Hall beat covered the ensuing fallout. Meanwhile, many men still carried on sexually as if nothing had changed. Before the year was over, one more adventure in paradise awaited Steve and Randy. Over a Christmas trip to Key West, the two basked poolside by day at a luxury resort, while pillaging the vibrant gay scene at night. In this small corner of the world, at least, the sexual revolution seemed to be happily carrying on.

Out at the clubs on a festive Saturday night, the two encountered a young couple giving off decidedly mixed signals. One definitely wanted to go home with them; the other didn't much care for the idea. The feeling, it seemed, was mutual: only the former, and not the latter, was invited to back to their place. As they stumbled back to the resort, Randy and Steve tugged at the guy they wanted, while he argued with his boyfriend. Reaching the gates, the younger couple erupted into a screaming argument, carrying on like feral cats as Steve and Randy tried to pull them apart. The only pause came when an older queen threw open his cabin door, shouting, "God damn it! I didn't pay $400 a night to listen to this. Go to bed!"

Seizing on the distraction, Randy and Steve yanked the young man through the gate, slamming it shut and leaving his lover behind. Once inside, the threesome went on well into the early morning, and when a pair of handcuffs appeared, the young man proved all too eager to try them on. Exhilaration soon gave way to exhaustion, however, when Steve, as he usually did, was the first to fall asleep. He'd only been dozing for a few hours, however, when he awoke to someone's foot softly kicking him. Their guest, now wedged uncomfortably between the two passed-out lovers, was still locked in the handcuffs.

No problem. Steve rolled out of bed, stumbling to his luggage and digging out the key. Returning, he bent over the naked, sex-drenched guest, who turned obligingly to be unlocked—*Oh shit.* Still shaking out the cobwebs, Steve stared unbelievingly at the half-broken key. As Randy slowly stirred, Steve got dressed and walked over to the pool, explaining the situation to the older, thong-clad gays who'd gotten up early to sunbathe. This was Key West, after all; someone had to own a pair of standard-issue handcuffs, right?

No luck. And calling a locksmith proved useless, as none were open on a Sunday morning. *Well.* Regardless of the situation, there was no need to be uncivilized. Steve ventured out for coffee and pastries, which he and Randy hand-fed to their guest. Finally, Steve managed to find a sleazy adult bookstore, where the manager had a key that he thought might work. When the young man was set free, he thanked them for a lovely time and asked about coming over again that night.

In the meantime, word had raced through the resort like wildfire, the details growing more salacious with each retelling. Randy and Steve had kidnapped this poor boy back to their cabin! Well before the advent of cell phones, the Internet, or social media, the nation's gay gossip circles lit up faster than a church lady's prayer chain. So swift and far-reaching did the story travel that by midafternoon, they were fielding calls from San Francisco friends demanding, "What the hell is going on there?"

Randy loved every minute of it. In the twenty months since meeting Steve, he'd had a near-perfect run of good fortune, but he could hardly have known how distant and fantastical those days would later seem. In late December the *Bay Area Reporter* shared the story of a young man who, after developing KS lesions, had opted to take his own life instead of waiting for the illness to run its course. Back in San Francisco, Randy would quickly realize that not even a burgeoning career or a near-perfect romance could shield him from the horrors that were beginning to unfold.

10 | 1983

FOR MANY, THE PARTY had continued well into 1982. By now, however, the disease had reached a stage where it could no longer be ignored. An illness some still associated with the sexual extremes was showing signs of dangerously high incidence in urban gay men. Assuming that AIDS would stay contained in any sexual subculture was as shortsighted as believing that the general population was insulated from what some regarded as the *H* disease: hookers, heroin addicts, Haitians, hemophiliacs, and homosexuals.

In San Francisco an impressive cadre of medical professionals, caregivers, and activists was beginning to dig in, thanks to city funding to fill the void left by a noncommittal federal government. "It was like being at the center of the forces of history," remembered University of California, San Francisco epidemiologist Dr. Andrew Moss. With his colleague Dr. Michael Gorman, Moss had undertaken the city's first AIDS surveillance study, finding that in neighborhoods with high concentrations of gay men, known cases had reached a startling incidence of one infection for every 350 never-married men.

Moss and Gorman had begun quietly sharing their data with local gay leaders who, from the outset, raised concerns around how to publicize it. The researchers were preparing a letter for the British medical journal the *Lancet*, which would take less time to review than a full research article. However, if the data was released prematurely, they risked not being able to publish it at all. Meanwhile, some gay leaders raised the specter of widespread panic within the gay community and attacks from antigay conservatives. Whether the two researchers liked it or not, their work had become undeniably political.

"I thought it was real important," Randy later remembered. "And then I found out that all these gay leaders had had this study for two months and they hadn't done anything to tell people about it. 'We'll release it through appropriate channels,' which meant the gay press. Or they have to have another meeting to decide about it." Bypassing Moss and Gorman entirely, he pressed the issue directly with the project's lead investigator, Dr. Marcus Conant. "He basically wanted the story," Moss recalled, "and thought it belonged to him."

Randy saw it differently. "Well, this was when everybody thought it was media hype and it wasn't real," he argued. "Everybody's out there getting fucked in the bathhouses every weekend, thinking that AIDS is media hype, and they weren't releasing this information." The English-born, Stanford-educated scientist did not appreciate the pestering of an aggressive young reporter. Moss declined to share the letter with Randy, but soon after, a draft began making its way through local medical circles, ultimately landing in the hands of Selma Dritz, who didn't give a damn about leaking it to the press.

The report included maps depicting the concentration of AIDS cases in San Francisco's densest gay neighborhoods, which, to Moss's irritation, Randy wanted to publish as well. "I thought that was a really bad idea," he remembered, "but also, I really didn't like being hustled. He was very aggressive, and very, it's all about him—very much, 'my story.'" Randy agreed to leave out the maps, but before it went to press, he recalled, several gay leaders told him that the story would only do harm.

Yet, he hadn't been alone in seeking answers. The Harvey Milk Democratic Club, led by Harvey's protégé Bill Kraus, was also demanding to know why the community hadn't been alerted. "Worst crisis ever," Kraus emphasized in late March remarks to the Milk Club. "We must take care of ourselves. Gay lib is not just sex, it's taking care of one another, having respect for one another. If there's a latency period and if it's sexually transmissible, then there's a real danger."

The next day, Randy's story appeared prominently in the *Chronicle*. While not directly challenging the researchers, it did question whose interests gay leaders were serving. After all, in just a few months, International Lesbian and Gay Freedom Day was expected to once again draw around three hundred thousand people, many of them tourists who risked taking the disease home to their far-flung communities. "These questions are simply too important to be ignored at a time when the gay community faces a plague that, at best, threatens to destroy our urban communities, or, at worst, threatens to destroy all of us," Randy insisted.

"I don't think there was anybody who wanted to hide it," Moss countered, "but quite a few people wanted to be really careful about it, and a lot of people thought there was severe danger of backlash." He and Gorman succeeded in publishing their letter and continued presenting the data during a period Moss remembered as the "rolling thunder" of early 1983. However, his relationship with Randy remained forever soured. While certainly a very good writer who could craft an interesting story, Randy, in his estimation, took too many liberties and showed little interest in, or patience for, the rigors of scientific research. "I think he was journalistically unreliable," the epidemiologist observed.

As new AIDS cases continued to climb, the political was now becoming undeniably personal. Privately, Randy was especially distressed when his friend Gary Walsh, a well-liked psychotherapist, began telling patients and loved ones that he, too, had been diagnosed with the disease. "Gary Walsh and I knew each other in the casual-yet-intimate way that many young gay men knew each other during the casual-yet-intimate 1970s," Randy later recalled. Gary had established one of the Castro's earliest counseling practices for gay men, and like Randy, he'd had a fondness for the cruising rituals of those carefree years.

"I would say that Gary celebrated sex among men, and casual sex," his lover Matthew Krieger remembered. For years, Gary had been working to normalize therapy to overcome the deep-seated traumas associated with gay and lesbian experiences. To be "casual yet intimate" meant that meeting someone sexually didn't preclude the possibility of a lasting friendship. Randy knew Gary Walsh to be one of the people who really cared, and now he was dying—not, however, without a fight.

Despite flagging energy and bouts of fever, thrush, KS lesions, and other illnesses, Gary confronted his diagnosis in ways that were becoming practically a ritual among certain gays: seeking out holistic remedies in another country, contemplating taking his own life before the disease could overtake him, and eventually coming to a place of powerful acceptance. Joining Bobbi Campbell and others who refused to go quietly, Gary embraced the role of patient-activist, insisting that people with AIDS be heard and respected by the public. Gary and Randy talked frequently throughout that year, affording an intimate glimpse of someone living with a purpose, even as his death became more inevitable.

For Randy, the experience of watching a good friend die was nothing short of hell. "The pain would grip me in the stomach and not let go," he reflected. While Gary and other activists were working to raise the disease's profile, including a nationally televised confrontation with Moral Majority leader Jerry Falwell, Randy became devoted to keeping the disease in the headlines. "He's living it in the sense of 'This is like being in Vietnam,'" Katy Butler recounted. "I remember him saying, 'When I come to work, nobody is living in the same world with me. Their friends aren't dying.'"

"He had to be very persistent within the paper," she added. "It wasn't like he had an editor above him who was saying, 'Jeez, this is really important.'" To the amazement of David Perlman, once Randy made AIDS part of his beat, he brought an impressive network of sources to it. "I mean, he was locked into the community," Perlman recalled. From City Hall to congressional aides, health care professionals to patients and activists, he just seemed to know everybody.

The community, meanwhile, remained locked in its own distracting battles. Locally, the year had gotten off to a rocky start, with San Francisco's gay Democratic clubs taking sides in the heated, and ultimately unsuccessful, "Dump Dianne" mayoral recall. At the same time, efforts to raise awareness and prevent new infections were meeting with resistance. While Randy's reporting hewed closely to local medical officials' concerns, both the *Bay Area Reporter* and the *Sentinel* continued to couch their coverage with disclaimers that the disease's sexual transmission had yet to be proven. In the *Bay Area Reporter*, editor Paul Lorch promised to "up the noise level on AIDS," signifying a turn in public discourse that even Randy initially applauded. Lorch's noise, however, quickly drew reactions of astonishment and horror. While the *BAR* did increase its AIDS coverage, Lorch's editorials adopted a surprisingly inflammatory tone.

Gay men's sexual pastimes had turned their bodies' "sewer system into a playpen," a joke that had now turned "rapidly sour," he commented. What's more, he postulated, the money that activists were demanding for medical care would lead to the "warehousing" of AIDS patients, while the doctors and researchers working to stop the disease had mainly their own interests at heart, including money, fame, and power. Local AIDS patients, including Gary Walsh, responded with an open letter in the *Sentinel* to Lorch and *BAR* publisher Bob Ross, calling for an end to the irresponsible commentaries and editorial "slander." Lorch replied in scathing terms, acidly mocking the activists and doubling down on his incendiary commentaries.

Consequently, San Francisco Public Health Director Mervyn Silverman hardly knew what he was stepping into when he held his first meeting in mid-May with gay business leaders and bathhouse representatives. To Silverman, the issue seemed uncontroversial: not enough people understood the underlying health problem, and the places where men were meeting offered an opportunity for education on how to protect themselves. "I was trying to get the gay community to close or to get the bathhouses to clean up, rather than this straight guy in the health department," he recalled. "Because I wanted it not only to be the action of removing an unsafe venue but [also to have] an educational impact."

Silverman left that first meeting assuming he'd accomplished what his public health training had taught him to seek: a consensus approach with buy-in from the affected community. Battle lines, however, were already being drawn. "How do we pursue a civil rights movement and still deal with the disease?" Randy later recalled. "The first reaction was, don't deal with the disease." As coverage dragged on through early June, letter writers in the gay papers took to assailing the entire affair, from Silverman's failure to include gay Democratic club leaders in the meeting to the increase in mainstream news stories tying AIDS specifically to gay men.

Randy's own take appeared soon after on the *Chronicle*'s editorial page, detailing how politics, in his view, had influenced Silverman's approach more than public health. "Mayor Dianne Feinstein's administration is closely aligned with the Toklas Club—which backed the mayor in the recall election while the Milk Club opposed her—and the health department's low-key approach to AIDS education may be more than mere coincidence," he wrote, overlooking the fact that Toklas leaders vehemently objected both to Silverman's meeting and the singling out of gay bathhouses. On the whole, Randy's point that AIDS was becoming politicized was correct. But lumping together the motives of Public Health, which wanted gays to take ownership of the response, with the that of the mayor, who wanted the baths closed, and that of her gay backers, who wanted them kept open, made little sense.

The arguing soon spilled further into the mainstream when journalists Peter Collier and David Horowitz, in a *California* magazine piece titled "White Wash," raised the question of whether gay leaders were perpetuating a conspiracy of silence while AIDS raged uncontrollably. Addressing the controversy around Moss and Gorman's surveillance study, the story seemed to broadly paint a segment of gay politicos as more focused on public relations than saving lives. Naturally, much of the controversy stemmed from Randy's reporting in the *Chronicle*.

"In eight years as a journalist, I've never been under such pressure to suppress a story," Randy told the authors. "People kept telling me it would hurt business in the Castro, hurt the Gay Rights Bill in Sacramento. My feeling is, what the hell—if you're dead, what does the rest of it matter?"

The gay press swiftly countered, but Randy stood his ground. "I just told them I don't get paid to not write news stories," he recounted. "To me, it was so obvious that the news value was there. It just made me so mad. Who were these elders of Zion, who were going to decide what gay people had a right to know or not?"

The shift in Randy's tone was becoming ever more apparent. Unlike Silverman and other officials, who lacked practical familiarity with gay politics, he knew the tendencies and self-interests of every figure involved. His skepticism of wealthy gay business owners, and especially bathhouse operators, dated back almost a decade. And what he perceived as political leaders' timidity only fueled his suspicion that certain power brokers were more concerned with consolidating power than saving the lives of ordinary people.

"There was a lot of stress on us," Steve Newman recalled. "Of course, our friends were dying. It was the worst of times. I don't think there has ever been a worse time in my life than that." As the story unfolded, Steve remembered, "it became clear more and more men were going to die. [Randy] thought it was Armageddon, of course." These long workdays were leading to increasingly fraught evenings at home, with Randy sobbing privately to Steve, "We are all going to die . . . all going to die."

As the ordeal continued, Steve was growing alarmed at how hard his lover was taking it. Maybe, he suggested, it was time to move on and cover something else and let the science reporters cover AIDS. At the very suggestion, however, Randy became incensed. "You don't understand," he seethed during one of their arguments. "I am the only one who can do this. There is nobody else that is going to warn us. It has to be me!"

Inconsolable moods weren't the only changes Steve was noticing. For him, some wine with dinner and a nightly joint had always been enough to take the edge off, but he had no way of knowing about the pot Randy was smoking on his daily commute, the lunch-hour cocktails he needed to get through the afternoon, or the lines of cocaine, snorted discreetly in a TV station's locked restroom. For years, Randy had kept his social circles mostly compartmentalized, so that he and Steve each had their own friends, with only a handful they shared in common. Although Linda Alband had moved to Seattle, Ann Neuenschwander was now a fixture, along with ex-lover Dan Yoder, friend Bill Cagle, and a handful of Ann's girlfriends from college. The more he saw Randy come home wasted, the more Steve would fume at what he saw as those friends' enabling, never seeing how often Randy had been the initiator or how he'd even taken to drinking apart from those friends.

Unsurprisingly, Steve's pleas to cut back proved a nonstarter from the get-go. It would, however, provide the fodder for Randy to later accuse his lover of acting not out of protectiveness or concern but out of jealousy and possessiveness. In this new reality, the habits that helped him cope in the past were proving stubbornly resistant to change. To see Randy stumble down the street in search of his car may have prompted some to wonder if he had a problem. It wasn't his behavior in the streets, however, that was raising eyebrows.

By mid-1983, some of the city's more illustrious bathhouses were beginning to feel the strain, and one of its largest, South of Market's popular Hothouse, was going out of business. Not long before it closed, however, journalist Mark Thompson, who'd worked with Randy at the *Advocate*, visited the one-time Victorian boarding house. At the top of its majestic staircase, he was startled to find Randy, naked except for a 49ers jersey. Making eye contact, Randy stammered and beat a hasty retreat. "I didn't disapprove of him being there at all," Thompson later wrote, "only his taste in fashion and apparent two-facedness."

Soon after, Randy recounted the Hothouse's liquidation sale as "the kinkiest garage sale in San Francisco history," complete with leather slings, mirrors, heavy chains, and washing machines. While bothered by Randy's lack of candor, Thompson still professed admiration for his one-time colleague's courage and dedication, calling him "a fellow advocate of exceptional talent." Others, meanwhile, were embracing a less charitable word: *traitor*.

———————

A San Francisco morning in late June doesn't look that different from any other day: overcast and foggy, with a slight chill in the air. The five o'clock alarm told Steve it was time to get up, leaving Randy to sleep a little longer while he prepared his morning weather forecast. Steve was still half-asleep when the phone rang, but what he was told quickly jolted him awake. Hanging up the telephone, he crept gingerly into the bedroom, where his lover lay entangled in the warm folds of their bed.

"Your family called," he began, pausing so Randy would comprehend.

"What did they want?" Randy sleepily replied.

There was no good way to soften the blow. "Your mother died." In the middle of the night, a massive stroke had taken the fifty-nine-year-old Norma.

Randy bolted upright, a look of panic in his eyes as he stammered, "I have to get back to writing."

That entire morning, he never shed a tear while finishing work on several stories. Steve booked his flight to Michigan, offering a warning as Randy hurried out the door. "Of all the times in your life, this is the one time you should not drink." By the time he touched down in Grand Rapids, Randy was so drunk he nearly fell down the steps of the plane.

He'd tried to scribble out an obituary, focusing only on the good. Norma Shilts had raised several sons from "humble rural Michigan roots," he noted, who'd gone on to distinguish themselves in journalism, physics, and law. "Mother was a down-home woman from the sticks of Michigan who never got her name in the newspaper or had her 15 minutes of fame," he scrawled. "But she gave us the values and the spark to make—" For once, the words escaped him. "Always urging us to do what—" He'd reached another dead end. "To strike our own paths and follow our cons— . . . the best . . ." Randy never finished the sentence.

The surrealism of the week was inescapable. When Randy finally found the words to describe it, they came in a piece published weeks later in the *Chronicle*, relating his experience to the industrial Midwest's lingering recession and decline. "From my California perspective," Randy wrote, "Michigan had long ago become a clichéd metaphor of the American recession, told and retold stories of Depression-level unemployment and decaying urban slums. But there are no clichés in the faces of parents, aunts, uncles, and cousins who have had the rules by which they lived irrevocably transformed."

His father now had sole responsibility for teenage son David, and to Randy's surprise, he noticed people discreetly slipping Bud some cash in lieu of flowers. "At home, Dad wept as he looked at the $500 pile of fives, 10s and occasional 20s," Randy recounted. "His tears came from gratitude, knowing that most of the money was from people who didn't have much more than he did."

Following Norma's burial, the four adult brothers found themselves alone together in the family's backyard. With Reed now living in Boston, Denny in West Germany, Gary in Illinois, and Randy in California, such reunions were rare. All week long, Reed wondered to himself, *Why did Randy seem like he was almost happy about their mom's death?* Pulling a joint from his pocket, Randy lit it, took a deep drag, passed it around, and began singing: "Ding! Dong! The witch is dead."

"Which old witch?" his brothers chimed in.

"The wicked witch. Ding! Dong! The wicked witch is dead!"

It seemed odd to Reed, but he joined in anyway. "Ding! Dong! The witch is dead! Which old witch? The wicked witch. Ding! Dong! The wicked witch is dead!"

They caused such a commotion that when family friend Patricia Hart stopped by to offer Bud some help, she could clearly hear it from the front yard. Years later, Patricia, who eventually became the second Mrs. Russell Shilts, related the story to Linda Alband. She had no idea the boys had that kind of relationship with their mother.

Back in San Francisco, the never-ending bickering quickly cast a shadow over Randy's homecoming. Fallout from recent AIDS stories had made him a prime target for criticism within the community, but when the gay rags did take issue with Randy's journalism, it often seemed to be around issues of semantics or tone. The *Sentinel*'s news editor, Gary Schweikhart, alluded to him as "the *Chronicle*'s most famous token, whose exploitative articles about AIDS have only added fuel to the flames of hysteria that are engulfing our community." But in defending the politicos accused of "suppressing" the Moss and Gorman study, even Schweikhart conceded they may have spun the findings a certain way.

However, in the same issue, Randy Alfred's column assailed the "White Wash" authors but raised questions about the outsized influence of bathhouse advertising on gay publications. "Why," he noted, "did it take five months from the release of early data on sexual transmissibility until gay media started printing explicit recommendations to cool it sexually?" Liberation, Alfred continued, didn't have to be an all-or-nothing proposition. "Counseling moderation in the face of unknown risks is not anti-liberation," he wrote. "Until science learns more about those risks, using ourselves as guinea pigs is anti-liberation in the deepest possible sense, because it is anti-life."

For his part, Randy later recounted that he didn't start out believing the bathhouses should or would be closed. "I just thought it was an issue you had to talk about. You couldn't talk about this disease and not talk about bathhouses. I used to go there. I know what happens." His high-profile position made him a lightning rod for scrutiny, however, especially during local AIDS forums.

"I would see him all the time at these huge community meetings that were really emotional and lots of screaming," remembered Laurie Garrett, at the time reporting for National Public Radio. "And I think our analysis of the problem was quite similar, except that I was coming at it from science, he was coming at it from advocacy." Privately, Laurie had misgivings about how Randy spoke during those unruly forums. "There would be a long prelude that would be laying out his analysis. And then, there might be a finding at the end."

The world he knew was beginning to shrink, leaving fewer spaces where AIDS didn't invade every anxious thought or conversation. The attacks were coming with greater regularity from people who, like Randy, were struggling to cope with the senselessness and scale of AIDS. "People who are politically committed, no matter what movement or cause, they do not appreciate independent analysis," he later complained. "All they want is their party line presented, and especially if you are from within the group and you criticize it, or even question it or even present another point of view . . . you become worse than a straight person who does the same thing."

No matter how hard he tried, Randy never completely shook off the hurt feelings. "I don't get any better," he later lamented, "but then, the other part of me thinks, well, I think the reason my writing is good [when] I do the important stuff is that the sensitivity comes out." Steeling himself to the criticism, he feared, would make him less responsive to the gravity of the subject matter. "I want to be the kind of writer who still connects to people on a human level."

At a protest in early October, Randy took interest in another kind of voice, which stood out amid the usual assemblage of demonstrators: the singularly sorrowful cry of a mother, grieving for her recently deceased son. "AIDS is not politics, AIDS is not gay—AIDS is just a killer," Gloria Rodriguez stated. Hearing a friend say that her son, Jes, deserved to die had led her to attend the demonstration, she said, clutching photos she kept in her wallet. Like Norma Shilts with her youngest child's autism, Rodriguez was turning her grief into advocacy, hoping that her only son's ordeal had not been in vain.

Describing her efforts, Randy offered more than just a point for under-scoring urgency. In the absence of leadership, and with the best available evidence muddled by gamesmanship and groundless speculation, too many people seemed to react protectively out of fear and indignation, instead of common decency and kindness. Even in health care settings, some providers appeared more interested in ridding themselves of AIDS patients altogether.

In the same week Randy relayed Gloria Rodriguez's story, another dispiriting bombshell landed at the San Francisco AIDS Foundation. Lying on a gurney, too weak to lift his head, twenty-seven-year-old Morgan MacDonald had been flown by chartered jet from Gainesville, Florida, and delivered by ambulance to foundation staff, who immediately had him taken to San Francisco General's Ward 5b.

The story attracted national attention, with city leaders condemning the high-profile "AIDS dumping," and Mervyn Silverman announcing plans to bill the Florida hospital for the entire cost of caring for their abandoned patient. Dianne Feinstein, herself a former nurse, denounced the action as setting terrible precedent, forcing a weakened patient to choose between being thrown out on the street or flown across the country for treatment.

In response, Gainesville officials had defended their actions as "humanitarian," as if sending a gay man with AIDS to die with his own kind was better than caring for him themselves. When MacDonald's heart gave out two weeks after his arrival, Feinstein commented, "It is sad that a young man had to spend his final days as a medical outcast."

The entire ordeal compounded a sense of dread among those on San Francisco's frontlines. The city's funding commitment already surpassed that of the federal government, Feinstein noted, resulting in a model for AIDS care the rest of the country could emulate. Instead, here was the worst possible alternative: other jurisdictions simply passing along the problem, instead of modifying their practices.

Just two weeks later, insult was added to injury as Randy mingled in the fraternity of the San Francisco Press Club awards. The *Chronicle* was beginning to earn some well-deserved recognition for its AIDS coverage, which was far outpacing the efforts of other major dailies. Randy, with colleagues David Perlman and Charles Pettit, collected an honorable mention that night for one of those AIDS features, but the accolades meant next to nothing once the guest of honor stood up to speak.

"What's the hardest part about having AIDS?" asked Bill Kurtis of *CBS Morning News*. "It's trying to convince your wife you're Haitian." Out in the banquet hall, Randy sat fuming. This disease had been no laughing matter for Morgan MacDonald or the other patients of Ward 5b, not for Gloria Rodriguez, and certainly not for Gary Walsh, who'd begun to consider taking his own life. But among mainstream journalists, supposedly the vanguard against abuses by the powerful, the entire epidemic was still seen as something of a dirty little joke, to be batted around with a wink or an elbow to the ribs. In later years, Randy would cite the cringeworthy joke as influential to his writing. For the time being, however, the storm was going nowhere, and Randy's year in hell was far from over.

––––––––––––––

"Maybe we should have seen it all coming, the deadly hangover after the heady and often hedonistic decade that gays had enjoyed in the 1970s." The word processor projected a cold, indifferent glow as Randy sank deeper into thought. With the bleakest of years tumbling toward its darkest, briefest of days, this uninspiring mid-November afternoon was doing little to boost his spirits. Every facet of gay life he'd previously covered now seemed tainted by the scourge of this new, AIDS-tinged reality.

The *Chronicle* was planning to devote an entire mid-January issue of *This World*, its Sunday newsmagazine, to AIDS, with Randy as its major contributor. Ahead of its release, he was working on a commentary addressing questions around the disease's impact on the larger cause of gay liberation. "If a group of social engineers had consciously set out [to] create an ideal breeding ground for the proliferation of a deadly, sexually transmitted disease, they couldn't have done any better than gays did for themselves over the past 10 years," he wrote.

The revolution had been a sexual one, after all, and it would be difficult for someone not to reconsider their own past behaviors, given recent events. Call it shame or repentance or hysteria, but now even the slightest sign of fever or an unexpected bruise could trigger waves of panic and second-guessing. And for that, Randy laid the responsibility, at least partly, on gay elites for their devotion to pushing an agenda of respectability and economic clout.

"As part of the campaign to gain social acceptance for what had long been considered a deviant lifestyle," he charged, "the gay political leaders argued convincingly that homosexuals certainly were not the old stereotypes of depraved, drugged-out, alcoholic, promiscuous, sex-obsessed men with a penchant for kinky sexual acts. Even as the politicians proselytized, however, entire subcultures and business networks grew up in major cities, catering to drugged-out, alcoholic, promiscuous, sex-obsessed men with a penchant for kinky sexual acts."

Even if just a minority of gays were living full-time in the fast lane, their sexual subcultures weren't exclusive from each other. People dabbled. "Mainstream gays who led more conventional lifestyles at first took comfort in early data which indicated that the first victims came from the all-nighters with histories of drug use and esoteric sex," he observed. "It was only happening to them, not the typical homosexuals. But, it turned out, the disease was just picking off the stragglers first."

It was clear now that the incubation period from infection to AIDS-defining symptoms could take longer than was first believed, meaning the window to proliferate might well have spanned the entire period of gays' ascendance in San Francisco. "When the clean-cut Castro men donned their cashmere sweaters and wandered to the Pacific Heights gay bars, they took AIDS with them," Randy postulated. "Within months, it was evident the disease spread quickly from the fast-lane into every segment of the gay community."

Collectively, it added up to one dispiriting conclusion: "The party is over now." And if it wasn't, Randy continued, then it should be. So said the doctors and scientists who vented their frustrations to him, both on and off the record. To their consternation, however, patronage at the bathhouses, which had dipped earlier in the year, was climbing back to previous levels, prompting Selma Dritz to complain that AIDS patients were still having casual sex in those establishments. In reporting this development, Randy did try to be fair, noting that the baths provided more for their customers than just easy sex.

"You have to remember that some AIDS patients live in terrible flophouse hotels and they use the baths as a place to clean up or watch television," one volunteer told him, making them cleaner, warmer, and more welcoming than the places where many otherwise homeless persons with AIDS would end up. Regardless, Selma countered, "We've got to work this out on a community basis. We can understand that they're trying to get everything they can when they have a life-threatening disease, but they shouldn't be taking other people down with them."

And here, for Randy, was the problem as 1983 was drawing to a close. A journalist's job, as he saw it, was to present all sides of an issue and let the community argue it out. But the more he was criticized for even writing about the baths, the more he came to embrace the position of medical experts who asked why they were still open. "I had health people saying, 'We've got to close these bathhouses,'" he later recalled. "And I remember one of my editors said, 'They should be closed.' And I said, 'Oh, it's never going to happen.' I was just convinced. And then, the more they argued against closing them, then I started coming to the point of view that gee, this is all stupid. People were acting out their denial."

Randy once confided to his brother Gary that in his freelancing days, he'd taken to writing up some of his more debauched encounters on Folsom Street, changing a few details, and selling the stories to gay stroke magazines. But even during those decadent times, the evidence of a community flirting with disaster had been there all along, just as Randy had reported during those times. Casual sex had been pervasive to gay life long enough to make changing those behaviors difficult, even when the consequences were now acknowledged by many to be deadly.

"Every time I've had risky sex in the past eight months," *BAR* contributor Paul Reed confessed, "I've vowed the next day never to do it again, even taken a red felt pen and marked a large red 'X' on my calendar. Now, to look back over that calendar is almost chilling. To think that each red X indicates an unsafe trick that was vowed to be the last such encounter is unsettling."

Even with efforts to promote safe sex workshops and condom use, many were now left with the stark impression that the only safe sex was no sex at all. To replace the fraternal comfort of the baths, some men were organizing private parties where they would strip, watch porn, and stroke off in front of each other, while minimizing any contact by which fluids could be shared. In the final version of his commentary, Randy mentioned these efforts; it wasn't that men weren't trying, but navigating this new terrain could be exhausting, especially when self-protecting thoughts could be easily overridden by the impulse to just do what came naturally.

A few weeks before the special issue of *This World* went to press, the *Chronicle*'s Leah Garchik, the section editor for the Sunday magazine, called a meeting to make decisions on content. Overall, everything was taking shaping quite nicely, as David Perlman was writing an update on the disease's medical mystery, while other contributors addressed issues of stigma and fear within the general population.

Randy, meanwhile, had been busy. His lead story would highlight the sometimes off-beat, always compassionate goings-on of Ward 5b, while in a piece examining the political response to AIDS, he made use of a trove of Freedom of Information Act documents to show how the Reagan administration had forced Centers for Disease Control (CDC) officials to cobble together a barely adequate AIDS response using other budget lines. And accompanying his social impact commentary was a shorter piece rehashing the politics of regulating the bathhouses, which noted how San Francisco was well ahead of other major cities in committing resources to epidemiology and AIDS care.

Randy had delivered a compelling range of articles, but, it seemed, he didn't know when to step back and let others do their jobs. "In the course of that," Leah recalled, "because Randy cared so much about this, he was kind of directing traffic; he kind of took over." Leah knew how the magazine should be assembled, and here was Randy telling people what to write and where their stories should go. "And so, I felt at some point that he had usurped my authority," she explained.

After the meeting, Leah pulled him aside for a discreet word. In more than a decade at the *Chronicle*, she'd learned to keep a long fuse, but the way he'd walked all over her had been unprofessional. "Randy, I'm the editor of this section," she told him. "You may be the principal contributor to it, but it's my section."

What happened next was like nothing she'd ever seen, before or since. Like a little boy who'd been scolded by his teacher, Randy caught his breath. Unable to summon the words, his brown eyes began to swell, unable to hold back the tears. "He started crying," Leah remembered. "I was shocked." She hadn't been abusive or vulgar, just firm. "It was so shocking to me," she repeated, "talking to a colleague who started crying."

———————

Christmas in San Francisco didn't look that different from any other time of the year: overcast and foggy, with a slight chill in the air. With no travel plans, Steve and Randy decided to throw a small party on December 24, inviting a few friends over for drinks. As usual, the cocktails were flowing freely, and

Steve and a buddy decided to go buy some cocaine. When they returned, the two boarded the elevator alongside an eye-catching specimen: a stunningly handsome leather daddy, about their age, and perfectly outfitted. "He was dressed the part," Steve remembered. "He was impeccable in his leather design."

Steve and others knew the man as a fixture in the leather and S&M scene. His name was George, known as Father George in local street ministries, where he did outreach with homeless gay youth. Naturally, when the elevator reached their floor, Steve invited him to come join the party. At the end of the night, the unexpected guest sat between Randy and Steve, chatting amiably on the sofa. Sensing it was time to go, Father George stood up, only for his hosts to pull him back down: where did he think he was going?

The action frantically accelerated once they moved into the bedroom. Entwined in the pile of naked bodies, Steve tried his best to keep up, but as usual, he was fighting fatigue. Taking a break, he leaned back against the pillows, expecting to admire the scene. What played out next, however, caught him completely by surprise. "For some reason," Steve recounted, "Randy decided he wanted to be topped by this guy, and he had drunk quite a lot by that point. The three of us partied a little bit, and Randy wanted to do this particular thing."

Father George was only too happy to oblige. The action from here played out in almost trancelike fashion, with the sculpted, confident alpha positioning Randy to his liking, before bearing down to penetrate his lubed and waiting supplicant, with nothing in between to inhibit their joining. It looked like one of those porn movies from not so long ago, rendering Steve too hypnotized to interfere. At first, he tried to join in, but realizing he was too fucked up, he lay back to watch instead. The impulse to put a stop to it, or insist they use a condom, remained foggy and elusive, as if trapped in some inaccessible part of his brain.

Drifting in and out of consciousness, Steve saw the two going full-force over the next few hours. "I would wake up and they would still be at it," he remembered. "I'd fall asleep and wake up again and they were still at it." Well into the early morning, the inebriated Randy allowed himself to be fully dominated. In the end, only the inevitable exhaustion seemed powerful enough to separate them. "He had a good time," Steve remembered. "I was standing back in awe of what was going on that night."

Waking to a foggy Christmas morning, Randy and Steve quietly closed the door behind their guest and said little about what happened. The encounter, however, would haunt them well beyond their relationship's dissolution. For Steve, the memory became a never-far-off companion, reminding him of what he saw as a failure to be Randy's champion and protector. But just as Steve and Father George made choices, so had Randy. He'd professed to quitting the baths and embracing safe sex early in the pandemic, despite privately telling friends that in his worst episodes of blackout drinking, he couldn't remember what he'd done. The implications now were unmistakable. "By 1983," he later wrote, "it would be very difficult to be at the receptive end of semen deposition and not get this virus."

In the future, they would speak of that Christmas Eve on two more occasions, the first after finding Father George's obituary. The second conversation came later. "I apologized to him, and it came many years later," Steve admitted, "that I was not sober enough to protect him from that happening. You forget what was happening at the time." In hindsight, they would both agree that it was likely the night when Randy crossed the line, becoming more a part of the pandemic than just another worried bystander.

11 | GAY TRAITORS

THE STRAINS OF "LET IT BE" offered a somber, yet comforting note to the celebrants who quietly filled San Francisco's Pride Center. Like Randy, Gary Walsh always had a soft spot for the Beatles. In the age of AIDS, some would end up attending a funeral nearly every day. Gary himself even appeared in a taped television interview, recorded before his passing in late February. Those in attendance seemed comforted by the dying therapist's description of a woman in white, beckoning him to cross over. Randy, however, left the service with an uneasy feeling.

"It's not beautiful when a young man dies at thirty-nine," a friend complained as they exited the center. "It sucks." In the *Chronicle*, Randy personally penned Gary's obituary. To him, it seemed like many gays were now retreating into a kind of self-enshrouding spirituality, as if resigning themselves to hoping for a beautiful death like Gary's—passing quietly, loved ones by his side. "He probably had hallucinations," the friend added. "And everybody wants to talk about his beautiful death. It makes me want to puke. Everybody's gone crazy."

Randy shushed his companion, warning that by speaking out of turn, he could end up being labeled a traitor. As it turned out, he had good reason to be wary. A couple weeks later, the *Sentinel's* pseudonymous gossip columnist "Octavia Hayes" related an attempt by two unnamed activists to embarrass Randy that night by spreading rumors of a fake, Gary Walsh–recorded "enemies tape," castigating certain figures for their alleged AIDS hysteria and betrayal of the community. Acknowledging that "many people are upset by Randy's one-man crusade to close the bathhouses," Hayes admonished, "this last stunt to make a fool out of him was still a bit much."

Early 1984 so far seemed to offer little more than rehashing the same fights, even as AIDS cases continued to climb. Locally, the parole of Dan White brought protesters out on Castro Street, but gay leaders were now contending with myriad new issues since the ex-supervisor's incarceration. Among them, the question of what to do about the bathhouses loomed large, especially with the Democratic Convention coming in July. And within San Francisco's gay press, much of its AIDS coverage was turning into a running commentary on Randy's reporting.

Among some of his contemporaries, those efforts were still well-received. In a letter to *Chronicle* editor William German, the *BAR*'s Allen White described Randy's work on *This World* as "important and needed to be said." Although at times depressing and unpleasant to read, he wrote, "Randy Shilts was brutally frank in stating that truth." The animosity among others, however, was just beginning to peak.

In early February Randy again questioned the effectiveness of Mervyn Silverman's efforts, as an uptick in rectal gonorrhea indicated that unprotected anal sex was once more on the rise. Consequently, he noted, local and national leaders were questioning what was leading so many gay men to still put themselves at risk. The answers, naturally, were difficult to distill into a simple answer. As Randy had previously emphasized, many men were trying to adjust their sexual habits, but the temptations of familiar environments made it difficult to stay perfectly safe.

In a study by local therapist Leon McCusick, Randy noted, more than 60 percent of men who frequented the baths agreed with the statement "Sometimes I get so frustrated that I have sex I know I shouldn't be having." The availability of AIDS posters and condoms around these establishments was a good start, but as the research findings noted, almost half the men reported not even seeing them. If anything, Randy's writing cast more judgment on those with the power to influence larger changes in these environments than on the men who frequented them.

On this point, he was hardly alone. "I was good friends with Bill Kraus and the folks who put together that brochure *Can We Talk?* for the Milk Club, which was the first educational effort that people did," journalist Larry Bush recalled. Working at the time for Assemblyman Art Agnos, Larry favored education over closure. Others, however, feared that even those educational efforts were being stymied. "We discovered that the bathhouse owners not only were not helping," activist Michael Housh recalled, but also "were trying to camouflage the whole problem that was there, in a way that was particularly unfortunate."

Predictably, the backlash against Randy was led by the *BAR*'s Paul Lorch, who mocked his reporting as an "attack to close down the bad breath parlors." Even while acknowledging that nothing had changed over the past year, Lorch insisted the issue shouldn't even be discussed. "The logic runs: Gay men have death-dealing sex in these homosexual playpens," he wrote. "They cannot control themselves. If they can't keep themselves healthy, we must deny them an opportunity where they might become unhealthy."

"Randy Shilts wants to close the baths," Lorch declared. Casting Randy as the foil gave detractors the power to make the entire affair personal, allowing the unpopularity of the messenger to overshadow the substance of the message. "Like a backyard clothesline, he digs around until he can find shreds and tatters to hang on it." Lorch's attacks were obscuring a very urgent need for a conversation on how to navigate risk-taking in sexually charged environments. "It's sex that Shilts and [Harry] Britt and the frustrated doctors want to stop," Lorch charged. "Stop sex and you'll stop AIDS and you'll stop people dying. Oh no, they'll say—it's safe sex we want people to have. That is permissible. It's the dirty sex we're out to stop. The unsafe kind."

Practically speaking, there was no good way to win this kind of food fight. "That was horrible," Ann Neuenschwander remembered. "People spit on him. All these gay men hated him, and lots of things were written about him being a traitor to his community, and it was just really terrible. He was, as he would say, crestfallen." The epidemic had rendered Randy and everyone around him powerless in unprecedented ways, leading to an explosion of inflammatory responses. "It was so hard because all he's trying to do is help them," Ann added, "and they were just so cruel to him. It was just sad."

———————

Following the Christmas he'd rather have forgotten, alcohol and pot had remained stalwart companions, but after learning that Gary Walsh had passed away, Randy took himself on one final bender. And then on February 23, 1984, after waking up to the hangover to end all hangovers, he summoned the determination to make a different choice. The recovery communities he'd first written about in the mid-'70s had continued their growth, to the point where San Francisco's lesbians and gay men could find an Alcoholics Anonymous meeting virtually any hour of the day, any day of the week, in nondescript church halls, empty office suites, and community centers across the city. Although Randy never had much trouble making conversation, the experience of having to listen to other people's stories and tell a roomful of strangers, "I am an alcoholic" posed a different kind of challenge.

It would hardly be an overnight transformation, but the twelve-step model offered the kind of tough love Randy needed. Having to unlearn certain thoughts and behaviors meant examining long-held beliefs and assumptions, airing them openly, and being receptive to hard feedback. Whenever Randy needed a meeting, he could find a space to sit, talk, and listen. As difficult as working the program could be, gay AA meetings offered him a crucial touchstone, right at the time when he needed it most.

The intensely personal nature of the attacks had taken Randy by surprise. "It's like I became wrapped up as some kind of authority power figure," he later reflected. "I've lived my whole adult life being open about being gay, and then I get people hassling me for being an Uncle Tom or something, or being a self-hating gay. And I just think, *My god, these people who've never had anything comparable to living the kind of very public gay life that I have.*"

Around the city, Steve Newman remembered, gay maître d's would take to greeting the couple with "Shilts party! Table for Randy Shilts!" Even worse were the strangers who'd harangue Randy in public, calling him a self-hating homosexual who'd betrayed his own community. "There were people yelling at him at parties," Steve recalled. "I hated going to parties." The sight was more than Steve could bear: "I would just get in the action and start yelling at people. . . . I would just let them have it in front of everybody."

With their home life growing ever more tenuous, it was one way for Steve to remain on his lover's good side. But as the scene kept repeating itself, the ugliness only added more pressure to their fragile relationship. In mid-March, despite Steve's best efforts, Randy packed his belongings and moved out, a decision he hoped would redefine, but not necessarily end, their flagging relationship.

"I think [Steve and I] might make it if Steve loosens up," he told himself while unpacking. Almost a month removed from his last drink but still smoking pot, he'd begun to experience a renewed sense of clarity, and with it an uncomfortable tug between wanting his independence and stealing glances at Steve's weather forecasts on TV. Though his lover was trying to hold it together, the cheerful on-air persona could hardly mask the sadness in his eyes. "He pulled away," Steve remembered. "He pulled away, and it was just so frustrating."

Randy's move had left Steve shattered. "I loved him so much, and he wouldn't let me in. I was in despair," he recounted. "I could just see that we were getting further and further away, and no matter what I did, I felt power-less against it. I had hoped that whatever was causing this would get better." In couples counseling, Steve found himself on the defensive, as the therapist seemed to immediately accept Randy's version of events over his. The main issue, in Steve's mind, had been the drinking. If quitting drugs and alcohol would help heal their broken bond, then he was willing to do it. But now in therapy, he was shocked to hear himself cast as jealous and controlling.

In the bigger picture of Randy's life, he picked one hell of a time to blow up his relationship. As if confronting his alcoholism and separating from Steve weren't enough, he'd begun to fear for his own safety. Thanks to the bathhouse controversy, even an attempt at lighter news, a mildly campy account of Sheriff Mike Hennessy's recruiting efforts at a South of Market leather bar, provoked accusations of homophobia and betrayal. Apparently for some gays, Randy's suggestion that patrons might already know how to handle a pair of handcuffs, own their uniforms, and know their way around a dungeon was the last straw.

"Randy Shilts is a perfect example of how a bad reporter who lands a job with a big city daily newspaper because he happens to be gay can carelessly and viciously turn on his community," *California Voice* editorialized under the headline, "Shilts—Gay Uncle Tom." The paper made no secret of its disdain for "a third-rate reporter covering gay events for a second-rate daily newspaper," blaming him for the veto of a recent gay rights bill and suggesting he be "run out of town on a rail."

So intense was the vitriol that as the year progressed, Randy was getting hate mail from both extremes, with antigay zealots calling him a "sweetheart faggot" and a "cocksucker," at the same time gays were angrily condemn-ing him. "You are a traitor to your own kind," began one anonymous note signed by "A Pig in Paradise." In a greeting card captioned "Just wanted you to know that you're at the very top of my̶ OUR list," the writer added, "You are a Judas. You have betrayed your gay brothers and sisters for silver by

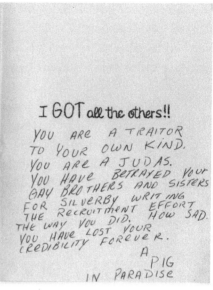

Anonymous mail sent to Randy Shilts, March 14, 1984.
Courtesy of Shilts Copyright Trust, c/o Hill Nadell Literary Agency

writing the recruitment effort the way you did. How sad. You have lost your credibility forever."

Responding to the *Sentinel*'s "Octavia Hayes," Randy retorted that the gossip columnist hadn't bothered to even ask him about the Gary Walsh "enemies tape" rumors. The attacks on one reporter, when there was clearly now a larger battle to fight, had him wondering if people were even taking AIDS seriously. Unlike many of the activists who'd attended Gary's funeral—who, Randy charged, were beginning to flock to AIDS memorials as a bizarre sort of social event—he was actually there to mourn a good friend of six years. "In case these unnamed people . . . didn't notice, they were at a funeral service that night," Randy continued. "That means someone died. In fact, lots of people are dying of AIDS. The problem here is not Randy Shilts."

Turning to the characterization of his so-called one-man crusade, he added, "Please show me one piece of paper on which I have written that I think the bathhouses should be shut down. I'd like to see it. Lacking that, I have to assume you are suffering from hallucinations." In a handwritten postscript, he concluded, "Just imagine how you'd feel if you learned somebody had pulled a stunt like that on you."

Randy never sent the letter, but he did agree to sit down with the *Sentinel* to tell his side of the story. Concerning the police article, he offered an apology but maintained, "I thought it was funny, I really did. The people who are maddest are those gays who are very concerned about how straight people view them." Turning to AIDS, Randy insisted, "Quoting people who are for shutting the bathhouses does not mean I am for shutting them."

Still, he acknowledged, his combative questioning could certainly give that impression, especially since he found many of the arguments for doing nothing to be insulting to gays' intelligence. "I think the leadership of the gay community and the public officials have been very, very remiss in playing hear-no-evil/see-no-evil when it comes to the bathhouses, because they are clearly a major problem with AIDS," he insisted. "The gay leadership may be willing to lie to gay people about the bathhouses, gay people may be willing to lie to themselves about bathhouses, but I'm not going to lie to them."

AIDS was not making him famous, Randy protested, nor was it driving up the *Chronicle*'s readership. Reporting on a disease that was killing his friends and lovers wasn't bringing him any satisfaction, and certainly no one was encouraging him to bash his own community. If people would look at his career with a little perspective, Randy pleaded, they would see a journalist who'd fought for gay issues to be taken seriously for nearly a decade, even when it had set back his career. After all the acrimony, he still hoped that people would see him as "a newspaper reporter trying to do his best in a real difficult situation."

In late March the issue seemed to be coming to a head when plans were announced for a petition drive, putting the issue on a citywide ballot. Facing the prospect of losing the popular vote, a group of gay political leaders, businessmen, doctors, and activists hastily composed a letter to Silverman supporting closure of the baths, at least until the epidemic had subsided. From the outset, the public health director had been wanting the community to agree on a solution.

As the story leaked, however, the number of committed signers began to shrink. By the time Silverman received the public letter, the final tally of signatures had dropped from around fifty, as Randy had first reported, to sixteen. Moreover, the city attorney had advised that, a city order to close the baths would likely be overturned, leading Silverman to delay his decision for two more weeks.

"It was fraught with peril," explained Cleve Jones, who found himself con-flicted but left with little room to maneuver because of Randy. "He's trying to box in Merv Silverman. He's confronting all the activists. He's trying to force everybody to take a position. He was very black and white."

For his part, Silverman respected Randy's thoroughness but felt that he was letting his own views drive the story. "And I remember a couple times calling up his editor and saying, 'Randy ought to be on the editorial page, because he's sort of writing opinions, not reporting,'" he recalled. For a period, the two lived near each other in the Upper Ashbury neighborhood and would still greet each other cordially on the street, even after the director briefly banned him from the health department's offices.

The resulting theatrics included a press conference protested by men wearing nothing but bath towels and a public forum where moderator Randy Alfred—dressed in a whimsical, referee-inspired outfit, complete with whistle—was rushed by angry audience members, who had to be restrained. Those who'd signed the letter faced a virulent backlash, while Randy took heat for prematurely reporting Silverman's decision. Declaring that the letter signers had nearly "killed off" the entire movement, Paul Lorch insisted gays should "remember those names well—if not etch them into their anger and regret."

Subsequently, the director announced that the bathhouses and sex clubs could remain open, but sexual activities on the premises were banned. If inspections found sex occurring, he said, they would be closed. The constantly changing storyline left outsiders struggling to keep up, but for those who'd followed closely, the debate around bathhouses had taken too long to even happen. "The last two weeks' general debate about AIDS and the baths . . . is about eighteen months overdue," Randy Alfred wrote in the *Sentinel*. "Delay has cost us many options."

Peppering his comments with some well-placed jabs and queenly innuendo ("The gay movement has come from 'Oh, Mary!' to Typhoid Mary in just fif-teen uneasy years."), Alfred argued that changing one's behaviors in response to a virus that knew and cared nothing of political correctness could hardly be considered "ideologically impermissible." Those who'd objected to even talking about the baths had little credibility, in Alfred's view, when it came to labeling their opponents as turncoats and homophobes. "There has been no treachery here," he admonished, "and those who speak of 'traitors' do nothing but betray their own foolish irresponsibility."

"To speak only of civil liberties is to ignore that AIDS is no longer a matter of private consent, but of public health," Alfred continued. "In short," he added, "it's time to grow up. We are now in the fifth—not the second—year of this epidemic, and we have known it is contagious since July 1982. From all reports, AIDS kills slowly and painfully, and there is no gay liberation in the coffin."

Not long after, Shilts and Alfred had a chance encounter in public. Since their spat over *The Mayor of Castro Street*, both had devoted themselves to covering AIDS, at considerable personal cost. Until now, however, they'd found little cause for mending their chilly relationship. As they spoke, Randy brought up Alfred's bathhouse stance, observing that it seemed they were on the same side. For Alfred, the encounter marked a return to at least some civility, if not a particularly close friendship. It would not occur to him until years later that Randy, in keeping with the tenets of twelve-step recovery, may have been trying to make amends.

Letting go of past grievances, however, didn't make it any easier to cope with the turbulent present. Determined to rekindle a sense of closeness, Steve Newman suggested a getaway to Mendocino, where for at least a few days, the curative powers of a hot tub overlooking the Pacific seemed to ease their conflict.

After they reentered the city, however, the tensions promptly returned, as Randy insisted that they stop at the first newsstand so he could read the *BAR*'s latest attacks. "He couldn't wait a day, until the following morning," Steve lamented. "He had to see right away. It was very frustrating in dealing with someone who is that sensitive and couldn't relax, couldn't divorce himself from turmoil, even for a day."

Even the late April news that the National Cancer Institute had isolated the virus causing AIDS seemed incapable of displacing the warfare over San Francisco's bathhouses. Silverman, Feinstein, and the Board of Supervisors quickly fell into a monthslong argument over delays in issuing bathhouse regulations, while the *New York Native* reported that leaders of the Alice B. Toklas Democratic Club had formally denounced Randy Shilts as "homophobic."

For all the sound and fury, it would still appear that nothing had really changed, except for the widening gulf between Randy and his own community. For the moment, he turned his focus toward election-year politics, the upcoming Democratic convention, gays' political gains in the heartland, and speculation around Feinstein's chances for the vice presidential nomination. Away from the *Chronicle*, however, he still had plenty to say about AIDS, the bathhouses, and gay politics.

"Traitors or Heroes?" asked the *New York Native* in a midsummer feature. In a commentary for the Big Apple's preeminent gay paper, Randy charged that "a homosexual McCarthyism" had overtaken San Francisco's gay community. Ever the debater, he framed the issue around two somewhat simplistically defined groups: the ardent liberationists, who viewed their sexuality as "central to the male homosexual experience, a fundamental civil liberty which needs to be defended," and the pragmatists, "who see the gay movement as a broader, psycho-social phenomenon encompassing issues of self-conception, personal identity, and long-term social change."

Gay liberation's political history could not be separated from its sexual history, Randy argued, no matter how hard its leaders had tried to pretend otherwise. Back in 1969, he wrote, "Everybody could kick free of the Apollonian establishment and partake of some good, old-fashioned Dionysian hedonism." The gay leaders and media who'd obscured this fundamental debate, he charged, had now effectively risked the extinction of gay men as biological organisms. Even as those leaders sought to sanitize the homosexual image, Randy added, promiscuity had become practically an article of faith. With more gays flocking to major cities, the humanistic view of gays' sexual liberation had to contend with "an entire subculture and business network . . . catering to drugged-out, alcoholic, promiscuous gay men with penchants for kinky sexual acts."

Despite political gains, he continued, gay culture had stagnated on a plateau of repetitive, unoriginal cruising rituals, conforming to a dress code that had remained unchanged well into the '80s. The community known for trendsetting was proving stubbornly resistant to change, believing that its still-nascent culture and hierarchies must be defended at all costs. There was no greater example of this obstinacy, Randy wrote, than the community's response to AIDS. In holding its political ground, a core segment of the movement had grown reactionary, he contended, attacking not only the mounting scientific evidence but also any health official, activist, politician, or journalist who cited it to suggest that something must change.

Raising the question of what it meant to be a community, Randy asked, "Are we talking about sexual freedom, or a wider, humanistic vision of how people should live their lives?" To drive home the stakes, he took a rare personal turn, recounting his "casual-yet-intimate" friendship with Gary Walsh and the ordeal of helplessly watching a good friend suffer and die. "One thing about Gary, he liked being alive," he marveled. "He stood up for himself."

Recalling his friend's televised confrontation with Jerry Falwell the previous year, Randy mused at how, on one hand, gays could rally to reject a mysticism that condemned them to divine retribution, while, on the other hand, embracing an equally mystical retreat from the difficult existential questions AIDS had raised. Inspiring spiritual overtones, no matter how comforting they could be, were not going to keep the virus from killing more people.

Falwell was always, unapologetically, going to be Falwell—capitalizing on fears toward an unpopular minority group to gain and consolidate his power. In the meantime, Randy noted, Dianne Feinstein had quietly accomplished more for lesbians and gays than any other politician, despite her infamous prudishness. In Randy's opinion, attacking her for politicizing the baths, as if making gay sex a public issue would somehow boost her career, made no sense.

In discussing the issue privately, he noted, the mayor's voice would become uncharacteristically vulnerable, causing him to remember that Feinstein, a former nurse, had plenty of experience watching people die. "I don't like how political this has become," she told him. "People are seeing hobgoblins where there aren't any, talking politics when people are dying. People are dying of this, you know." Despite the mayor's past run-ins with gay activists, Randy saw no reason to doubt her sincerity about saving gay lives.

Contentious as the headline made it seem, Randy's tone reflected more a sense of somber frustration than blistering anger. Focusing on the bigger picture of gay culture, political posturing, and his fears for gays' extinction, he named none of his antagonists by name. In closing, however, he described how in San Francisco, an influential gay editor kept an enemies' list of the AIDS activists who'd dared to challenge his commentaries. Whenever one of those activists passed away, Randy explained, the editor would cheerfully take out the list and cross off the deceased's name. The question, it seemed, was whether it was more homophobic to take an unpopular position for the community's survival, or to cheer for the deaths of other gays as part of some petty, never-ending schoolyard rivalry.

Whatever he'd hoped to accomplish, Randy had put his position on the record. By the time his commentary reached newsstands, the gay press was turning its attentions toward the 1984 election and implications for AIDS treatment, now that the causal agent had purportedly been found. Even his depiction of Paul Lorch was left unchallenged by the *BAR*, which by midyear had dispensed with the caustic editor and his scorching, narcissistic commentaries. The only response of note came in a letter to the *Native* from the estate of Bobbi Campbell. The original "AIDS poster boy" had passed away in mid-August, and just as he had with Gary Walsh, Randy personally penned Campbell's obituary, noting his contributions to early AIDS funding and the emphasis on self-empowerment among persons living with the virus.

Taking issue with what he called the "simplistic reductionism" of Randy's commentary, Campbell insisted that "AIDS partisans are not either 'traitors' or 'murderers'—or 'heroes.'" Given how the *Native* had titled the piece, it was easy to overlook that Randy had, in fact, used no such terms to label anyone. Emphasizing the complex nature of risk reduction, Campbell insisted that the people working on AIDS had good intentions but were frustrated, a point on which Randy would likely have agreed. However, Campbell added in what was likely his final public statement, "It is a disservice to all of us, and especially to those of us who have AIDS, to present one's own personal viewpoint in the cloak of moral absolutism."

In the larger picture of Randy's life, the bathhouse controversy marked a period of both intense conflict and painful self-reflection. Whereas Campbell had rightly called it a complex situation, in casting Randy as a purveyor of "moral absolutism," he was reinforcing another oversimplification in a debate where opponents had tried to paint each other into easily definable corners. "Nobody was being kind in any of these fights," Larry Bush remembered. "It was soul killing, and there are some friendships that will never come back together. Nor should they."

The issue lingered well into the fall, as Silverman and the Board of Supervisors continued to clash over bathhouse regulations, until a Superior Court judge ruled that the businesses that hadn't permanently closed would be able to operate under strict restrictions, which included monitoring patrons' behaviors, removing the doors on private cubicles, and strictly prohibiting unsafe sex "as defined by the San Francisco AIDS Foundation."

Dating back to before AIDS, Randy had lamented how gay liberation seemed to be falling short in taking care of its own. Overshadowed in the movement's political gains and the disproportionate growth of pleasure-focused businesses was an underaddressed need for, as he put it, more "humanistic" elements: spaces for gays to work on self-acceptance and learn to care for each other as more than just objects of sexual convenience. And on a personal level, as he kept counting the days since hitting rock bottom, Randy could recognize just how critically he'd needed more of those supports in his own life.

One silver lining of the pandemic would be the opportunity to address that imbalance, as a nationwide movement of homegrown AIDS organizations was springing up to offer comfort, education, and advocacy. But Randy, in calling attention to the environments where some men still risked their own and others' lives, now found himself permanently alienated from segments of his community. In late 1984, when the Oscar-winning documentary *The Times of Harvey Milk* premiered at the Castro Theater, a glimpse of Randy in the background of two brief scenes was enough to prompt some audience members to erupt derisively in boos.

12 | THE BIG BOOK

IN AN IDEAL WORLD, the practice of scientific research relies on the careful collection of verifiable, bias-free evidence, unencumbered by individual aspirations or political winds, from which discernable patterns lead to rigorous experimental designs for testing new hypotheses. Realistically, however, such standards remain vulnerable to a host of social pressures and manipulations. Decisions around what to study, which methods to use, and who to involve can easily fall victim to innate biases and blind spots, while funding considerations, publication priorities, and peer-review invitations can be subject to a decidedly unscientific web of rivalries and egos.

As cases continued to climb, Randy's imperative for writing his second book was becoming ever clearer. Thanks to Michael Denneny at St. Martin's, some of the first AIDS medical research was now appearing in popular nonfiction, but no book so far had penetrated the public's consciousness to marshal the wide support that AIDS-afflicted communities needed. Such narrative would require a balance between scientific accuracy, political intrigue, and emotional resonance.

Among those considering the task, journalist Frank Robinson was imagining a sociological approach, detailing how younger gays were especially vulnerable to certain risk-taking. A close friend and former speechwriter for Harvey Milk, Robinson had signed the much-maligned public letter calling for gay bathhouses to be closed, yet to his amazement, he never endured the same vilification as Randy. Robinson had even calculated how many miles of intestinal tract were likely connected on any given night in San Francisco's bathhouses, surely an eyebrow-raising figure if it had ever made its way into print.

Robinson quickly changed his mind about writing a book, however, after Randy told him, "I'm going to follow the money." By the end of 1984 Randy's AIDS journalism was entering a new phase, with increasing coverage of national and international stories as his colleagues took more of the local beat. What had once fallen mostly to him and David Perlman to cover now required the attention of an informal "AIDS team," including Katy Butler, Susan Sward, and a handful of others.

As general guidelines go, "follow the money" can be useful when it recognizes multiple forms of self-interest, including power, wealth, and fame. Details of how leaders put their own interests ahead of the greater good had underlaid much of Randy's AIDS reporting so far. In late 1984 a series of trips to New York, Atlanta, Bethesda, and Paris had unearthed a web of stories supporting that central premise. Randy's working idea for the book, he told his brother Gary, came from visits to elite government laboratories, where he heard a staffer complain of their rival French researchers, "They can't get it—this is our Nobel Prize!"

"I think it was just the next step," Steve Newman remembered. "It was just the next thing that needed to be done. He thought it would change the way AIDS was being dealt with." In December 1984 the *Chronicle's This World* magazine again devoted a cover story to the disease. Tracing investigators' steps back to early 1981, Randy noted, "The story of the AIDS investigations at the CDC is, to a large extent, the story of how the deadly and terrifying epidemic has unfolded in America."

While the agency's track record with disease outbreaks was less than perfect, its staff had scrambled to do exactly what it was trained to do. Dr. James Curran, picked to head the CDC's fledgling office on AIDS, traveled frequently to the Bay Area in those first few years and came to know Randy as an ever-present figure. During the bathhouse controversy in 1984, Curran came to San Francisco to meet privately with Mervyn Silverman, only to find Randy waiting for him at the gate when his flight landed.

"It's unusual for reporters—particularly nowadays but even then—to be knowledgeable," Curran remembered. "Randy was one of those people who knew everything, and that was really helpful." The CDC's early outreach to gay physicians had indicated that the disease was already spreading far and wide. The most formidable obstacles the agency faced, Randy reported, were institutional: resistance from Reagan administration budget officers and indifference by the news media.

As early studies sat unfinished and field investigators called for additional labs and equipment, the administration was still publicly insisting it had all the money, facilities, and equipment it needed. Thanks to his congressional sources, however, Randy knew otherwise. Meanwhile, one frustrated CDC staffer complained, "It was the only story I've been involved with in which we felt the need to sell it to people. Reporters' reaction would be that they couldn't sell their editors on it."

Running parallel to these stymied efforts was the intercontinental race to solve the mystery of the virus, or as Randy put it to his brother Gary, "The Quest for the Nobel." Detailing how Americans had hampered French efforts to publish and present their findings for a year, he leaned hard on the premise that showmanship and ego had outweighed scientific merit at key junctures of the discovery process. While Dr. Robert Gallo of the National Cancer Institute had insisted that the Pasteur Institute's methods had not been sufficiently rigorous, Randy pointed out what other scientists considered the flaws in Gallo's own assumptions.

One reason why Gallo's lab had taken so long to find the virus in AIDS patients' T-lymphocyte cells, he explained, was that the virus had already killed off those cells and thus couldn't be found in the samples collected. By examining the blood of patients with less severe, "pre-AIDS" symptoms, the French had found the virus more expediently, in the lymph nodes of a gay man from New York with lymphadenopathy. "It was very easy to find the virus," Dr. Luc Montagnier told Randy. "No long stories of difficulties. We looked and it was there."

Gallo had also continued to lump this retrovirus together with the leukemia retroviruses he'd discovered in the 1970s, but it does not, in fact, behave like leukemia. Unconcerned with political niceties, the Pasteur team freely aired its grievances to Randy, who noted that CDC staffers were privately agreeing that the French had found the virus first. "Scientists are human beings—they are not saints," Montagnier ruefully admitted to him. In the months ahead, science journalists would begin to scrutinize irregularities in Gallo's work, even as the Reagan administration seemed to be ignoring the implications of impropriety.

"The Year of the Plague," as dubbed by the *Chronicle* in a year-end special section, was giving way to a new year with a widening expanse of issues. Evidence of the virus's routes of transmission and potentially long incubation period was beginning to make heterosexuals nervous, Randy noted. Since late

1984, news of AIDS diagnoses among men who'd had sex with female sex workers had begun to draw attention, and over the new year, Randy reported on the case of a woman with AIDS-defining symptoms and a history of sex work and injection drug use, for which police were demanding that she be tested. Setting aside the fact that testing was still experimental, doctors protested the idea that law enforcement could arbitrarily force anyone to be screened, while social services were scrambling to find her a means of survival, other than turning tricks in the Tenderloin.

Early 1985 did bring promising news about testing, although it seemed that with each new development, another round of complications would arise. Initial plans to limit it to blood banks raised concerns that they would be overwhelmed by people anxious to know their status, but the federal government was resisting calls to pay for screening in private doctors' offices and public clinics. Up to this point, Randy reported, at least seventeen of the Bay Area's AIDS deaths had been attributed to blood transfusions, including one case dating back to 1979. Faced with evidence that the disease could take longer to manifest symptoms than had originally been believed, medical officials and transfusion recipients waited apprehensively to see how far the virus had actually traveled.

Meanwhile, a new debate was raging among gays over whether to take the test, with many arguing that learning one's diagnosis could provoke unnecessary anxieties and lead to civil rights abuses. For every gay man who insisted he was dying to know, Randy reported, others were expressing concerns. "It would kill me to find out that I had been infected—I couldn't handle it," one downtown businessman told him. "I'd worry about it all the time."

In the background of all this, Randy and Steve's relationship was lurching toward its painful dissolution. When Randy finally ended it, he opted for expedience, typing out a tersely written farewell note like the draft of another news story. For Steve, nothing cut quite as deeply as this flat, businesslike rejection letter, compared to the multitude of love notes he'd saved from earlier years. While he still clung to the possibility of friendship, Randy was developing his own minor obsession, questioning mutual friends over whether his ex-lover had been tested, once screening became available. Still hurting from the breakup and annoyed by the implication that he'd been the less-than-faithful partner, Steve refused to say. If Randy had concerns about the virus, he'd have to swallow his pride and get tested himself.

Parallel to these developments, Randy was quietly working on his book proposal. In addition to a growing number of East Coast trips, his frequent conversations with Michael Denneny helped anchor the narrative of what he hoped would be more than just another dry chronicling of AIDS, the medical phenomenon. From those conversations, Michael knew they were both concerned about the general lack of urgency. "Our major thing was to break the silence and get people putting it on the agenda," he recalled, "so we knew we had to get the media, and we knew we had to get the scientific establishment. And the scientific establishment was really hard."

At Michael's suggestion, Randy adopted the title *And the Band Played On*, using the refrain of a popular old waltz to implicate a scandal of indifference, malfeasance, and political squabbling while the disease had spread. The book would address the hypothesized origins of AIDS in colonial Africa and extend through 1985. Centered around San Francisco but drawing a blistering contrast with New York's response, he promised a chronology that would "weave the warp of the human dilemmas of key characters to the woof of a thoroughly documented account of how this plague unfolded in America," leading to "provocative conclusions about how AIDS became so entrenched in America before public and private resources were aimed against it."

The political dimensions of his argument were bolstered by a *Mother Jones* story by Larry Bush and David Talbot, who characterized the Reagan administration's nonresponse to AIDS as a combination of budgetary obstinance and deceptively optimistic messaging, reinforced by disinterest among scientific elites around working with the gay community. But in his proposal for *Band*, Randy was trying to pitch a story that would transcend the disease's medical and political complexities to connect with readers around a universal human condition: the struggle to overcome a shared existential threat.

"People died," he charged, as budget officials stubbornly adhered to Ronald Reagan's "no new social spending" admonition, despite pleas from worried CDC epidemiologists. "People died," he repeated, as prestigious scientists slow-footed their efforts in response to what was viewed as a homosexual problem. "People died and nobody paid attention," he added, because news organizations were too embarrassed to describe gay men's sexual habits. And, he emphasized, people died because public health leaders failed to explicitly tell the public how to avoid infection, a stance made all the more obstructive by gay leaders who'd waffled on supporting unpopular precautionary measures.

"Because the story will be told through the lives of a core of characters," Randy wrote, "AIDS at last will leave the realm of dry science writing and become firmly enmeshed in the lives of flesh-and-blood people." His list of major characters included familiar names like Bill Kraus, Cleve Jones, and Merv Silverman, in addition to a handful of locals, including Gary Walsh. Also joining the cast were James Curran, Luc Montagnier, and New York's Larry Kramer, while the disease itself would also be a major character, Randy promised. "As the book progresses," he wrote, "the masks that have hidden the face of this enemy fall away as more becomes known about AIDS."

Minor players would include Robert Gallo and Edward Brandt Jr. at the federal level, Dr. David Sencer in New York City, and, representing the oppositional view on AIDS and its sufferers, the Reverend Jerry Falwell. Curiously, Randy proposed another major character, heretofore unseen in any of his reporting: Dr. Thomas Ainsworth, "a typical gay community doctor" in the Castro, who was well liked by many gay patients, including Randy himself. As the disease had taken hold, he wrote, Ainsworth could find himself on any given day with half a dozen dying patients, inflicting himself with a staggering degree of grief and inner conflict as he tried and failed to save lives.

When Randy broached the idea with his personal physician, Ainsworth vetoed it. The early years of AIDS had already exacted a heavy toll on the popular doctor, and he had no desire to revisit the ordeal. With several years' experience treating venereal disease, Ainsworth's office was used to handling a high volume of lab work, so that when anonymous screening became available, his patients generally got their results within a day or two. At the time, the only test available required a blood draw, which Ainsworth himself would carry out. If the patient requested it, brief counseling would be offered, with results delivered in person or over the phone. Most significantly, all transactions were done with cash, to prevent patients from being outed to their insurance companies.

Not long after screening procedures were established, Randy went to see Dr. Ainsworth. He wanted to be tested but asked the doctor to hold the result until he was ready to learn it. Ainsworth agreed, drawing blood from Randy's arm and labeling it with the necessary lab codes. When the result came back, Ainsworth quietly filed it away, keeping his promise to say nothing until his patient was ready.

By midyear, it seemed that 1985 was shaping up to be no less chaotic or con-flicted than its predecessors. While attacks against Randy in the gay press had ebbed to some occasional sniping, the *Bay Area Reporter*'s Brian Jones still found cause to blame him for an antigay assault in Buena Vista Park, where illicit sex had long predated the bathhouse fight and still continued after many had closed. On top of everything else, by midyear it appeared that gay bashing in the city was surging, with reports of new attacks both on the streets of gay neighborhoods and on public transit routes.

Yet, in the final days of June, a quarter million celebrants were expected once more in San Francisco's downtown for International Lesbian and Gay Freedom Day. The parade caught a newly clean-shaven Randy in a contempla-tive mood, having spent the past couple weeks covering the United Nations' fortieth anniversary. The modern gay movement was almost as old as the UN itself, and in the city where it was founded, gays and lesbians had established their own enduring stronghold.

"Nobody knew exactly what we were creating, or where it was going," Randy reflected, "but we knew it was very new and very different, that [it] had never been done anywhere, and there was a real excitement." In a city known for its countercultures, he saw parallels between the rise of gay power and the earlier beatniks and hippies. "You had something new going on, something that was going to change the culture that was centered on one little geographic strip."

For Randy, the idea of an empowered gay community taking its political place was as American as it could get. "There was something very serious going on in the late '70s, and that was a whole generation of gay men who had accepted themselves and were creating a political force," he added. Har-vey Milk had shown that old fashioned ward politics—organizing neighbors around their common concerns, registering voters, and getting them to the polls—could work for gays just as effectively as any other group. "That's what power is about, and that's what gets you respect, and people tend not to give you your civil rights out of the kindness of their hearts. You have to show them that you have something to give them, or something to withhold from them."

In the not-so-distant past, Randy reminisced, a good portion of the com-munity had resembled "a bunch of sailors on shore leave" more than an orga-nized political force, an era he characterized as "the culmination of sex without consequences." Thinking back to those earlier times, Randy observed, "I think gay men could sort of comfort themselves with the notion that we weren't being any more promiscuous or sexually active than heterosexual men would be, if they had the same opportunities."

The warning signs had been overlooked in part because so many men were having such a good time. Even Randy, who'd reported back then on the calamities bombarding gay men, had been caught off guard. "In retrospect," he reflected, "after writing these stories I sometimes think to myself, *Why didn't I see it coming?*"

The 1985 parade, however, was giving him hope that a stronger, more resilient community was emerging. The leather-clad sex radicals, whose ranks had been hit hardest in the pandemic's early years, marched with their norm-defying kinks still proudly on display, only many groups were now handing out condoms to enthusiastic bystanders. Some of the loudest applause, Randy noticed, were for the frontline medical and social service workers, alongside a legion of proud people with AIDS (PWAs) and volunteers. And, Randy noted, a surging contingent of lesbians and gays in recovery filled the streets, the word LIVING SOBER emblazoned on their placards, T-shirts, and banners.

The coming weeks brought more cause for optimism, as local gays Victor Amburgy and Jack McCarty, held hostage with several other Americans in Beirut, were safely delivered home. Despite having to conceal their relationship, the two survived in part, they told Randy, because McCarty, a volunteer for the Shanti Project, had drawn on his experiences with AIDS patients to help keep the other hostages calm. Arriving at Andrews Air Force Base, Randy noted, the couple walked arm in arm from the airplane to be greeted by the president and First Lady.

Up to this point, Randy's vision for the book still lacked an ending. A chronology of the first five years of AIDS would pack plenty of intrigue, but the virus's discovery really only signified the end of the beginning, without effective treatment. The story still lacked resolution, but in late July, the American AIDS narrative would take its most dramatic turn so far. The rumblings started when it was revealed that Rock Hudson was seeking medical treatment in Paris at the Pasteur Institute. In the *New York Times*, an Associated Press headline read ROCK HUDSON IS ILL WITH LIVER CANCER IN PARIS HOSPITAL as the fifty-nine-year-old actor's publicity team offered shifting explanations for his hospitalization.

THE BIG BOOK | 149

Randy responded with a lengthy profile of San Francisco's "AIDS exiles," all of whom were seeking help from the French doctors, alluding strongly to the reason for Hudson's hospitalization without actually saying it. Within twenty-four hours, Hudson's representatives publicly confirmed his AIDS diagnosis. Almost immediately, the scuttlebutt seemed to say that if the embodiment of American masculinity had somehow contracted AIDS, then nobody was safe. Although the revelation sparked a renewed interest in the disease, the media's embarrassment around discussing gays and their sex lives was threatening to undermine this opportunity for marshaling public support.

Despite generally disfavoring the outing of public figures, Randy and colleague Perry Lang reached out to his friends who knew Hudson well, Armistead Maupin and Ken Maley. The two spoke on the record about the actor's open secret, depicting a man perfectly at ease with his sexuality but who'd followed the rules of Hollywood in maintaining a gentleman's discretion. As far back as 1976, Armistead shared, he'd encouraged Hudson to speak publicly about being gay, to which the actor had replied, "One of these days, I'm going to have a lot to tell."

When it became clear that he was too sick for further treatment, Hudson chartered a flight home to California, where television cameras captured his unresponsive body, shrouded in a white hospital gown, being wheeled by stretcher to a waiting helicopter. For Cleve Jones, living at the time in Maui, the moment represented a turning point. "So, I have this image in my head of Rock Hudson, this fucking closet case, and this aerial shot from this helicopter," he remembered, "and . . . I thought, *You know . . . the networks spent more money to get that shot than the Feds had spent on this disease.*"

That flash of anger told Cleve it was time to return home to San Francisco. In the aftermath of their interview, Armistead and Ken faced backlash from the gay press for outing their friend, while Randy emerged for once with relatively little fallout. More annoying to him was the news media's newfound interest in the pandemic. "It should not have taken the diagnosis of a movie star to nudge the nation's television networks, newsmagazines, and national dailies into serious AIDS coverage," he scolded. "By anybody's standards, more than 12,000 Americans dead or dying from a disease nobody even heard of just four years ago is a giant news story."

Hudson's revelation allowed for previously uninterested editors to finally treat AIDS as a serious concern, but the fact that it had taken this long revealed a bitter truth about the media's priorities. "The reason for the lack of coverage is not hard to fathom," Randy continued. "The groups most victimized by Acquired Immune Deficiency Syndrome are not exactly an honor roll of America's favorite minorities."

The cinematic turn gave Randy the ending he needed for *And the Band Played On*. Working with San Francisco literary agent Fred Hill, he'd begun shopping the proposal to publishers, even as Michael Denneny worried that perhaps it was still too soon. "I probably would have waited another year," Michael reflected. "I thought he was pushing it a little early, but he had his reasons for it." With Michael's encouragement, Hill sent the proposal to a dozen different publishers, but as house after house kept turning it down, Randy came back to St. Martin's as his best option.

Michael had used his editorial position to give some AIDS-afflicted authors a reason to hang on, even if their books weren't expected to make money. "There were a number of cases where I brought up books, and I said, 'My main argument with this book is, if you sign this contract for $4,000, this guy will live for another year,'" he remembered. "'I mean, I know writers, and he will live until he finishes his damn novel.'"

Michael won a fair share of those arguments, even when he worried that a finished manuscript might never arrive. To his surprise, many of them did come in, and in quite good shape. But even the will to finish wasn't enough to keep some of those authors alive much longer. "I was publishing these books," he lamented, "and again and again, the author would be dead by the time I was just editing the book."

As Michael suspected, bringing *Band* to his publishing board would be a fight. Even though editor after editor praised the quality of writing and the importance of the subject matter, they questioned, even in the wake of Hudson's bombshell, whether Randy was trying to sell a story that still lacked an ending. Once everyone had said their piece, CEO Tom McCormack glanced around the room. The editorial department in its entirety had called it the best proposal they'd ever read, he noted, but they'd all voted to turn it down.

"I also want to point out to you," he added, "that if we don't sign this book up, then Michael's going to kill us." McCormack overturned the decision, but with low commercial expectations, St. Martin's only offered a minimal advance of $16,000. Although Randy would need to continue working while writing the book, the money afforded him the means to continue his research and purchase a home computer. In early September, the *Chronicle*'s Herb Caen told readers, "Newsman Randy Shilts has signed a contract with St. Martin's Press for a book on the AIDS scene here that will crucify—or at least nail—a few guardians of the public health for being asleep at their posts."

After a late November vigil commemorating Harvey Milk and George Moscone, Cleve spoke with Randy about an exciting new idea. All through his time in Hawaii, the two had stayed in touch. "He was encouraging me to go to AA," Cleve recounted. "He would say things like, 'You know, maybe you're not quitting drinking forever, and maybe you're not quitting drugs forever. Maybe you're just giving yourself a break, and that's good. It's good for your liver, girl.'" For the vigil, Cleve had encouraged everyone to carry signs with the names of friends who'd died and then pin them to the federal building's wall. "And that's when I looked at that patchwork of names, and I had the idea."

"Randy," Cleve told him, "Say the word *quilt*. What does it evoke?" More than thirty years later, the memory still sparked Cleve's passions. "It's the Conestoga wagons crossing the prairie; it's the slaves stealing the remnants and creating something of warmth and value; it's the different textures and colors; it's a comforter. What word evokes American folk culture more than *quilt*?"

"[Randy] understood it," Cleve remarked, "and talked about the power of it." With his friend's encouragement, Cleve held tight to that vision, persuading a handful of intimates to begin stitching quilt panels bearing the names of loved ones lost to AIDS. As both men dove deeper into their respective projects, Cleve began to notice how Randy, the frumpy, disheveled friend who'd lived in notorious squalor, had undergone a transformation of his own.

"I go to see him," Cleve marveled, "and everything is in its place. And on the wall, I think, was the book." Randy had laid out every storyline on his walls using index cards, arranging the various threads into a unified, continuous chronology. "Here's the Bill Kraus line, the Marcus Conant line, the Cleve Jones line, the Dr. Dritz line," Cleve recounted. "I'm looking at that and really being like . . . 'Oh, this is how you write a big fucking book!'"

To be sure, Cleve added, even in sobriety Randy would always still be "just so fucking full of himself." But his ambitions had now come into clearer focus, bringing order to the chaotic story and prompting a bit of introspection into the forces behind his more destructive impulses. In January 1986, a story appeared in *San Francisco Focus*, profiling the struggles that many high-achieving thirtysomethings were experiencing with addiction. In a rare departure for Randy, the first-person essay was credited to "Martin S.," a pseudonym that few were likely to recognize.

"The Pepsi generation has matured into the coke-and-chardonnay set," he wrote, "falling into the age-old trap of substance abuse." The experience of bottoming out had become so common among the city's young elites, he observed, that certain AA groups were gaining an upscale aesthetic, replacing simple spreads of cookies with health-conscious foods and gourmet coffee. "The emphasis on anonymity is not based on fear of exposure," he continued, "but on the fact that recovery works best once we strip ourselves of our precious identities and learn to deal with ourselves as people again, not as job titles or Porsche owners."

Having space to safely share and learn from each other's stories remained as therapeutic in the materialistic 1980s as it was in 1939, when *Alcoholics Anonymous* (i.e., the "Big Book") was first published. Thinking back on life before sobriety, Randy wrote, "I remember the evenings two years ago when, in the throes of melancholy, I'd smoke a joint and think of how misunderstood I was. I knew myself to be caring and warm-hearted, a nice guy who people would like if they only got to know the real me." Without the use of chemicals, he noted, "I occasionally get a glimpse of that caring and warm-hearted person I used to think about. At times, I feel myself becoming, finally, the person I always wanted to be."

In early April, Randy was rummaging through some belongings when he came across his old journal. Reading those entries with weary, sober eyes, he paused. All that history, the idealism of Harvey and the movement, and he'd mostly obsessed about "career and sex," and whether or not he'd ever be successful. *Jesus, what a head trip*, he thought. *Was that really me?*

Of course it was. The young freelancer who'd dreamed of working for a major newspaper was now focused on the Pulitzer Prize, and while casual (safe) sex could still be fun, he longed for a lasting relationship. The absence of alcohol and drugs, he added, "has helped me see how success is my drug too, and how I've been trying to have an applauded today replace a childhood [in] which I was beaten and emotionally abused."

The memories made him want to set down the diary. "Suffice it to say, that somewhere, I hoped to have a hand in making a better world and (most lately) in saving some lives," he wrote in its final entry. "Life gets so much more serious than we ever expect it to be, and all our youthful scheming can look pretty petty in retrospect. I hope I do a better job of all this life business in my second 34 years."

13 | THAT NEBULOUS COMMODITY

A JOB'S A JOB, right? As long as Wes Haley was getting paid, "If you tell me to stand in the corner and pick my nose standing on my head . . . okay, I'll do it." Wes had landed at the *Chronicle* in 1985 as an editorial assistant, working the early shift each morning before the newsroom got busy. "When I started at the paper, [Randy] had just gone into the prima donna stage, where he didn't want to work in the office," he remembered. "He wanted to work from home or other places. And of course, he had the reputation and the cojones to pull it off."

Whatever Randy had done to organize his home life, it clearly hadn't carried over to his job. "I mean, he was an effing slob," Wes continued. When an editor ordered him to clean Randy's desk, Wes set to work sorting heaps of paper and folders into bankers' boxes. No matter where he turned, however, he was confronted by an obscene infestation of paper clips, spilling over like an ant colony. Later that day, he wrote in his diary, "We could stop manufacturing paperclips everywhere in the world, and Randy Shilts could supply them."

When Randy returned, Wes remembered, it was "hugs, hugs, kisses, kisses to everybody, and fuck-yous to others," alternating blowing kisses with double middle-fingers. Suddenly, a shriek erupted: "GOD DAMN, WHO THE FUCK DID THIS?"

Wes quietly approached him. The two were close in height, but Wes's thicker frame gave the appearance that he wouldn't be pushed around. "I did," he replied.

Randy blinked. "Oh, okay. Did you throw anything away?"

"Randy, I wrote you a note and I sent it over to you," Wes answered. "I threw nothing away, except the recycled paper clips."

"Oh, I can get those back."

The passing moment cemented a new friendship, as Randy, himself an early riser, began calling every morning for some girl talk. "I really felt that through this period, Randy and I were really good, close friends," Wes explained, "because I listened to *everything* that he had to do, but we could dish. And yes, I felt that everything was so heavy in his life that I felt like I could be friends with him."

In Wes, Randy had found a gay office mate who wasn't direct competition, in whom he could safely confide without fear of gossip, envy, or sexual tension. "You and I never slept together, did we?" Randy once asked.

"Honey, please," Wes replied. "We're sisters."

"Every gay man somewhere has got someone in the family that they aren't going to diddle with," Wes explained. "And I said, 'Randy, I'm never going to go to bed with you.' He goes, 'Oh good, because I don't want to go to bed with you.'"

"Am I that disgusting?"

"Well, you're a little short."

"Well, fuck you."

After joining the *Chronicle* in 1986, newcomer Evelyn C. White quickly got to know Randy on Sunday evenings, when he held down the city editor's desk with a few rookie reporters. "With me being the only Black woman in the newsroom at the time, we gravitated towards each other, both of us being gay," she explained. "And during slow times, we would end up chatting with each other."

Evelyn's first impressions weren't dissimilar from other new gay and lesbian journalists in town. "He just exuded a certain kind of generosity," remembered Elaine Herscher, who began as a stringer before joining the newsroom. "He was very welcoming. He knew I was gay, and he was kind of, 'You're in the club.' Whatever he was doing, he would share it with me."

Because Randy truly had no direct local competition, instead of pulling the door shut, he'd offer advice and encouragement to those who were climbing the ranks. Even in the midst of the *Bay Area Reporter*'s harshest attacks, for example, he still wrote to its reporter Mike Hippler with praise and constructive criticism. And when broadcast journalist Hank Plante arrived at CBS station KPIX, Randy advised him to get good stories by letting people know he was gay, even though he was technically the competition.

At the same time, Randy was maintaining an unwavering commitment to the AIDS beat, devoting extensive time to medical conferences in Copenhagen, Paris, and Brussels, in addition to return visits to Washington and New York City. In total, he would count 519 interviews with 219 individuals for the book. But, he noted, a list of every AIDS-related interview he'd conducted would likely exceed 900 people. If Randy had any thoughts about the test results that sat waiting for him, they mostly stayed compartmentalized from his work—except, he mentioned to one of his sources, he didn't think he'd been infected, because sexually he was a top.

As Randy worked on *And the Band Played On*, he was coming across substantial new information, causing the narrative to shift in key ways from what he'd originally outlined. "To have a coherent narrative, when you don't have a single central character, is very difficult," Michael Denneny recalled. "He had half a dozen main characters, but [he was] braiding those stories in a way that kept people reading!"

In describing the failure to recognize and respond to a burgeoning health crisis, the central theme of *Band* was emerging without Randy explicitly calling it what it was: a major systemic clusterfuck. HIV/AIDS, as the disease was now being termed, had disrupted not only the formal systems for controlling new diseases but also informal systems with their own implicit boundaries, authority figures, and internal processes. Such disruptions could have been remediated sooner, however, once decision-makers had recognized and adjusted to the threat.

If corrections to these systems had occurred sooner, two public health strategies, treatment and containment, might have helped mitigate the pandemic's worst consequences. Effective treatment would require cooperation across multiple systems to support research on the disease's cause and potential treatments, in addition to population studies to better understand the needs of the afflicted. Additionally, as seen in San Francisco, community-based services were needed to reduce the burden on providers and stabilize patients' essential needs, like housing, food, income, and complementary therapies.

Recalling those early years, Dr. Paul Volberding observed, "Our first AIDS patients were stereotypically people who were the most socially disconnected. But what happened very quickly is that we discovered that there was a family, i.e., the gay community and organizations within the gay community. Very quickly, there was this organic kind of integration of the hospitalized care with the community-based care, and all that was around the gay community organizations."

Containment, meanwhile, required accurate ascertainment of the disease's prevalence and of how it was being transmitted, which would need to include researchers, contact tracers, physicians, community leaders, activists, and patients. Most important, containing the disease required strong federal leadership. As *And the Band Played On* would illustrate, the context in 1981 for mounting a quick, decisive response had not been ideal, but it hadn't been impossible.

Across *Band*'s many settings, Randy would assign much of the blame to attitudes, norms, and hierarchies that had influenced the workings of each particular system. Thus, the word *politics*, as he was using it, could be taken to have two meanings: first, the interplay of personality and power that influences just about every group, community, or workplace, and, second, the Reagan administration's use of political gamesmanship to delay multiple systems' responses.

"Government is not the solution to our problem, government is the problem," Ronald Reagan had famously declared. Yet, as Randy noted, the government had spent millions to investigate cyanide-laced Tylenol capsules in 1982, a mercifully brief scare that claimed only seven lives. Clearly, government hadn't been the problem when it came to that particular crisis, but with AIDS, those same systems had failed.

"CDC was just ready; [AIDS] was right down CDC's alley," Dr. Donald Francis remembered. "We'd worked with gay men for years. We were comfortable. We'd worked with IV drug users for years. Whatever was thrown our way, we were comfortable with. And we were set." With a background in global smallpox, ebola containment, hepatitis B, and feline leukemia, Francis seemed to have the ideal skills and experience to handle AIDS.

"I had, one, all the international stuff. Two, I'd worked with gay men for years. Here we had the laboratory work, [and] now I had my doctorate in feline leukemia," Francis explained. "It was all set up. You couldn't have plotted it better. Except we had Republicans who fucked everything up." When he submitted the CDC's first official AIDS budget, Reagan's budget officials bluntly answered, "Look pretty and do as little as you can."

"We are the public health service of the United States of America," Francis fumed, "and we were just told [this] by these assholes, who were our bosses, and it shook everyone. I had been trained by CDC . . . not to 'look pretty and do as little as you can.'" Francis's relocation to the Bay Area, where he would serve as AIDS advisor to the State of California, brought him further into Randy's circle and made him one of the more prolific sources during the book's later stages. What started as brief conversations turned into long sessions at Randy's apartment, surrounded by his raw materials. "He would have these manila folders lined up . . . vertical lined manila folders by day, and then he'd have a little tag when the year would change. But there might be six feet between that, depending on what was going on at that time," Francis recalled.

Even with hindsight, it remains no easy feat to explicate the failure of each system depicted in *Band*. But Randy would rely on figures like Don Francis to personify frustrations with how political games had stalled a timely, effective response. In that respect, Francis played a key role by helping Randy relate the larger consequences of AIDS to the personalities impeding certain efforts.

Moreover, by virtue of his position and years of experience, Francis offered a useful vantage point for connecting different actors across systems, from federal officials on down. The gamesmanship around funding and messaging represented only part of Francis's frustrations, as he'd also grown wary of what he perceived as the National Cancer Institute's manipulation to favor Robert Gallo's claims that the virus was a variant of his earlier discovery, the human T-lymphotropic virus type 1 (HTLV-1).

It's worth recalling that in his proposal, Randy hadn't even mentioned Don Francis and only considered Bob Gallo to be a minor character. But by taking on the work of isolating HIV, Gallo had assumed a vital role in understanding how the virus traveled and reproduced, which would be essential for rolling out an effective public health response. The attention garnered by Gallo's drawn-out dispute with the French, including evidence that he'd used the Pasteur Institute's isolates of the virus to grow his own prototype, had attracted scrutiny because of not only his methods but also the personality traits that made him difficult for others, including Francis, to work with.

Although Gallo was surely known to be gregarious and accessible, he could also come across as arrogant, dismissive, territorial, and hell-bent on securing his accolades. None of these characterizations originated with Randy. Journalists Larry Bush and David Talbot had described Gallo's rivalry with the French as "scientific competition at its most vulgar," with scientists "engaging in an unseemly race for individual glory," while Laurie Garrett regarded him as "full of himself" and incapable of saying anything "outside of whatever is in his personal interest to say." *Band* did not offer the final or definitive statement on Gallo, as a comprehensive account of his alleged misconduct would come later from John Crewdson of the *Chicago Tribune*. Outside the realm of science journalism, however, Randy's depiction would be the first to make a serious dent in Gallo's public reputation.

Decades later, Gallo continued to defend his work, insisting that he'd defined the field of human retrovirology in the 1970s. It is correct to say that even before HIV/AIDS was discovered, Gallo had made a substantial contribution to combating it with his discovery of reverse transcriptase, the biochemical footprint that provided evidence that human retroviruses were the underlying cause of certain cancers. It is also true that during the 1984 press conference announcing his discovery, Gallo had allowed that, if the French could prove their virus, dubbed LAV, was the underlying cause of AIDS, then the virus should be given that name.

With respect to Randy, Gallo's perspective would come to reflect both magnanimity and irritation. "I don't know Randy Shilts," he emphasized. "He seems like a nice guy, but he was bamboozled by somebody. And then he's not a scholar of science, let me tell you that. He did not know, understand, or do any degree of research related to the science of this problem at the time."

Critics would detail a number of errors in Randy's depiction of the science, but it's also true that Randy wasn't trying to write another scientific AIDS book. His purpose had been to "follow the money," with the complexities of scientific research providing one of many important contexts. To tell this particular story, Randy had to know just enough to translate the science for a general readership, and in conveying some of those details, he made mistakes.

At the same time, Gallo's characterization of Randy's work would also include some inaccuracies. His claim, for example, that Randy relied solely on Don Francis, a man whom he regarded as "not a scientist by any stretch of the imagination," is contradicted by a substantial number of interviews documented in Randy's papers, including many of the scientists working on retroviruses at the time. Gallo also protested that Randy hadn't bothered to interview James Curran, who readily acknowledged his role as a source.

Despite his grievances, Gallo reflected, "I guess he's a very good writer. I know he was dedicated to AIDS. I'm sure I would've liked him very much if I got to know him. Truthfully, I have no bad feelings related to Shilts. Just wish I knew him ahead of time and had a chance to talk with him." Here again, however, the record contradicts Gallo's recollections. In the source notes for *Band*, Randy listed a single interview with Gallo in April 1986, which is corroborated by a contemporaneously published account in the *Chronicle*, detailing a "wide-ranging, four-hour interview" in Gallo's Bethesda laboratory.

Given how frequently Gallo was engaging with the press, it may simply be that the encounter didn't merit any special memories. For Randy, however, it corroborated the personality traits of a man who would occupy an outsized portion of the narrative. Whatever else they may have discussed, Randy apparently had what he needed to defend his characterization.

Although some would complain that Randy was casting Don Francis as the book's undeserving hero, by Francis's own standards, his goal of getting new cases down to zero remained unmet. Conversely, while it would be tempting to paint Bob Gallo as a one-dimensional villain, he was also someone who'd worked his way to the top of a high-risk, high-reward profession, which incentivized the kinds of ambitious, territorial behaviors Randy and others would amplify. Ultimately, within the broader AIDS response, both Gallo and Francis held crucial positions within ill-fitting systems, which had broken down at crucial moments due to the competing priorities of territoriality, public recognition, and egos.

In crafting the characters who would drive *Band*'s narrative, Randy consistently gave sympathetic treatment to people who'd approached the crisis with earnestness and urgency, exemplifying traits like compassion, self-sacrifice, and foresight. Advocates like Larry Kramer would earn sympathetic treatment, as would Gary Walsh, whose decline had been painstakingly captured in the diary of his lover, Matthew Krieger. But if one had to choose a central character across the book's many interwoven threads, the strongest case would be for Bill Kraus.

Out of all of Randy's sources, no one spoke with Randy more on the record, and only Dr. Marcus Conant would come close to matching Kraus's mentions in the narrative. With his involvement across numerous systems and a story arc to rival any tragic hero, Kraus gave Randy a compelling link between several of the book's most stirring conflicts. After working for Harry Britt, he'd become Congressman Phil Burton's liaison to the gay community in 1982. A dogged pragmatist, known for favoring old-fashioned vote counting over soaring speeches, Kraus had risen to prominence at a moment when antigay forces were also on the ascent.

"Bill was a very interesting person," Michael Housh recalled. "I think, had he lived, there is no doubt that he would've ended up in Congress . . . and probably would've given Barney [Frank] heart failure." Michael and his lover Rick Pacurar had witnessed many of *Band*'s key events involving Bill Kraus. The couple moved to DC when Michael worked for Barbara Boxer and regularly hosted Kraus during his visits to Capitol Hill. Similar to Kraus, they provided Randy with documents and insider tips while connecting him with key congressional aides.

Bill Kraus's influence on Randy can be seen in how *Band* portrayed his efforts to fight both for his community and his life. His connections to multiple systems offered Randy an invaluable figure for marrying the accounts of political insiders with the flesh-and-blood stories he'd promised in *Band*'s proposal. Of Kraus's efforts with Timothy Westmoreland to secure the initial AIDS research funds, Randy wrote, "[It] is clear that virtually all the money that funded the early scientific advances on AIDS can be credited almost solely to these two gay men."

In 1983 Kraus spearheaded an old-fashioned pamphlet strategy, using congressional mailers to send a tamer brochure to all constituents while working with Milk Club leaders to craft a more explicit one for gay men. For taking such an aggressive approach, Kraus, like Randy, had experienced a painful backlash, including epithets like "sexual fascist" and "sexual Nazi." Adding to his frustrations were revelations that federal officials had been slow to disburse the research funding he'd secured and that the Reagan administration was grossly overstating its commitment by using the vague phrase, "studies relevant to patients with AIDS." But more pointedly, Kraus and Randy's extensive conversations brought focus to the existential crisis they were both facing.

Like Randy, Kraus had recognized the threat somewhat earlier than many, but not soon enough to rule out the possibility of infection. By intertwining the details of Kraus's political work with anecdotes of his on-and-off relationship with Kico Govantes, Randy would elevate the story of his demise to near-operatic magnitude. The definitive diagnosis would come in October 1984, when Marcus Conant found a purple lesion on Kraus's thigh. From this point forward, the narrative would veer away from his skillful political organizing to a frantic, futile effort to escape his fate.

Across the book's final 120 pages, Randy interspersed details of how Kraus, like Gary Walsh, had temporarily sought refuge in another country and dabbled in religious mysticism. Remembering Bill's passing in January 1986, Michael Housh simply said, "It was horrible." Randy, as he'd previously done for Gary Walsh and Bobbi Campbell, penned Kraus's obituary before providing a more intimate depiction of the death scene in *Band*'s agonizing final pages.

Of all the AIDS casualties to feature prominently in *Band*, Randy was leaning heavily on the stories of two close friends, Bill Kraus and Gary Walsh, to personify what he'd characterized as gay liberation's more pragmatic elements. While the former had sought to improve gay lives by strong-arming the political machinery, the latter had worked to foster self-acceptance among his clients, friends, and lovers. In elevating these two characters, Randy was offering examples of what gays had already lost; however, not every gay man in *Band* would meet the same demise.

Whenever possible, Randy tried to showcase gays who'd worked, mostly out of the public eye, to combat the pandemic in its earliest years. One such example, Dr. Donald Abrams, was completing his fellowship at University of California, San Francisco, when Randy first contacted him. "He called me, and he said, 'This disease decreases lymphocytes in the blood. What's a lymphocyte?'" Abrams remembered. After getting an explanation, Randy asked, "Can I say that you're gay?" No, Abrams told Randy, because it wasn't relevant to the story. In 1984 Abrams briefly caused his own mini-uproar by getting ahead of Bob Gallo's retrovirus announcement. In the aftermath, Randy called him to ask, "What's a retrovirus?" After getting an explanation, he again probed, "Can I say that you're gay?" Again, Abrams explained, he didn't see the relevance. When Randy interviewed him for *Band*, however, Abrams told him, "In the book, you can say that I'm gay." As they spoke, he noticed a tear rolling down Randy's cheek.

Similar to Abrams, Timothy Westmoreland hadn't considered his sexuality relevant to the story. As chief counsel to the House Subcommittee on Health and the Environment, Westmoreland considered himself to be openly gay, but "in a sort of soft-spoken way." In his position reporting directly to Chairman Henry Waxman, Westmoreland had stayed apprised on the latest AIDS developments, leading to his first face-to-face encounter with Randy on Capitol Hill in early 1985. "At the time, I thought [Randy] was a reporter doing background research," he remembered. "He was also trying to get a grasp on how Congress worked, and how Congress interacted with the executive branch, and how congressional legislation could lead to funding, and how hearings and publicity could lead to funding." From these encounters emerged substantial evidence that Reagan administration officials had favored ideology over public health.

In outlining his case, however, Randy made a decision that left Westmoreland feeling burned when the book was published. Although Westmoreland had specifically asked to not be named, he'd also made himself a publicly gay figure in 1983 by writing an AIDS editorial for the *Washington Blade*. By the time he learned that Randy had explicitly named him and his sexuality, the book had already gone to press. "Randy thought that it was important that it be a gay man working within the system," Westmoreland explained. "[While] I wasn't in any way closeted in my life, there was no particular reason for me to tell the Republican members and the Republican staff, 'By the way, before you think of anything about what I'm briefing you on, you should start thinking that I'm a gay man.'" Although the exposure would raise tensions for a while, Westmoreland still enjoyed the backing of his boss and would hold his position until 1995. Despite the initial fears, *Band* didn't destroy his career, and he remained on good enough terms with Randy to provide technical assistance on his later work.

If Randy had any qualms about partially outing one of his sources, it seemed that he placed a higher priority on showing how gay men were contributing positively to HIV/AIDS relief efforts. As the narrative was taking shape, it was clear that he would need those stories to balance his portrayal of the "no surrender" sexual revolutionaries, whose actions were sure to upend certain readers' sensibilities. His descriptions of packed, sweaty dance floors and widely shared party drugs provided plenty of tawdry details, which he easily could have mined from his own past.

In *Band*'s early chapters, readers would learn of exotic practices, like inhaling poppers and fist-fucking, through the innocent eyes of Kico Govantes, while in another brief scene, Gary Walsh patiently offered a tutorial on how to cruise. As the story progressed, Randy was able to relay the frustrations of Larry Kramer to contrast the New York and San Francisco AIDS responses, while providing background on the scorn Kramer had earned for his earlier novel *Faggots*. In a book packed with science and policy, these passages could be read as merely adding color, if they simply stood as isolated anecdotes. But it was Randy's return to Dr. Selma Dritz, now retired, which provided the material to fundamentally bind all these seamier elements into their own extensive plot line.

When Randy and Selma sat down in early 1986, the conversation began like two old friends. She'd landed in San Francisco in 1967, when public health was essentially still a "one-horse department," but in the midst of the most substantial influx of gay people the city had ever seen, she started seeing increases in rare infectious diseases among men ages twenty to forty. For her efforts, Selma had earned the affection of many locals, who dubbed her the "Den Mother of the Gays" and the "Sex Queen of San Francisco." But as fond as she was of these honorifics, Selma reflected, she knew she wasn't a gay man—she was a mother. And as more AIDS cases required tracing, the more it hurt, even as she tried to harden herself and save more patients than she lost.

There was never a question that it was transmittable, Selma continued. She'd used every available channel to sound the alarm, pleading with gay doctors to report new cases and warn their patients. The politicians could have said something about it, she lamented. Bathhouse owners were just businessmen, giving the customers what they wanted. Gay men found comfort in groups, she acknowledged, and they had every right to be there. But when it came to diseases, she insisted, they did not have the right to kill others.

"I became hopeless," Selma continued. Even with a few years' distance, she could still remember many of the cases. There was Bobbi Campbell, who'd looked so good on the second anniversary of his diagnosis but hadn't made it to his third. Another patient, a "tin god on wheels," had taught music lessons to work his way through medical school. After he'd died, she told Randy, his parents wouldn't even claim the remains.

And then, there was "Montreal." Selma had heard about the man back in 1982, when he'd been traced to eight different contacts in San Francisco, Los Angeles, and his own city. At the time, they were hoping he was already dead, she said, but he was still going to the baths. Selma herself had confronted him during a San Francisco stay, after callers to the San Francisco AIDS Foundation had reported a man with a French accent, telling sex partners that he'd given them gay cancer.

"It's none of your goddamn business," Montreal had told her. "It is my right to do what I want with my own body." When Selma's countered that he didn't have the right to endanger others, he responded, "It's not my duty to protect others."

"Not at the baths?" she'd countered.

"You know what goes on there," Montreal shot back. "I've got it. They can get it too."

Following that encounter, Selma called the city attorney. As she continued, Randy scrawled "Dugas" down the right-hand side of his yellow notepad. The conversation moved on to other topics, but when they parted, she loaned him some research articles. In an early CDC study examining a cluster of forty-one gay men with AIDS, Montreal had seemingly been designated "Patient Zero" because of his direct sexual contact with eight different AIDS cases in New York and Los Angeles.

At the time, the study had provided valuable evidence of sexual transmission. On a subsequent East Coast trip, Randy interviewed Dr. Linda Laubenstein at New York University's Langone Medical Center, who recalled that not only were all of her initial KS patients gay men, but many belonged to the same social circle. During that same visit, he also sat down with activist Paul Popham, whose friendship and firsthand knowledge of Gaetan Dugas added further intrigue to the tale.

As Randy's curiosity toward Gaetan grew, his editor took notice. "I remember when Randy was doing the reporting," Michael Denneny recounted. "At a certain period, he said, 'It's getting very creepy. I keep coming up against the same guy in city after city. It's like he's haunting me or something.'" The details, Randy told him, were always the same. "He's blonde. It turns out he's French-Canadian, turns out he's in airlines. I mean, he was slowly becoming aware of that, because he was running into people describing what he started feeling was the same person."

Returning to San Francisco, Randy wrote to Selma, "I'm going to nag you about Patient Zero, since he has such a unique role both in the epidemic and by epitomizing (in one body) so many of the public health issues which defied a knee-jerk response. What to do about a Patient Zero remains something the gay community has yet to face up to . . . and such patients will certainly arise again."

In March Randy interviewed four Vancouver men who'd known Gaetan personally, two of whom spoke on condition of anonymity. Across numerous conversations, a plotline was beginning to emerge. The following month, he spoke with Dr. William Darrow, one of the authors of the cluster study, who shared candid details of his team's tracking efforts. Gaetan's first contact with CDC investigators had come in August 1981, when Dr. Mary Guinan, another member of the field team, interviewed him at New York University School of Medicine.

Randy telephoned Guinan and shared what he already knew about that interview. The two were already acquainted from her time collecting case histories in a Tenderloin hotel room. Guinan had been amazed at how quickly Randy had located and spoken with the men she'd interviewed, even as she'd kept strict confidentiality. For her willingness to be an anonymous source, Randy had teasingly given her the nickname "Sore Throat." But despite their good relationship and her respect for Randy's reporting, Guinan recalled, "I told Randy that I could not tell him whether I did [interview him] or not. He said, 'I know you did.' I said, 'End of conversation.'"

Still, Randy had enough information to fill in the details. A native of Quebec City, Gaetan had worked for Air Canada since the early 1970s. In addition to his attractiveness, he'd stood out for his generosity, spontaneity, and wit; he was a natural life of the party with a loud, infectious laugh, who reminded friends of a glowing, Jo Anne Worley–type personality. He could make a bad situation funny, one friend told Randy, but above all else, Gaetan loved being gay, and for him, being gay meant having sex. Everywhere he went, Gaetan collected the names of men he bedded, writing them down in a fabric-covered book that he'd later share with CDC investigators. "Sex was a way of expressing himself," Randy observed. "Everything was sexual . . . the way he looked, talked, and dressed. Asking him not to have sex was not just asking him to give up sex." By late 1982, after repeated warnings from medical providers and public health officials, Gaetan increasingly found himself an object of panic, fear, and hostility.

"In many ways, which people don't often say about Gaetan, he really was sort of the ideal gay everyman of the '70s," Michael Denneny reflected. "And it was through his sexuality that he created his adult persona. So, sexuality was immensely important to him. And it is totally understandable why he would resist. But at the same time, looking at it, it was irresponsible. And it took him a while to get to that point. And he did have sex, and in fact he was driven out of several places by the community. This is before [Randy had] ever written the book. The community drove him out of two different towns because they thought he was spreading AIDS."

During Gaetan's last stay in San Francisco, Randy learned, he'd been bluntly confronted on Castro Street. And in 1983 Gaetan's Vancouver friends heard that local bar owners considered posting his picture as a warning. Randy learned that Gaetan had studied as much AIDS research as he could find, so that he frequently asked impressive questions about the latest findings and voiced concerns about fear and stigma toward AIDS patients. At the same time, members of the group AIDS Vancouver were strategizing how to bring Gaetan "out of circulation" by appealing to his sense of responsibility to the gay community. About halfway through his sixty pages of notes, Randy jotted down the words *Anger* and *Denial*, framing them in a felt-tipped box for emphasis.

When Gaetan returned to Quebec City in February 1984, it was clear that he'd grown weaker, more isolated, and frightened. As Randy noted, his passing in late March left behind an abundance of friends and lovers. At the time of Gaetan's death, the San Francisco bathhouse fury was still escalating, including the backlash against Randy. Although the flight attendant who'd commanded fervent attention in life had already exited the scene, his visage would haunt the narrative of AIDS in ways he likely never expected.

As he'd done with *Band*'s other plotlines, Randy surgically inserted Gaetan's story into his chronology, using these vignettes to underscore the perils of containing an infectious disease when someone is actively carrying it across a continent. The facts at Randy's disposal were, arguably, consistent with what he knew at the time in that Gaetan had, in fact, been among the first AIDS cases diagnosed in North America. He did travel extensively, amassing an impressive history of sexual partners. He was traced to a substantial proportion of the first cases collected by CDC researchers, and by his own admission, he'd continued having sex with new partners in multiple cities, well past the time he'd been asked to curtail his behaviors.

By sprinkling the term *Patient Zero* early in the narrative, Randy was fashioning a character to serve as both a cautionary example and a literary device. As Selma Dritz had explained, if one individual could give the virus to ten people, then those ten could give it to ten more, creating a tremendous hazard in transmissibility. The scenes involving Gaetan were faithful to Randy's handwritten notes, so that the portrayal of Gaetan's character appeared to be consistent with his sources.

"I think Randy was fascinated with him," Mary Guinan reflected. "He had followed him and his sexual behavior so thoroughly and [portrayed] him as he was." Guinan, however, was not pleased with Randy's embrace of the *Patient Zero* term. "As Gaetan said, 'Someone gave it to me,'" she insisted. "The results of the case/control study showed clearly that the number of sex partners greatly enhanced the risk of AIDS. Many of the men with AIDS reported over twenty thousand sex partners, many more than Gaetan. So, I feel Gaetan was singled out as the bad guy, which is unfortunate."

If Randy had stuck to simply portraying Gaetan as an example of basic epidemiology, he would've stayed on safer ground. But a case example alone likely wouldn't have done enough to press home his larger point that political preoccupations had given cover for HIV to proliferate. "Gaetan was the perfect—what's the word I want to use? The perfect—well, I better use it—the perfect spreader," Mervyn Silverman explained. "Here he was on flights, flying all over the world. He'd come into San Francisco; he's having sex with gay men in San Francisco. He's in New York, he's in London, he's in Paris. Patient Zero, I don't believe for a minute. But certainly, he facilitated the spread tremendously."

However, Randy's use of that loaded term, although it only appeared seven times in conjunction with the case and control study, still hinted at more than the evidence could deliver. "Whether Gaetan Dugas actually was the person who brought AIDS to North America remains a question of debate and is ultimately unanswerable," he wrote. "In any event, there's no doubt that Gaetan played a key role in spreading the new virus from one end of the United States to the other."

In making that leap from evidence to conjecture, Randy was taking a substantial risk. While it was true that the question of Gaetan bringing HIV to North America could never be confirmed, scientific research would eventually advance to the point where it could be answered with an emphatic no.

The notion of a single carrier, though tantalizing, has typically served more to distract, distort, and blame than to help contain a widespread disease outbreak.

"We had very strong disagreements about *And the Band Played On*," Laurie Garrett recalled. "And I told him that he wasn't understanding what an epidemiologist means when they say, 'Patient Zero,' and that Gaetan Dugas was not the source of AIDS." Moreover, as the saying goes, correlation doesn't equal causation. The fact that Gaetan had sex with so many men who turned up in early field research didn't prove that he was the source of their HIV infection, and as others pointed out, one of those lovers most certainly did pass the virus to him. However, given that investigators interviewed sex partners of Gaetan who had yet to experience symptoms, it is possible that he did pass HIV to men who were previously uninfected, both before and after he'd been urged to curtail his behaviors.

Regarding Randy's point that Gaetan had played a "key role" in HIV's migration, he knew that Gaetan wasn't the only carrier in that study cohort, but he had the most distinguishing features, an unforgettable name, and a charming disposition that stood in chilling contrast to behaviors that seemed especially callous. As a result, the sprawling landscape of *And the Band Played On* gained a compelling pseudo-villain, whose struggles lent credibility to the fears and frustrations of its beleaguered central characters.

"He had to construct a story, and it was perfectly appropriate to put Gaetan Dugas in that," Don Francis commented, "but Gaetan Dugas was [one of] about a thousand people that did the same thing." Francis had also briefly met Gaetan while he was alive and, like others, found him to be charming. "But to be honest, I think Randy did a good job on that, because let's bring it down to the real-world person, and if you asked him, 'Was [Gaetan] the sole spreader of AIDS in the world?' he would certainly say no. But [Randy] needed that, and it was fine."

The assumption would be that Randy had cynically seized on Gaetan Dugas as a way to give *Band* a bestselling hook. But there was no denying that Gaetan had distinguished himself in the research literature, in the recollections of scientists and medical officials, and in the accounts of his former lovers. Consequently, as Randy neared completion of *And the Band Played On*, there indeed was Gaetan Dugas, a comparatively late addition, woven into a story for which he wasn't originally intended, for purposes that would be debated for decades.

When it came to Gaetan the human being, Randy remained faithful to the notes he'd collected, capturing the full range, from generous lover and friend to unyielding sexual revolutionary to vulnerable, frightened patient. In the circles where he ran, Gaetan was popular and therefore powerful, affording him the sexual and social currency to get what he wanted. As for Gaetan the case example, Randy's notes showed how he fully understood Gaetan to not be *the* Patient Zero, but a man whose behaviors encapsulated several problems that couldn't be solved in simple, straightforward ways. That Randy saw the potential for future patients like Gaetan suggests that he considered it vital for gay communities to not downplay such cases when they came to light.

As time and further evidence would show, the intimation that Gaetan may have brought HIV to North America, no matter how carefully Randy worded it, went beyond the evidence. For sure, he had the backing of his editor, but even Michael Denneny understood the difference between a literary device and a literal interpretation. "I think the whole Patient Zero thing would be a whole book in itself," he said, and such books would eventually be written. It was not, however, the book that Randy had set out to write. In the finished work of more than six hundred pages, Gaetan received thirty-five mentions, with only seven concerning the Patient Zero designation. How the storyline would be received remained anyone's guess until the book hit the shelves.

In early 1987 Selma Dritz sent Randy a quick note. "After a long hiatus, I'm seeing your by-line more frequently recently," she wrote. "Does this mean you've completed your work on the proposed AIDS book?"

Indeed, with the final chapters completed, Randy had resumed his full-time beat in late January, telling the *Sentinel*, "[It's] been a year and a half since I've written a news story that's gotten me in trouble." In a lengthy interview, he promised a book that would detail "a massive failure of institutions who are supposed to protect America from such scourges as epidemics," teasing, "I have the life story of the first known western person to ever [contract] AIDS. There's a massive surprise in that story. So, for the first time, how AIDS enters the U.S. and spreads coast to coast is made very clear—with some very new information."

Randy Shilts at the *San Francisco Chronicle* news desk, November 1987.
Photo by Scot Sommerdorf for the San Francisco Chronicle / *Polaris Images*

In hindsight, that "massive surprise" raises questions about what, exactly, Randy thought he was selling. But for now, he was returning to full-time reporting as city politics was buzzing again around the influence of gay power. An upcoming special election would test that political muscle, as Harry Britt was running to challenge presumptive frontrunner Nancy Pelosi for the vacant congressional seat of Sala Burton. Meanwhile, Randy's coverage of national and international AIDS stories expanded to include an interview with Surgeon General C. Everett Koop, a stalwart conservative, who'd stunned his political overseers by distributing a report on AIDS bluntly calling for safer-sex education, condom use, and strong antidiscrimination laws to incentivize voluntary testing.

Even though *Band* was now in production, it would gain a stirring epilogue, tying its mid-1985 conclusion around Rock Hudson's illness to events surrounding the Third International Conference on AIDS, held in Washington, DC, in late May. As Randy would note, conference events signified the arrival of a new chapter in AIDS activism, as Larry Kramer, attending a fundraising dinner headlined by Ronald Reagan, unleashed a torrent of righteous anger toward the president who'd ignored a deadly pandemic.

The high-profile eruption, along with numerous protests around the city, made it clear that a new era of confrontation had arrived, with dramatic street theatrics and coordinated disruptions to the status quo, supplanting the earlier efforts of figures like Bobbi Campbell, Gary Walsh, and Bill Kraus. Six years overdue, AIDS was beginning to seize the spotlight, thanks in part to Randy's determination to keep it in the headlines. But on the issue of his own health, he remained publicly silent as the book neared publication.

———————

"I can tell you exactly when he learned it," Michael Denneny remembered, concerning Randy's HIV test results. "It was the day he finished the manuscript . . . and it wasn't until he sent the manuscript to me that he called the doctor and said, 'Okay, what are the results?' He did not want to know if he was positive or negative while he was writing the book."

Michael's estimation of when Randy found out put the window squarely in the early months of 1987. At the time, Ann Neuenschwander was still living in San Francisco and helping Randy organize his files, usually with *All My Children* playing in the background. "We were on our way up to Diamond Heights for a drive," she recalled, which would take them up to Twin Peaks. Randy had picked her up, announcing that he had something to tell her. "I was used to his dramatic statements," Ann said, "so I didn't feel that it was anything serious."

Like any other drive, they were singing along to the radio. "I used to always sing, 'People let me tell you 'bout my best friend. He's a warm cuddly boy,'" she laughed. "That was Randy. And he joked, and we sang in the car all the time, to all the music." Midride, Randy broke the news to his best friend. "I started crying," Ann recalled, but Randy bristled. "No! You can't cry," he told her. "Stop it. Stop it."

"I wanted you to be here because I wanted you to know," Randy added. "Don't cry." As Ann pulled herself together, a familiar tune came on the radio and they started singing, "Well, East Coast girls are hip, I really dig those styles they wear . . ."

"And we were singing our hearts out at this bad news," she added. "But he didn't want to talk anymore about it." For the time being, at least, Ann wasn't allowed to tell anyone.

Wes Haley was at his newsroom desk when he received an unexpected call. "[Randy] had called the newspaper to ask if our union insurance covered [HIV]. And of course, it came through my desk," Wes explained. "And I said, "Honey, call me tomorrow morning.'"

The next day, Randy phoned at the usual time and asked, "Well, what do you think?"

"Yes," Wes told him. "It's covered. Believe me. It's covered."

"Are you sure?"

"Yes, I'm sure. Don't worry about that." Wes added, "Are you OK?"

"Well, I'm as OK as I can be," Randy sighed. "Girlfriend . . . when news hits the fan, this shit's going to fly everywhere."

"Yeah," Wes replied. "Yeah. Yeah. It is." And then, somewhat startlingly, he asked another question. "I asked him if he had gone bug hunting," Wes continued, invoking a slang term for people who have condomless sex for the purpose of contracting HIV. For once, his friend was silent. "I wish it would have been in person," Wes reflected, "because I wanted to see his face. What was as telling as his face was the quietness. No bravado. No smart ass. No 'Fuck you, bitch,' because that's what he called me a lot. It was just like . . . I don't know how you write it. I don't know how you say it. There was just this . . . *pfft*."

"And I thought, *Well, I've fucked things up*. And then I felt bad, because I've insulted him or something," Wes recalled. "But I had said to myself, *There's no need to try to backpedal*. Because after you've already asked somebody if they've bug hunted, what do you say to them?" Following that exchange, Randy didn't call back for another two days. And when their daily conversations resumed, just like with Ann, it was back to business as usual.

14 | NO PRIZE FOR MODESTY

SINCE ITS FOUNDING AS the nation's capital, Washington, DC, had rarely witnessed a scene like October 11, 1987. With hundreds of thousands arriving from across the country, the daylong event echoed with raucous chants, whistles, singing, and speeches, accompanied by the sobering sight of wheelchair-bound men being pushed by their loved ones, while outraged demonstrators wielded placards bearing the slogan SILENCE EQUALS DEATH. On the National Mall, a band of activists organized by Cleve Jones unfurled the most stunning symbol of AIDS activism to date, marking the debut of his vision, the NAMES Project.

"The National March on Washington for Gay and Lesbian Rights was the largest gay protest ever held and one of the largest civil rights demonstrations in the nation's capital since the Vietnam war," Randy wrote in the *Chronicle*. "Although the demonstration was organized to support a host of gay issues, most of the signs and chants were focused on the AIDS epidemic," he added, "which has cut a broad swath of death through the gay community." At least for the weekend, he was back to being just a reporter on his beat. Profound forces, however, were already transforming his life.

Before *And the Band Played On*'s late-September release, Randy's reporting had taken an interesting turn when he accompanied Dianne Feinstein's eighty-five-person delegation to visit Abidjan, San Francisco's sister city in the West African Republic of Côte d'Ivoire. The six-day tour represented a political and cultural high mark to the mayor's time in office, with the travel list including a substantial number of Black community leaders. "He almost got killed on that trip," Belva Davis remembered, "because it was almost all

Black people . . . and Randy was doing a reporter's job by asking questions that were awkward about how [AIDS had originated]."

Randy was especially drawn to the city's extreme wealth disparities, which left its hospitals pleading for more resources. "People got angry and said, 'You're like everybody else. Now you're gonna try and dump this epidemic on Black people.' And he just kept being aggressive about trying to explain what he was trying to do," Belva chuckled. "And I finally had to say, 'Randy, just be quiet.'"

From Abidjan, Randy went to visit Uganda, in the heart of Central Africa, where transmission of HIV was primarily through heterosexual sex and childbirth. In reporting these experiences, he was beginning to articulate a link between the virus's origins and the vast expansion of roads and highways, which had brought new opportunities for rural villagers to find work and sexual liaisons in larger cities. "The hoofbeats of the coming Apocalypse echo along every dirt road in this sweltering part of the world," Randy observed. The region's medical experts were anticipating an explosion, with one Ugandan researcher telling him, "All we can do is try to salvage the next generation. This generation is lost."

Randy Shilts with unknown associates visiting Uganda, September 1987.
Photographer unknown, courtesy of Linda Alband

Back in the United States, galleys of *And the Band Played On* had caught the attention of Douglas Foster, the new editor of *Mother Jones*, who saw *Band* as a way to make a splash by threading together all the Reagan administration pieces to illustrate its scandalous dereliction of duty. Before going in, Foster was well aware of Randy's reputation as a "self-centered gas bag," but he'd come to view the public brashness as a form of self-protection. "Randy was a master at almost soap opera–like narrative structure," he remembered. "And so, there were some long nights where I think I got very quickly past that self-absorbed person I'd met at parties and to the kind of outrageously funny and sweet and tender guy."

Mother Jones would give *Band* a boost within progressive media, but in New York, Michael Denneny was experiencing his own frustrations. "When we went in, originally the sales department had slated the first print run of five thousand copies," he explained. "When we came out of that sales conference, they had changed it to thirty-five thousand copies. And my sales forces went out on a crusade. They were so emotionally involved with it. My whole career was at stake if we sold four thousand copies and didn't get the response that we wanted from the media, which was basically to break the wall of silence and get it on the public agenda, once and for all."

"At a certain point," Michael continued, "the publicist who was dealing with the book came to my office, virtually in tears, and said, 'We're getting absolutely a closed door everywhere. The *New York Times* has told us they're not gonna review it.'" Desperate for a solution, Michael phoned a publicist friend, who was between jobs at the time. "I said, 'I need you to read this nine-hundred-page manuscript and tell me if there's any way we can succeed with it,'" he recalled. "'You're the only person I know who has the time to read.'"

When Michael called the following Monday, his friend told him, "I can tell you how to make it a bestseller, but you're not gonna like it." Michael promptly invited himself over for lunch.

"So, I go over there," he recounted, "and he said, 'You can make it a bestseller the following way: you pull out the stuff on Patient Zero, and you present it as 'the man who brought AIDS to America,' and you pitch it to the *New York Post*.'"

The Rupert Murdoch–owned paper was the most homophobic national tabloid of its time, which had given antigay conservatives a platform to write about AIDS as God's punishment for homosexuals. "They'll take the bait," his friend continued. "And once they take it, the whole media will fall in line. The *Times* will cover it. I can predict, you're gonna have the whole front page of the *Post*: THE MAN WHO BROUGHT AIDS TO AMERICA."

That evening, Michael called his author. "He was horrified," Michael remembered. "He said, 'No, no, no.' And we talked every night until Friday." Granted, St. Martin's already owned the book, and for all practical purposes, Randy had no power to stop them. "So, I never had to make the decision of whether to go against him or not," Michael explained, "but he always knew that if he didn't say yes, I could still do it. So finally, that Friday, he said, 'All right. We'll do it.' But it took four nights of several hours on the phone, every night, to talk him into it."

St. Martin's went ahead with the press release, and just as Michael's friend predicted, the *Post* responded with the headline THE MAN WHO GAVE US AIDS splashed across the front page, five days before the National March on Washington. "Randy never comes close to saying that," Michael reiterated. "We in the press release to the *Post* said that. And . . . so if you're going to blame anybody, you have to blame me, not him."

While presenting an unseemly dilemma, the publicity angle also offered a critical opportunity. With Gaetan Dugas attracting all the attention, Randy would have to double down on the larger systemic failures that *Band* had painstakingly highlighted. The following day, the *Times* published an Associated Press account that stuck with Randy's emphasis on Gaetan "playing a key role," while tying the out-of-control pandemic to larger societal and political failures. As Randy left the National March for an eighteen-city book tour, the media swirl was already underway.

"[Gaetan is] in no way representative of the people with AIDS," he told *USA Today*. "He's a rare case. People with AIDS have been very responsible, ringing the bells of alert, but I wanted to tell the whole story. Patient Zero is a very small part of the story." If there was a villain to be found in *Band*, he emphasized, it was the Reagan administration. "Quite frankly, I think the role of Patient Zero can be exaggerated," he added. "AIDS would have spread rapidly without him. You have to understand it was a looser time, when the commercial sex industry was at its height."

Still, there's no denying that Randy had contributed to the hype as much as anyone else. When *California* magazine published the Patient Zero plotline that same month, the story appeared with the headline PATIENT ZERO: THE MAN WHO BROUGHT THE AIDS EPIDEMIC TO CALIFORNIA, tying Randy that much closer to a claim he couldn't substantiate.

Backlash from the Canadian press came almost immediately, with *USA Today* detailing how Randy walked out on a Montreal television interviewer, who characterized the story as a "cheap publicity stunt."

In offering an apology for any pain he may have caused Gaetan's family, Randy shared, "And I'd feel very bad if my book caused people with AIDS to be harassed. But I'm not pointing a finger. In scientific research he was a link. He played an important role in understanding the disease. He didn't even know for much of the time what he was doing."

In San Francisco, the gay media's initial responses stayed largely positive, with the *Sentinel* calling it "the most thorough, comprehensive exploration of the AIDS epidemic to date." And despite Randy's scathing portrayal of Paul Lorch, the *Bay Area Reporter* called it "a watershed in the course of the AIDS epidemic," which was "clearly headed for the bestseller lists, and, therefore, into the consciousness of mainstream America."

Noting the balance Randy had struck between criticizing gay leaders and lauding the community's sprawling mobilization efforts, *BAR* reviewer Paul Reed emphasized, "The theme of waiting until it was too late is the major focus of the book. The reasons for this deadly reticence were, as the book amply demonstrates, purely political, not medical." Only briefly noting the "chilling" story of Gaetan Dugas, he concluded, "The book is both an enraging expose and a deeply moving tale of heroism."

The *New York Native* offered a mixed response, with publisher Charles Ortleb calling it "not an objective work of a journalist. Randy has the amusing habit of calling himself a 'reporter' or 'journalist,' as though the rest of us who have written on the epidemic were lost in a web of our own subjectivity." However, the *Native*'s media critic Ed Sikov initially praised *Band* while criticizing the *Post* for its distortions. "The gay community is getting a bad rap because of Shilts's book," Sikov wrote, "and no doubt there will be some angry readers who blame Shilts for attacking the community when so many others are more deserving of criticism. From what I've read, the book is both more complex in argument and subtle in presentation than major media reports care to allow." However, two weeks later, he pointed out that Randy and St. Martin's had yet to push back against the *Post*.

"Randy was not pure," acknowledged friend and legal activist Benjamin Schatz. "He understood the game element of the media game. And I think some people were pissed off at him for not being pure." Schatz developed a friendship with Randy after becoming the first attorney to work full-time on AIDS-related impact litigation with National Gay Rights Advocates' AIDS Civil Rights Project. "[Randy] needed a hook if he wanted this book to get mainstream attention and to get the broader point across," he explained. "You have to know, particularly when you are part of a marginalized minority that nobody wants to hear about, that you've got to go for the hook. I often didn't agree with the hook, but there was a sense that we were all on the same side."

"I never saw what Randy was doing as trying to pin blame on anybody, which is how some people took it to be," Larry Bush reflected. "I didn't see that what Randy had done should be faulted in any way by anyone, because he was not inventing anything. He was creating an explanation that at least led away from that we are all to blame for being ill."

Some reviewers, however, saw it differently. In a generally positive appraisal, the *Chicago Sun-Times*'s William Hines wrote that Randy had attributed the virus's spread "to the unusual mobility of gays in search of new pals and new pleasures, jet setting recklessly across the globe, sowing the seeds of death in whatever orifices might be found." By conflating Gaetan's behaviors with those of gays as a whole, such reviews lent cover to longstanding homophobic attitudes. "ALL THEY GOTTA DO IS QUIT TAKING IT UP THE FUCKING ASS—SHILTS!! RIGHT??" read one piece of anonymous mail Randy received during his tour.

As the tour continued, Randy himself became more the subject of media attention. "Homosexuals debate whether the author is a hero or a traitor," wrote Robert Reinhold for the *New York Times*, rehashing old arguments about Randy's coverage of gay leaders and the bathhouses. By insisting that some leaders' PR fears had impeded the community's response, Randy seemed to hit a nerve. Still, Reinhold noted, the national spotlight had made him either more "exuberant," or "strident and abrasive," depending on one's point of view, adding, "He will win no Pulitzer Prize for modesty."

Aided by a Book-of-the-Month Club selection and extensive coverage in national news magazines, *Band* reached the *New York Times* bestsellers list by mid-November. Soon after, it was reported that an NBC miniseries was in the works. Another significant boost came from CBS News' *60 Minutes*, which brought in Selma Dritz and one of Gaetan's former lovers to expand on the Patient Zero story. As in previous interviews, Randy couched his comments by calling it "a horrible combination of circumstances" before pivoting to the political story.

"AIDS did not just happen, AIDS was allowed to happen," he insisted. "This disease did not emerge full-grown on the biological landscape, and I don't think you can look to medicine in order to understand how AIDS was able to spread so quickly across this country unimpeded. I think you have to look at the politics of AIDS."

In appearance after appearance, Randy more or less repeated some version of that script. "I believe in moral absolutes," he told his hometown newspaper, the *Aurora Beacon-News*. "To me, what is morally wrong is not being kind to your fellow man and ignoring situations in which you can help out. Some people may think a gay has no right to say anything about morality. But I don't think homosexuality is a moral issue."

The attention endured for months, thanks to Randy's willingness to talk extensively on the lecture circuit. Before *Band*'s release, Michael Denneny had introduced him to lecture agent George Greenfield, who specialized in representing people at the vanguard of current events and social issues. "I always felt there was the opportunity in representing people on the cutting edge of critical issues to provide a wider audience," Greenfield explained. "Randy's speaking engagements reached many thousands of people. It was not uncommon for audiences to be eight hundred, a thousand people."

From college campuses to medical conferences, Randy was connecting with audiences around the world, bypassing the national press and speaking directly with local communities. "[He was] intensely focused on his mission to tell the story as he knew it," Greenfield remembered. "I also felt that he was very gracious with his accessibility and his passion to tell the story from the podium, and to be available for people who were interested in knowing more."

After reading *Band*, Selma Dritz wrote Randy a brief congratulatory note, telling him, "I'm pleased with you, and VERY proud of you in a collegial way, and in a maternal way. I don't need to say 'keep up the good work'—you can't do less. You're <u>really</u> good." From Atlanta, Mary Guinan wrote, "Your book is a beautiful book, beautifully written. In its essence it reveals your love of humankind. I grieved again for each of the people I knew who died and those I didn't know whom you described."

Randy Shilts posing next to a graffiti mural, San Francisco, June 1988.
Photo by Bill Burke for Esquire, courtesy of Bill Burke

As the first CDC researcher to interview Gaetan, Guinan had fielded an abundance of phone calls when the book was released. "I decided that I had to read the book immediately in order to defend myself," she told Randy. "After I finished the book, I decided I didn't need to defend myself."

At the CDC, James Curran took his portrayal in stride. "I think the method in which it's written, the chronologic method, both tells the detective story, and it does it in a reportorial style, which is an unusual style," he reflected. Randy had sent Curran two autographed copies, for himself and his mother, thanking the beleaguered public health official for having "the worst job in the world."

Other members of the cast took a less favorable view. Despite his relatively positive portrayal and despite regarding the work as both "a good book" and "the only book" from that early era, Dr. Andrew Moss strongly objected to the Gaetan Dugas hype. Still, in a letter calling for Randy and William Darrow to repudiate the Patient Zero story, Moss noted, "Mr. Shilts, to give him credit, does not overstress Mr. Dugas' role."

Robert Gallo, meanwhile, was alerted to the book by his colleague, Dr. Howard Streicher. "I said, 'I have no concern about it,'" Gallo recalled. "'It's going to probably be read by half a dozen people in New York or San Francisco that are in the gay community. They want to write what they understand and what they know, but I don't care.'" But Streicher showed Gallo what he characterized as sixteen pages of errors, "and they were almost comical errors," he added. "That's all I can tell you."

Years later, journalist John Crewdson's book on Gallo would note nearly a page and a half of historical and scientific errors in *Band*, such as misidentifying certain research discoveries, incorrectly describing a handful of meetings and meeting participants, and misunderstanding federal patenting regulations. However, Gallo's most vehement objections seemed to arise less from the book than from its subsequent adaptation as an HBO television docudrama, which compressed and embellished numerous events to fit a two-hour time frame and featured an especially unforgiving portrayal of the embattled scientist by actor Alan Alda.

On the policymaking front, Tim Westmoreland also noted a number of errors. "I think [Randy] confuses a budget resolution with a continuing resolution," he observed. "But one resolution was the same as another resolution for Randy. He confuses fiscal years and calendar years and whether an authorization actually conveys money." Nevertheless, Westmoreland added, "I've always said the story is true. He got a lot of the facts wrong. But the overall story, the point of the book, it's true. I know that there are people who have other objections to it. But the stuff that he writes about Washington and the executive branch, NIH, CDC, and how the Congress works, yeah, it's pretty true."

Even reviewers who highlighted *Band*'s flaws and indulgences still emphasized its larger importance. "It is a book that I want to like and recommend because I agree with a main conclusion Shilts reaches—that the response to AIDS by the public and private sectors has been fragmented, inadequate, and characterized by a 'business as usual' approach although a different response was, and still is, required," reviewer Sandra Panem wrote in *Science*. However, Panem noted, the book risked overemphasizing the influence of homophobia while making "a depressing free-market analysis" of the AIDS response. "It is perhaps the picture of a self-aggrandizing scientific community, detached from the realities of dread disease, that should most interest and disturb the readers of *Science*," she added.

When Laurie Garrett came to Randy's first book event in Los Angeles, she learned he was trying to avoid her. "He was nervous that I was going to trash him," she explained, "and several people at the party told me, 'Randy's afraid to talk to you.'" Similar to Randy Alfred with *The Mayor of Castro Street*, Laurie seemed to be one of the few journalists whose opinion really worried him. "And I had to really think carefully what to say publicly," she added, "because there were some huge inaccuracies there."

In addition to Patient Zero, Laurie felt Randy had overstated the importance of Don Francis, while shorting lesser-known contributors like Dr. Jay Levy at University of California, San Francisco, and especially Françoise Barré-Sinoussi at Pasteur Institute. "And there were just too many aspects of the science that he didn't understand correctly," Laurie added. However, she did agree with Randy that the United States had overstated its role in discovering HIV, that Gallo's conduct merited closer scrutiny, and that crucial efforts, from protecting the blood supply to expediting medical research, had been slow-walked.

"And where he got a paper trail, he dove in," she enthused. "He was there all the way down to the weeds. And it's in there. And the parts that are right are *Go baby, go*. And it's real exciting to see it. He was absolutely right about the role of the Reagan administration, and he tore into them with full teeth, and that's great."

"And so, though his instinct was right," Laurie continued, "in telling that tale, he got a lot wrong. And I had to decide, which is more important? To correct the errors, or to promote the big message? And I opted for the latter." For her, *And the Band Played On* blurred the boundaries between advocacy and reporting. "I would never have written that book that way," she added.

Randy had tried to emphasize that *Band* was not written to be the *definitive* story of AIDS but an *important* one, with characters who were illustrative of larger themes, and that it shouldn't be taken as the final word on every person who contributed. Yet, Laurie countered, because of the book's size and density, those intentions weren't obvious to casual readers.

In balancing her criticism, however, Laurie raised two key considerations for understanding *Band*. First, she emphasized, "[HIV/AIDS] has been the most thoroughly documented epidemic in human history," noting how, beyond journalism, there was a substantial creative outpouring by artists, musicians, authors, and playwrights. Unlike any prior pandemic, HIV had emerged in an era of unprecedented mass media expansion, providing an opportunity for the afflicted to convey their experiences in real time to wider audiences.

"It's all there, and it's all emotional, and it's all part of the record," Laurie continued. "But Randy's book stands at the top as the one most likely to be cited by everybody as the history and the real document. And as I say, that's fortunate, in the sense that it captures the outrage, and unfortunate, in terms of the inaccuracies. Heroes create it, and devils create it."

Second, Laurie noted, HIV/AIDS had exacted an undeniable toll on practically everyone it touched, including journalists. "My life would've probably been a lot happier, and a lot easier, if I hadn't committed myself to covering HIV," she reflected, "Traveling to watch this nightmare unfold, you feel parts of your soul being eroded. And seeing that much death—such a death toll."

Symptoms of AIDS-related post-traumatic stress have been noted almost from the beginning, leading some in the HIV community to eventually coin the term AIDS survivor syndrome, or ASS.

"And you've never really talked about the fact that you went to war, you were in the war, and you all have PTSD," Laurie added. "And every one of you, you've gone through alcoholism, you've gone through outrageous drug abuse. You've all gone through suicidal [ideation] . . . all of this."

However one views *And the Band Played On*, it was nevertheless the response of a person deeply affected by events inflicted on him, and his contemporaries, over several uninterrupted years. On one level, the narrative tied together a host of systemic injustices across a broad political landscape, while on another, it essentially retraced the pathways of Randy's own traumas, investigating their complexities as far back as he could take them.

Individual responses to trauma can differ substantially, but it undeniably alters one's perceptions of events in ways that others might view as contradictory. "Nobody should be telling me what the truth of AIDS was; I was there," he told William Darrow, who objected to some of *Band*'s more subjective elements. Nonetheless, Darrow called it a "tour de force," detailing a thrilling medical mystery while documenting the devastating consequences of political self-interest.

Adding to those pressures was the aftermath of Randy's HIV diagnosis. When publicly asked, he usually sidestepped the truth by exploiting general ignorance about HIV, telling interviewers that no, he didn't have AIDS. "The only people who have the right to know my antibody status are the people

I'm going to bed with," he told *San Francisco Focus* in 1989. While some in the HIV community would regard Randy's lack of candor as a betrayal, it's also true that within prominent segments of that community, he didn't exactly have cause to think he would ever be accepted. Simply put, there wasn't a lot of trust to be had there, going back as far as the fights around bathhouses.

Randy did, however, express appreciation for the recovery community, admitting his past struggles with alcoholism in several interviews. In *Band*'s acknowledgements, he included a thank you to "the friends of Bill W. who sustained me with their experience, strength, and hope," and at his first book signing at San Francisco's Zuni Café, he promised that all proceeds would go to the Castro-adjacent counseling center, 18th Street Services.

For both author and publisher, *Band* represented a substantial commercial success, with hardcover sales exceeding one hundred thousand copies. On top of numerous awards, *Esquire* included Randy on a list of "24 Men Who Matter," alongside other "good guys" like Paul Newman, Ted Koppel, Robin Williams, Mario Cuomo, and H. Ross Perot. And at the highest levels, *Band* came close to winning the National Book Critics' Circle Award for General Nonfiction, ultimately falling short to Richard Rhodes's *The Making of the Atomic Bomb*.

Aside from commercial success, one of *Band*'s lesser-acknowledged achievements came in giving people a way to reckon with their own losses. From its discovery in 1981, HIV/AIDS would claim more than seven hundred thousand Americans over the next four decades. For many, the book became intimately linked to memories of a cherished loved one. In her congratulations to Randy, Mary Guinan wrote of a friend whose twenty-year-old son had come home to die. "I recommended that she read your book," Guinan told him. "I believe it will help her—maybe it will make her angry or help her grieve."

Subsequently, the book remained essential reading, not just for students of public health but also for the workers who were creating AIDS service organizations around the country. "There were a few things that really made a difference in terms of changing the narrative," Benjamin Schatz explained, "and the change of the narrative got increased funding, and increased funding got increased research. And increased research and increased funding got meds, and meds kept people alive. So, there are people who are alive. There are people who've made extraordinary differences, or who've been completely mundane in their lives, but they've lived them."

Outside of New York and San Francisco, it seemed that many communities had experienced their own version of *Band*, if one took Randy's example and followed the money. Randy himself would applaud the growth in community services, and in turn, some of those frontline workers would invoke his legacy, so that even decades later, older staff at an AIDS organization could be heard telling newer colleagues, "If you want to understand why things are the way they are around here, you'd better read *And the Band Played On.*"

15 | GHOST STORIES

THE DRIVE FROM SAN Francisco was relatively easy: cross the Golden Gate Bridge and take Highway 101 north, head west on River Road, and follow the winding Russian River to the tiny resort town of Guerneville. With a quick right, the main drag would quickly disappear. Another quick right, and a long gravel driveway brought visitors to a hollow hemmed in by steep slopes of ancient redwoods, enfolding the renovated, suburban-style ranch dwelling that became the first home that Randy truly owned.

Henceforth, to friends and family it would be known as Chez Rondey, a chic-yet-relaxed dwelling with tall front windows, a large living-room skylight, stone fireplace, and exposed beams. The property offered a prime location for gatherings both small and large, the most memorable of which was Randy's annual birthday party, now officially known as Shiltsmas. Though the term itself had been around for almost twenty years, August 8, 1988, marked what many considered to be the first Shiltsmas celebration. It was Ann Neuenschwander's idea to make it a White Party, with balloons, cardboard eights all over the yard, and all-white attire. The occasion gained further legitimacy when Mayor Art Agnos declared it Randy Shilts Day in San Francisco, with friends Rick Pacurar and Michael Housh presenting him the proclamation during the festivities.

Chez Rondey would gain a number of eclectic items, the most memorable being a massive stuffed Kodiak bear, towering on its hind legs near the front entryway. "Scared the fucking shit out of me," Wes Haley remembered. "God, that thing was huge." When Wes pressed for details, Randy would only tell him, "I had my phase." In fact, several changes in Randy's decorating and fashion sense could be attributed to a new relationship. His media tour had ushered in a "serious" look, featuring pinstripes, suspenders, and dress slacks.

For those wondering why he'd started dressing like a gay Republican, the truth is, he was being dressed by one. Randy's newest boyfriend was a quiet, conservative New Englander named Richard, who worked in antiques after serving in the military.

While a number of Chez Rondey's pieces had come from Richard's collection, friends also credited him with giving Randy his most important birthday present that year. On the other side of the driveway sat a miniature dwelling fashioned to resemble the remodeled house. Of course, nobody remembered it actually being used, because its occupant, a young golden retriever named Dash, never slept there.

"Dash was his baby," remembered Linda Alband. After eight years away, she was at loose ends and ready for a change, right when Ann was getting married and leaving for the Peace Corps. That summer, Linda returned from Seattle to become Randy's business manager, working with him for hours at a time and taking care of Dash whenever he was away.

The significance of Dash's arrival did not escape those who cared for Randy, including one who'd been frozen out of his inner circle. The previous year had been momentous in its own right for Steve Newman, who now occupied a place in the *Chronicle* newsroom as the founder of Earthweek, a syndicated weekly column devoted to news about the planet, significant weather events, and climate change. Steve felt proud of his ex-lover's accomplishments, but once again, through no fault of his own, he'd found himself competing with Randy for the spotlight. "It was pretty hard." Steve remembered. "He would go stiff when we would see each other in the newsroom."

On the advice of his newest lover, Steve adopted a puppy named Skye from the same breeder and invited Randy over for a play date. Alone together in Steve's backyard, the two were able to talk for once without becoming defensive. "I would not call it a friendship," Steve clarified. "It wasn't that close. It was more a tolerance of each other."

While there would still be some strained moments, they did achieve a measure of familiarity. Randy and Dash came over when Steve threw Skye a birthday party, and Randy began including Steve in parties at Chez Rondey. "I'm so glad that it happened—a reconciliation where we could be at least civil and confide in each other," Steve reflected.

Meanwhile, Randy's success had brought substantial pride to the Shilts family. On a family visit to Chez Rondey, his brother Gary recalled, their father

Has Dash Gone Hollywood?

"Has Dash Gone Hollywood?"
Shiltsmas invitation, 1990.
*Linda Alband Collection of Randy
Shilts Materials (collection no.
2003-09), courtesy of Gay,
Lesbian, Bisexual, Transgender
Historical Society*

"Five *percent* of gross? You tell that slut Lassie that
she'll work for 5 *percent* of net or she'll never work in this
town again!"

leaned back and gazed in amazement at the surrounding redwoods. When the Penguin paperback version of *Band* came out in October 1988, Bud told the *Detroit News*, "We have never been ashamed of the fact that Randy is gay. Here is somebody from a small town who has been a tremendous success. He worked his buns off to get where he is. What more can I say as a parent? We have achieved our goal."

Randy, however, was feeling less than satisfied. "Here I was chastising the media in the book for avoiding public policy matters, and look what they latched onto," he complained. "I'd hoped with the book to shame the scientists into mobilizing. I'd hoped the national media would be ashamed of how they behaved. I thought the White House, once subjected to the ridicule they deserve, would change. Never have I had so much success, and never have I failed in such a large way."

In early 1989 Randy's work took a new turn with the debut of a weekly AIDS column, affording him the flexibility to cover a range of topics, including treatment news, syringe exchange, political disputes, and safer-sex promotion efforts. In a piece detailing the disproportionate impact on Black communities, for example, he described how conservative churches were hindering awareness-raising efforts, predicting a perilous outcome if their disapproval of homosexuality remained at odds with the very real threat posed to Black families and communities.

After more than a year of media tours, the grind was starting to take its toll. The demand for Randy never seemed to ebb, however, whether it was appearing on serious news programs, tawdry daytime talk shows, or radio call-in shows wherever he was visiting. One health conference even rescheduled to match Randy's availability, George Greenfield marveled. "That's the only time in my career that ever happened."

The work of repeatedly answering the same questions, even while nothing seemed to change, was turning life in the spotlight into its own ordeal. "The bitter irony is, my role as an AIDS celebrity just gives me a more elevated promontory from which to watch the world make the same mistakes in the handling of the AIDS epidemic that I had hoped my work would help to change," he wrote in *Esquire*. "When I return from network tapings and celebrity glad-handing, I come back to my home in San Francisco's gay community and see friends dying. They die in my arms and my dreams, and nothing at all has changed."

Instead of prompting a society-wide self-reckoning, *Band* had become part of the political arrow-slinging, leaving Randy to doubt how much longer he could continue. Still, he worried about stepping away from a role he'd effectively created for himself. With these nagging doubts and frustrations, Randy prepared for what was essentially his valedictory moment as the world's most famous AIDS journalist.

The Fifth International Conference on AIDS in Montreal would be remembered for not only a breakthrough in grassroots activism but also its co-occurrence with major world events, including Tiananmen Square and the Ayatollah Khomeini's death. At the start of each day, Randy and David Perlman would meet up in the press room, where admirers and detractors alike would gather as David was trying to work. "I finally had to say to him, 'Randy, for Christ's sake, would you get your goddamn fan club out of here? I gotta write!'" Perlman remembered.

Unsurprisingly, the decision to give Randy this platform met with some resistance. "There were many in the organizing committee who objected just on the grounds of 'Why should we have a journalist talk in the front room?'" Laurie Garrett explained. "And then, of course there were those who bitterly disagreed with Randy's book. And they just felt like, 'Well, if you're going to have a journalist, that's the wrong one.'"

After a full week's work, his closing remarks to an estimated twelve thousand attendees were pure Randy, framing a gravely serious message with plenty of sass and gas, earning both applause and boos. On a number of high-level points, he and AIDS activists seemed to agree, yet he took strong exception to many of their tactics, especially those directed by White protestors from the AIDS Coalition to Unleash Power (ACT UP) toward Black African health officials. "Some [of their] actions were strategically pertinent to the matters at hand, such as a well-articulated ACT UP proposal for streamlining AIDS drug development," he wrote in a post-conference commentary. "Other actions, however, were downright rude."

With more gay men likely to test positive in the coming years, he predicted, "[civil] disobedience is bound to play a growing and potentially constructive role in the world of AIDS. The problem is that many of these fledgling protesters don't know how to put their anger to the best tactical use." In that vein, he wanted public outrage to produce substantive results, rather than simply expressing anger for anger's sake. While the outrage was certainly justifiable and cathartic, Randy added, in the context of modern-day politics, it was simply "infantile, and sometimes counterproductive."

Hosting an hourlong special for KQED News, Randy laid out his take on the social complexities of AIDS, beginning with a rundown of recent disruptions by local militants. For the activists, Randy observed, any action that got AIDS to the top of the national agenda was considered acceptable, even if it didn't align with their self-professed standard: "Does it stop the dying? And does it do it now?"

As one of the activists profiled, ACT UP San Francisco member Waiyde Palmer characterized his experiences with Randy as "combative and limited." Although a number of protesters were White and from privileged backgrounds,

Palmer acknowledged, a split formed between those who wanted to focus narrowly on AIDS-specific issues and others who related HIV/AIDS to racism, sexism, homophobia, poverty, and other structural injustices. Randy, in Palmer's opinion, clung stubbornly to the pursuit of respectability politics, reveling in his status as "the representative voice of the LGBT community" and adopting a contrarian view to position himself above the militants.

"Sometimes he was more conservative, and sometimes he was more mainstream," Benjamin Schatz allowed, "and sometimes, I feel like he was selling out, but it wasn't because he was selling out the community to be famous. He had his own perspective." Where Randy saw the usefulness of activism directed at changing sympathies, laws, and policies, he also derided efforts to confront people's word choices and semantic differences as "AIDS speak," diverting valuable energy from larger battles simply to assuage the "bad feelings" of movement activists. Moreover, he panned the activists who disrupted mass at major Catholic landmarks as alienating to ordinary churchgoers, whose sympathies were needed in the voting booth to effect larger political changes.

An almost-daily bombardment of bad news, compounded by the onslaught of obituaries and funerals, made it easy for diverging views to harden into suspicion, resentment, and occasional bursts of outrage. As Palmer remembered, on one occasion when Randy came to cover an ACT UP meeting, he was booed and shouted out of the room with chants of "Get out." Given that animosity, one can only imagine the reaction if activists had learned that in the telephone directory, he'd listed his Chez Rondey number under the pseudonym, "Zero, P."

For a brief moment on October 17, 1989, it must have seemed like the earth itself had stirred to match the heated social discord. With evening rush hour well underway, the region's largest earthquake since 1906 shook the ground from Santa Cruz all the way to Oakland and Marin, collapsing part of the Bay Bridge and devastating entire blocks of San Francisco's neighborhoods. For Randy, it was another starring moment, with colleagues recalling his energy and focus under extreme conditions.

The next day, he shared the lead story with Susan Sward and soon after was tapped to write the epilogue in the *Chronicle*'s commemorative book. Combining vivid imagery of the day with a blistering rebuke of the Reagan and Bush Administrations for their years of slow-walking federal infrastructure spending, Randy emphasized, "Read the logical conclusion of such political theology in the girders twisted like spaghetti above the Oakland landscape and among the boulders of concrete that entombed 1½ miles of rush hour traffic."

He could just as easily have been talking about the federal AIDS response. To see such an immediate outpouring of humanitarian relief had to strike a nerve with those who were struggling on the frontlines of HIV/AIDS, still waiting for a comprehensive, government-led response. In 1989 alone, the United States recorded more than fourteen thousand deaths from AIDS; by comparison, direct and indirect fatalities from the Loma Prieta earthquake would total sixty-three.

———————

As the weariness of AIDS journalism continued to weigh on him, it was becoming clear that Randy's future considerations couldn't be put off. By mid-1989, his relationship with Richard was already waning, while on the health front, he'd started azidothymidine (AZT) fairly early. The first-generation HIV drug was already showing only limited effectiveness, however, as well as harsh side effects. Elaine Herscher recalled seeing Randy in the newsroom, mixing the drug in powder form into a glass of water. "I said, 'You're looking like you lost some weight.'

"And he was very clear, to be absolutely crystal clear on this point: 'That's because I was trying.'"

The psychological effects of living with the virus began to manifest outside of Randy's professional work, as he spent much of 1989 making another attempt at writing fiction. From a collection of hand-scribbled notes came the treatment for an unpublished novel titled "Ghosts," which tumbled from his mind in a blur of familiar names, images, and landscapes. Filled with menacing shadows and unwelcome echoes, the story conveyed a jumble of conflicting feelings toward gay culture, AIDS, and Randy's own fragile existence. The cast of characters even included familiar, quasi-parental character types named Bud and Norma, along with an extra-sensitive golden retriever called Dash.

The story offered hints as to how Randy was reckoning with this crucial juncture in his life, down to the caustic mentions of AIDS activists and their strident tactics. The narrator, who'd inherited substantial money from a wealthy older lover, had come to Northern California seeking property to open a transcendental meditation center. At the heart of the tale stood an abandoned Russian River resort he hoped to buy, where the gay men who'd once ruled over the property now haunted it with raucous nightly sex parties.

Each evening, the apparitions would come to life beneath the rising moon, walking out of a riverbed strewn with bits of cremated ashes, their AIDS-ravaged bodies growing young, strong, and healthy again. Whenever another casualty's ashes were sprinkled at the riverbank, the recently deceased would rise up to join the debauchery. "Though they were dressed with remarkable similarity in lusty costumes of leather and [Levi's]," the narrator observed, "I was struck by how these men did not have the spent, aged appearance of the people who wore such attire now. They were fresh and full of life, of promise."

In the most startling moments, Randy's protagonist would confront and try to reason with the partiers but ended up seduced, not once but twice, by the same sturdy, hitchhiking leather man. "My mind raced with confusion, as I lay there naked and helpless on that cot," he confessed. "I was so weak, so overpowered . . . that I felt unable to resist when [he] lifted me from the cot and placed me in the confusing array of straps that soon nestled me." Overpowered by his Master, he succumbed to a long, brutal fucking as a crowd of leering, lusty men jeered them on.

"I didn't care," he wrote. "I only wanted to give myself over. . . . Again and again." Thoroughly satiated, yet dazed and disturbed, Randy's narrator canceled the purchase agreement and fled the area. Years later, however, he received word from a dying friend that the otherworldly leather man had been seen waiting for him by the river, believing with absolutely certainty that they would soon be reunited.

Randy shared the story with Michael Denneny, who diplomatically told him that it lacked the intrigue and compelling characters that made his journalism so effective. As a window into Randy's state of mind, however, "Ghosts" offers a stirring artifact from the time in which it was written. The narrator's conflicted feelings of revulsion and fascination echoed Randy's own past struggles that, when combined with the allure of readily accessible, uninhibited carnality, had proven too powerful and possibly contributed to his own infection. Where his narrator sought tranquility and repose, instead he was overpowered and taunted by men he both resented and desired. Moreover, the story revealed a preoccupation with notions of a living death after AIDS, embodied by the ghosts' determination to carry on each night, so envyingly virile in their supernatural state.

For whatever reason, even as Randy kept trying to develop other creative projects, "Ghosts" never went any further than this rough treatment. At the end of 1989, he announced a sabbatical from AIDS journalism, admitting, "I'm totally burned out. I'm feeling completely depleted." The pressures of covering, speaking, and arguing about the disease, all while coping with so many losses and managing his own health, had finally caught up with him. "In my dreams I was wandering around funerals, screaming, 'I can't take it anymore,'" he added. "I've spent eight years recording the decimation of my generation. I need a break."

For the first half of 1990, Randy's journalism appeared only sparingly in the *Chronicle*, as he briefly relocated to Los Angeles, living in the guest house of his film agent, Ron Bernstein. "I think his time in L.A. was fairly quiet," Bernstein shared, recalling how they'd meet in his garden every morning and discuss current events. Although Randy seemed to have ambitions of breaking into Hollywood as a screenwriter, Bernstein never saw any prospective scripts.

Randy Shilts on vacation, 1990. *Photo by Bill Cagle, courtesy of the photographer*

In late June, Randy returned to cover the Sixth International Conference on AIDS in San Francisco, but not with the same intensity as previous years. That summer, a bipartisan congressional majority passed two bills of consequence for people with HIV, the Americans with Disabilities Act and the Ryan White CARE Act, but in news coverage of the legislation, Randy's byline remained conspicuously absent. By fall, however, readers would learn about his next investigative target.

16 | THE FAMILY

THE WALK-UP AT FIFTEENTH and Market had creaky wooden steps, Jennifer Finlay noticed, as she hobbled upstairs to a badly needed meeting. For the recently sober young lesbian without health insurance, healing a herniated disc without pain meds had made the past year a nearly impossible ordeal. San Francisco at that time had the best AA groups, Jennifer believed, because of HIV/AIDS. "It was a mortal crisis," she remembered. "You could see that in the faces, and you could hear that in the stories, you could hear the humor. All those men in those rooms knew they were going to die, and they wanted to die sober. More than anything in the world, they wanted to die sober."

With her state disability aid running out, Jennifer had recently attended a support group for job seekers, when it had suddenly dawned on her: "I want to be a research assistant for nonfiction authors. I think I'd be good at it." Subsequently, she spilled her guts at that mid-December AA meeting, all except the part about wanting to be an author's research assistant. It wasn't her home group, but she recognized several faces in the crowd, including *his*. After getting sober, Jennifer had read *And the Band Played On* from cover to cover, recognizing in its voicing the "pink cloud" surrounding someone in his first few years of recovery.

"[Randy] came to see the bathhouses as an addiction problem," she explained. "Because you get really judgy when you first get sober. You become holier than thou because you're sober, and those other people aren't. And that's pretty common. 'We're arrogant, egotistical, and self-centered' is what they'll tell you in a meeting."

Afterward, as people hung around with their coffee and cheap cookies, Randy pulled Jennifer aside. In a moment of pure coincidence, she recalled,

"He came up to me after that meeting and said to give him a call, because he needed some help with research."

When Jennifer phoned him, Randy said he was looking for an assistant to research several library collections for documents concerning gays and the military. Two days before Christmas, he stopped by with a box of materials, writing a $450 check to cover her first thirty hours. "He was going to pay me $15 an hour, which, honestly, in 1990, [was] a lot of money," Jennifer recounted. "And the generosity of that . . . this man saved my life. There was no way I could take a real job at that stage. Not having to go do a regular office job, at that minute of my life, really saved me."

As far back as the *Advocate*, Randy had been aware of gay servicemembers' plight. In *Mayor*, he'd noted San Francisco's high concentration of gay former servicemembers who'd settled there rather than return home with the stigma of a less-than-honorable discharge. Moreover, Randy's long friendship with Leonard Matlovich had sharpened his sympathies for those deemed unfit, simply because of their homosexuality. During his brief stay in Los Angeles, Randy had struck up a dog-park friendship with publicist Howard Bragman, who'd recently started his own PR firm. When Randy shared that he'd been pitched the biography of billionaire playboy Malcolm Forbes, Howard told him, "You're Randy Shilts. I think it's kind of cheap. I don't think that's your brand." Howard was representing Joe Steffan, a midshipman suing the Naval Academy over his discharge. "A lot of us in the community felt this was the next big fight," he recalled. "And Randy and I talked about this ad nauseam, because this was my client and what I was working on."

"He made a very strong case to me, and that's when I first started realizing there had been a totally separate historical development," Michael Denneny remembered. "It was a totally separate gay movement within the military for thirty years that was so disconnected, because we were all leftists and they were all in the military."

In his proposal, Randy wrote, "There is a country where citizens are ushered into interrogation rooms for long hours of questioning, threatened with the removal of their children, with the censure of their parents and with prison, if they do not cooperate." In this country, he continued, individuals were pressured to name their friends and lovers, testify against them, and risk total ruin for admitting not even improper conduct but just having improper thoughts. "That country is America," Randy wrote, "and in America, this happens every day."

THE FAMILY | 201

Pressed by Michael, St. Martin's made a million-dollar offer that, unlike Randy's earlier books, provided substantial up-front support. Key to that research would be Linda Alband, whose prior work with military people would help Randy better understand the story's political, cultural, and structural complexities. "People in the military were outside the Constitution," Linda explained, "so it was a much clearer picture of how being gay affects them, because they could be tried and jailed based on personal, private acts or just rumors. He really wanted straight people to understand what it was like to be gay in America, and it was the way that he thought that he could tell the story more clearly."

In October 1990, Randy reported on the case of army colonel Edward Modesto, whose investigation was triggered when another gay man offered up his name while under interrogation. Such betrayals weren't unusual, as it was common for investigators to offer leniency if the person named names. By November, when Herb Caen broke the news of Randy's next book in the *Chronicle*, the public's interest in military matters had increased substantially with the commencement of Operation Desert Shield in the Middle East. When bombing commenced in January 1991, Randy was already well-immersed in his investigations.

"In the first few months it was just background," Jennifer remembered. Randy would pay for her rental car and travel expenses, so she could visit any California library or document repository with relevant military records or law journals. Understanding what exactly he was looking for, however, could be a challenge. "He would just rush through, I guess they call that a stream of consciousness," she reflected. "I never quite knew sometimes what he was looking for. But I don't know if he knew exactly what he was looking for."

Although the Uniform Code of Military Justice labeled homosexuality as "incompatible with military service," in reality the ban had been inconsistently enforced, and at times blatantly ignored. Consequently, individuals often found that, despite exemplary records, they were deemed unfit solely on the basis of homosexuality. In the lead-up to Desert Storm, the Pentagon had issued a "stop-loss" order, meaning any individual who was under investigation for "indecent acts" or who'd subsequently come out of their own accord, still faced court-martial and separation once hostilities had ceased. "It was such an insidious injustice," Howard Bragman commented. "During the war time, you'd say, 'I'm gay.' They'd say, 'We don't give a fuck, go put your ass on the line.' You'd get shot or killed. You'd come home, and then they'd kick you out for being gay."

For *Conduct Unbecoming*, Randy would lean on local sources like Cliff Anchor, a former lover of both Leonard Matlovich and Vietnam-era hero Dr. Tom Dooley, who'd settled in Guerneville in the late 1970s. All three men would feature prominently in *Conduct*, along with Perry Watkins, a Black gay inductee who, despite being completely candid about his sexuality and performing in on-base drag shows, had been allowed to reenlist repeatedly due to his exceptional record. Although Watkins had fought his mid-1980s discharge and won multiple lawsuits against the army, the ban on gays and lesbians remained in place.

Aided by Jennifer's research, along with the work of gay historians like Allan Bérubé and Jonathan Ned Katz, Randy was able to trace inconsistencies in the military's treatment of homosexuality from colonial times through the mid-twentieth century. These initial chapters would help Randy establish a context for the mistreatment of gay and lesbian servicemembers since World War II, when the government had leaned on the fledgling field of psychiatry to adopt a policy that shifted focus from punishing homosexual acts to investigating innate homosexual traits, in whatever way they could be identified.

To find people who were currently serving, Randy established a hotline that was advertised in alternative papers around the country. One of those ads caught the attention of Steve Robin, who was living in West Hollywood after recently leaving the army. Although Steve's own experiences had been problem-free, he candidly shared his recollections in what would become part of the chapter "Lesbian Vampires of Bavaria." Within the larger story, his accounts corroborated the snowballing of rumors and innuendo into vast conspiracy theories, such as reimagining the casual, longstanding gay slang "family" as a sinister cabal of homosexual servicemembers.

More interesting to Randy, however, was Steve's background as a military police investigator. As Steve described the training and protocols for conducting interrogations, Randy would interrupt with questions. "He was relating back to me other things that people said in regard to having run-ins with military police," Steve recalled. "And I was telling him, 'That's not how those things happen.'"

Subsequently, Steve shared his military police training materials, so that Randy could separate the outlier cases that appeared to violate regulations.

After Steve moved to Oklahoma City in early 1991, Randy asked him to go to Dallas to conduct interviews, out of which came a work arrangement where Steve would travel around the country to interview as many sources as he could, shipping the tapes back to Randy overnight. Eventually, Steve began staying at Randy's new Duncan Street condo for weeks at a time to review his interview tapes while Randy kept writing. On weekends, he'd bring his laundry up to Guerneville and stay over in Randy's guest bedroom.

That research was aided by attorneys working with the few national organizations helping gay and lesbian servicemembers, who would encourage their clients to call him. "I think that any impact-litigation firm wants to have a symbiotic relation with sympathetic news reporters, because you want somebody who cares about the issues, understands the issues, and can report fairly from a point of understanding. And Randy certainly was that person," explained Amelia Craig Cramer, a Lambda Legal staff attorney during this time.

Even getting the issue on the national gay activist agenda was an uphill battle, Craig Cramer noted. "Pacifism was very closely tied with anything that was considered to be liberal or progressive or radical policy, and most of the gay and lesbian rights movement was along those lines," she recalled. "But this was predominantly White, middle- and upper-middle-class people leading the movement, who also didn't have a lot of lived experience, in terms of the socioeconomic motivators for joining the military."

"Gay-lib-type folks didn't know quite what to think of us," Captain Carolyn "Dusty" Pruitt shared. "We were militarists, according to them." An army reservist and ordained minister, Pruitt had casually mentioned her sexuality in a 1983 *Los Angeles Times* interview, triggering an investigation with terrifying encroachments on her Constitutional rights, as army investigators began surveilling her congregation and monitoring her sermons. Pruitt's First Amendment lawsuit resulted in a historic ruling that servicemembers had a right to sue the US military.

In San Diego, activist Bridget Wilson would also provide Randy with a vital link between military discrimination and a host of issues involving clients she'd personally counseled, including HIV/AIDS cases and lesbian witch hunts in the navy. Much of what Bridget provided came from stories of ordinary people who'd sought help at the local gay community service center where she worked. "What Randy got from me was the network," Bridget explained.

In contrast to Randy's previous books, *Conduct* was bringing him closer to the lives of working-class lesbians and gays, especially those of color, for whom military service had offered opportunities to leave home, go to college, and pick up a skilled trade. In the case of Sergeant Sam Gallegos, coming from a Catholic military family, it was a given that he would join the army. "I was a young kid; all I wanted to do was to serve," he recounted. "But I've got a hell of a lot of anxiety going on, [because] I'm gay."

For Desert Storm, the army had shipped Sam to California's Fort Irwin, where he'd confided in a few people he thought he could trust. Soon after, when asked directly by his commanding officer, Sam recalled the recent case of Paul Starr, an air force junior officer who denied being gay, only to be charged with lying to investigators, who were already following him. Terrified of what they might already know, Sam told his CO the truth. "Next thing you know, I was under arrest, [and] things started to fall apart."

One saving grace was Sam's position in the public affairs office, where it wasn't unusual to contact various newspapers. With nothing to lose, he went ahead and called the *Chronicle*. When Sam heard from Linda Alband, he hung up and called her back from a pay phone, suspecting that the line was bugged. "I knew they were following me," he continued, "but now, what I was telling my command the whole time was 'Yes, Randy Shilts and I are friends. So, you guys are screwed.'"

After Desert Storm, Sam was separated with a less-than-honorable discharge, untreated mental health problems, no benefits, and only a part-time security job. He'd turned to heavy drinking when, in a subsequent conversation, Randy said to him, "I need somebody to do some work for me in Colorado. Would you be interested?"

After hanging up, Sam immediately called a friend and said, "You'll never guess who asked me to come work for him: Randy Shilts." Sam's job was to be Randy's eyes and ears in the Mountain West region, especially Colorado. "God, I was able to do this research, I was able to work with local reporters in Colorado Springs and in Denver," he enthused. "I was a young kid. I'm working for Randy Shilts!" The pay was better than any job he'd ever had, and when Randy put him up in a hotel with a pool and jacuzzi, Sam thought, *I'm in heaven.*

"Randy, God love him," he reflected. "He was so cool. Talk about a cool cat." Sam's knowledge of the scene around military installations proved to be a major asset. At local gay bars, he remembered, it only took a little time to get to know people, and soon they would open up. "A lot of what I did was old-fashioned gumshoe—gay gumshoe, if you will—to put together what happened."

Those efforts soon drew attention from the Colorado Springs police, which Randy took to mean he was onto something. Throughout the entire time he worked on *Conduct*, Randy remained convinced that he was under surveillance from military investigators. As a precaution, he had every document photocopied and held for safekeeping with his and Linda's mutual friends, Annie and Barry Biderman.

Whereas Sam personified many of the threats gay servicemen encountered, lesbians were forced to deal not just with homophobia but also sexism and sexual violence. "It was a horrible environment for women," remembered Penny Rand, who at age eighteen wound up at Idaho's Mountain Home Air Force Base. "They would give us these seminars, where the base preacher would come and basically tell us that our purpose there was to keep the GIs happy and that we needed to go out on dates. And then there were other people who would come in and explain how we could do makeup and look appealing."

It wasn't uncommon for women who refused men's attentions to hear "fucking dyke" muttered in their direction, but the consequences for rejecting these advances could be far worse than simple name-calling. While male harassers faced minimal sanction, the women who rejected them risked terrifying rounds of surveillance and interrogation when there was the slightest whisper of homosexuality. Although she'd effectively withstood accusations of lesbianism, Rand was eventually separated for her antiwar activism. When longtime friend Linda Alband contacted her about *Conduct*, Penny readily agreed to be interviewed. "I was naive thinking that [military service] would give me skills and also VA benefits," she reflected. "But I didn't have resources."

Tanya Domi faced similar harassment for suspected lesbianism, speaking up against sexual harassment, and defending the rights of other servicemembers. "I still think I would do it again," she reflected. Soon it was apparent that Randy's challenge wouldn't be a lack of sources, but an abundance. To Linda, he marveled at how well-prepared his military sources were, providing pristinely photocopied documents and always showing up on time. "Gay and lesbian soldiers, they outperformed," Domi marveled. "They always did—really smart."

For Colonel Margarethe "Grethe" Cammermeyer, the time between late 1989 and mid-1991 had been a prolonged ordeal of suffering in silence. At the apex of her long career, she had been up for a promotion requiring a security clearance investigation. When asked on a questionnaire about homosexuality, she chose to tell the truth, triggering a lengthy investigation leading to a discharge hearing in July 1991.

"I did not want to leave and ended up with attorneys fighting my discharge," Cammermeyer explained. However, once a discharge became inevitable, her attorneys offered to contact Randy. "Talking to Randy might not make any difference for her case," remembered Jon Davidson, counsel for both Cammermeyer and Dusty Pruitt. "But it was going to make her case to the general public in a way that could be helpful for sort of the longer aims of seeking justice."

Cammermeyer's story appeared in August 1991, falling between two other controversies concerning gays and the military. First, Randy had reported earlier that summer on an internal army memo urging reversal of the longstanding ban, in anticipation that federal courts may overturn it. While officials insisted that the document only represented one man's opinion, advocates hailed it as a sign that serious, evidence-driven debates were finally occurring. Defense Secretary Dick Cheney had called the policy an "old chestnut," Randy noted, even as investigators continued to pursue gay and lesbian servicemembers, including recent Desert Storm veterans.

Second, the rift between Randy and gay militants surfaced again in August, after the *Advocate* published a story outing Pentagon spokesman Pete Williams. The arguments around outing had simmered since the previous year, when journalist Michelangelo Signorile had publicly revealed the late Malcolm Forbes's homosexuality. As the *Advocate*'s publicist for the story, Howard Bragman considered himself a participant in Williams's outing, believing, like Signorile, that the ends justified the means in Williams's case. "I think [Randy] was absolutely against outing under any circumstances, and I was against outing except when there was utter hypocrisy involved," Howard explained. "I participated in that way, because I knew the effects and the pain [Williams] and Cheney had caused."

While criticizing the military and mainstream journalism for treating homosexuality like a shameful secret, Randy characterized outing as "a dirty business that hurts people," calling it hypocritical for gays to claim a right to privacy in their personal lives, while threatening to ruin the lives of those who didn't agree with them. As he'd done previously in critiquing ACT UP,

Randy's depiction of the core issue essentially aligned with his detractors, even though he objected to their tactics. Signorile, however, concluded that Randy had let himself be used by mainstream news organizations, similar to right-wing women who went on TV to bash feminists.

Although Randy's focus by now was almost entirely on the military, the media storm surrounding basketball star Earvin "Magic" Johnson's HIV diagnosis momentarily brought him back to AIDS journalism in late 1991. "In the past, the only time the government has gone into action against AIDS has been when people felt either that they were at risk for AIDS or that the epidemic affected people they knew," Randy wrote. "Although it may be only from a television screen, tens of millions of Americans feel they know Magic Johnson, and it is the hope of beleaguered AIDS organizers that Americans will show they care about stopping the disease that now threatens his life."

A month later, the media's obsession with the plight of "innocent" AIDS patients fixated on the case of Kimberly Bergalis, who was believed to have contracted HIV from her dentist. This led Randy to pen a *New York Times* commentary lamenting the media's implicit distinction between "good" AIDS cases and "bad" ones. "AIDS has spread without a concerted Government response because so many Americans believe that only people who have done something 'wrong' get the disease," he wrote. "Ms. Bergalis and many others might be alive now if those fighting AIDS did not also have to fight this prejudice."

Unable to escape the virus in his daily life, Randy had no choice but to press ahead with his work. Although the odds remained decidedly unfavorable, he still had a great deal left to do, and an uncertain amount of time left in which to do it.

Randy Shilts at his Guerneville home with Dash, date unknown. *Photo by Linda Alband, courtesy of the photographer*

17 | FOOLS AND BIMBOS

"DASH, GO GET LINDA. Go get Linda!" The early summer party had barely gotten underway when Linda Alband grabbed her camcorder and started recording. To celebrate Dash's fourth birthday, the humans were grilling out while he enjoyed an entire pizza and play date with his border collie friend, Wendells. Out on the hardwood deck stood Jennifer Finlay, holding a Diet Pepsi as the birthday boy drooled over his squeaky toy. "Look in the lens. This is your life!" Jennifer told the dog. Turning to the camera, she mugged, "Look at the lovely lesbian Birkenstocks," modeling her fashionably crunchy sandals.

"Look at Randy cook! Get this on film," an off-camera voice exclaimed as he brought out a bread bowl filled with spinach dip. As he and Linda stood talking, the camera swerved to catch Jennifer in a torrid water fight with Steve Robin. "I can shoot farther than you!" she taunted in her drenched pink T-shirt and khaki shorts.

"Aww, did we pee our pants?" Steve shot back. "I told you to get the ones with the wings!" Turning, he trained the Super Soaker on Dash, who jumped up and scurried over to Linda. As the dog flopped down and started rolling on his back, she swung the camera around.

"Dash never goes in this house. Look at all the cobwebs!" From the unused doghouse, Linda zoomed in closely on a car bearing the red-white-and-blue sticker: CLINTON '92.

Randy looked good that day, trim and relaxed in his striped polo shirt and khakis, with what appeared to be a recent haircut. Lately, however, he'd grown worried about the upcoming election. Two weeks earlier, he'd drafted a letter to Howard Bragman, who'd gotten involved with a gay political group supporting Democratic frontrunner Bill Clinton. "My life, I feel, depends on Clinton getting elected president," he wrote. Randy had avoided disclosing his HIV diagnosis, he explained, because it would change the way people viewed his journalism. "Besides," he added, "there's not much news value in it—I don't think anybody will stop the presses at the news that a 40-year-old gay man in San Francisco is HIV positive."

Countless people would die, including himself, Randy wrote, if the delays in research funding continued under a second Bush Administration. "Again, saying this aloud will have wide repercussions for my career as a journalist, as well as for my personal life," he added. "I'm willing to deal with that if I can be of service." Howard, to his recollection, never received the letter.

Even as work continued on *Conduct Unbecoming*, the year had gotten off to a somewhat rocky start for Randy's other projects. HBO Pictures had picked up *And the Band Played On* after NBC's option expired, but work had stagnated when director Joel Schumacher stepped away in late 1991. These production problems overlapped with Randy's struggles to turn *The Mayor of Castro Street* into a big-budget film, for which the activist group Outrage San Francisco was assailing Warner Bros. and director Oliver Stone for, in their words, "not consulting gay people directly, other than Shilts."

"Those people in Outrage don't know what they're talking about," Randy complained. Not only were *Mayor*'s producers gay, he added, but every gay person close to Harvey had been consulted. "I'm getting really sick of it being trashed on the basis of stupid rumors by people who don't know shit about what's going on."

This latest dustup with the militants lasted well into midyear, when Randy was preparing to address the National Lesbian and Gay Journalists Association's inaugural meeting. Despite past run-ins, he'd at least acknowledged the need for radical activism, even if he considered the rhetoric and tactics to sometimes be silly. However, his remarks included a blistering attack on what he characterized as "lavender fascists," whose efforts to control the community's thoughts, actions, and appearance amounted to little more than a temper tantrum.

The comments further cemented some activists' feelings that Randy must himself be a self-loathing gay person. His speech, however, would have lasting significance for someone else entirely. "He was one of the speakers at the event, and he gave up a portion of his time and asked me to speak," remembered Grethe Cammermeyer. Cammermeyer's fifteen-minute talk proved to be a personal game changer, as her case soon exploded in the national press. "That was essentially the beginning of my public speaking events," she reflected, eventually leading to her own memoir and an NBC docudrama starring Glenn Close. "He let me tell my story, and I'm forever grateful for the publicity that began as a result of his efforts."

The pressure to finish *Conduct* was already mounting when Clinton promised to end the ban if elected. Originally slated for a 1992 release, the book was already taking longer than expected to finish, adding more stress to an already precarious situation. When Randy's teenage nieces returned from a visit, they told their father about a trip to the hospital for pneumonia. "They said Randy would say it's no big deal, it's just a little pneumonia," Gary recalled. "I remember thinking, *A white wealthy man that is not lying on the ground— how does he get pneumonia?*"

"I blame AZT for a lot of people [dying], to be honest," Jennifer Finlay reflected, adding that Randy also dealt with persistent diarrhea and KS lesions. At their regular breakfast meetings, she'd always start with lengthy updates on her romantic life. For as much as she shared, however, she never heard Randy say much about himself. When it came to his health, Jennifer took her cues from Linda, who always treated it like Randy had a cold. In early 1992 Linda had helped him draft a will that would appoint her and ex-boyfriend Richard as coexecutors, while bequeathing his papers to the San Francisco Public Library. For taking care of Dash, Randy specified that the dog, along with $5,000, should go to Richard, with Linda and Howard Bragman next in line.

In recent years, Randy had come under the care of Dr. Lisa Capaldini, who maintained a small but popular practice in the Castro. "I met him as someone who was starting to get sick from this disease that killed everybody," she remembered. "When he first came here, by my recollection, I had not known him when he was fully healthy, but he didn't look like someone who was sick." As a patient, Randy was determined to enroll in every research trial he could find. "I knew he was very willing to try things that either might not work or might involve discomfort," Capaldini added. "And then, shortly after that period, we got into that cycle you got in with people with HIV, where they got one opportunistic infection, and then six months later, they got another one. And then four months later, they got another one. And two months later, they got another one."

Few people were better connected to AIDS treatment research than Randy, but part of the problem was his own take-charge personality. Instead of focusing on reducing stress, eating better, and conserving his energy, he seemed to want it all, embracing certain holistic practices while aggressively pursuing every new treatment. Capaldini's willingness to go along with him frustrated Linda, who wanted him to slow down. But from Capaldini's viewpoint, AIDS mortality was still 100 percent. If this was how a dying man wanted to handle his disease, she wasn't going to argue.

Compounding the issue was Randy's longstanding tendency to compartmentalize relationships. Although his friendship with Linda dated back more than twenty years, she was also his employee, who saw him apart from other friends. Moreover, details of Randy's personal life didn't necessarily get communicated from one group to another. Consequently, no one could exactly pinpoint when, in early 1992, college student Barry Barbieri began staying at Chez Rondey. The known details were relatively simple: Barry was from the Russian River area. They'd met at the Rainbow Cattle Company in Guerneville, and he quickly became a quiet, but ubiquitous, presence in Randy's life.

"So, Randy had a lesbian relationship," Jennifer quipped. "Randy didn't talk much about him to me, except for the musical taste differences and the youth." With an age gap of about twenty years, it would be the most incongruent relationship of Randy's life, with respect to experience and education. Linda's efforts at polite tolerance would gradually harden into irritation, as she experienced Barry as somewhat withdrawn, lacking in skills, and exhibiting what she perceived as jealousy toward Randy and others, including Dash.

Whether it was, as Linda believed, due to Randy being a "total wuss" with uncomfortable issues, or if there was a deeper bond that she just wasn't seeing, this new relationship endured far longer than anyone expected. At that year's Shiltsmas party, snippets of which she again captured with her camcorder, it was obvious that Randy's voice had grown raspy, and his stamina had weakened. Still, at day's end, he crashed contentedly into an outdoor deck chair, smiling as he opened presents. The gift pile had grown even larger and more eclectic, thanks to his military sources. It would, in fact, be the last Shiltsmas party Randy ever attended.

Within a few days of his forty-first birthday, HBO signaled a renewed effort to get *Band* moving again with the hiring of director Roger Spottiswoode.

Condensing the book into a compelling screenplay required substantial creative liberties like scrambling the chronology, embellishing dialogue, and casting celebrities who bore no resemblance to the real-life characters they played. "What was shocking was when the book went into a movie," recalled Don Francis, who served as a creative consultant. "As a scientist," he laughed, "that's not the way it was! I mean, read the book. That's the way it was. And they said, 'No. If we went and did every paragraph in that book, within fifteen minutes of that movie, you'd walk out.'"

By fall, Jennifer had wrapped up her library research and was beginning to write source notes. It was difficult to tell what Randy was wanting, however, as he was becoming less available to ask. "I provided maybe eighty percent of the research information, but I didn't know the interviews as well," she recounted. Work that may have lasted two weeks for someone who knew how it all fit together was taking much longer. Adding to the burden, Randy was also running out of money.

"He was going through the advance," Linda recalled, "but the anticipation was [that] he'd get the book in and get the last hundred thousand dollars." Randy was paying out of pocket to continue his health insurance while on book leave from the *Chronicle*, adding a substantial cost burden, as his medical needs were climbing. He always had to fight the insurance company to keep his therapist, Linda remembered, telling them, "I could potentially die of a really horrible disease. I think I need to see a psychiatrist."

In midfall, facing diminishing reserves and a looming deadline, Randy made a decision that would greatly impact his health, his finances, and his future. Accompanied by Barry and journalist friend Katie Leishman, he traveled to Germany at the end of October. Leishman, who'd written about AIDS in several national publications, had been friendly with Randy over the years, even though she'd shown a tendency to pursue certain dubious theories about the disease's underlying causes. "Katie goes to Germany with them because Randy wanted somebody there to speak German," Linda explained, "so his deal with her was he would pay all the expenses."

To Linda and Jennifer's recollection, the plan was for Randy to visit a German specialty clinic that was testing alternative treatments for AIDS patients. "I'm almost 98 percent positive there was a theory afoot that you could take your blood out and have it centrifuged, reheated, and put back into you, and that would kill all the HIV," Jennifer recounted, describing what was likely a treatment known as hyperthermia. The procedure had been panned by leading AIDS researchers, but to Linda's dismay, Randy decided to risk it.

"And so, they went away to Germany for a month," she remembered. "It was a horrible month for Randy. Randy was almost broke, and it cost him thousands and thousands and thousands of dollars for the three of them to go." When they returned, his condition had clearly worsened, as he again came down with pneumonia. On Christmas Eve, Linda spent the night in Guerneville, watching Randy stuff stockings by the crackling stone fireplace. Not long after she'd gone to bed, Barry came to wake her, saying, "Something's happened."

In the living room, Randy lay resting on the sofa. There was a popping in his lungs, he told her, but he felt okay. Since nothing else seemed to be wrong, they decided not to go to the hospital. On Christmas Day, Linda returned home while Randy took Barry and his mother to the airport and headed to his condo on Duncan Street. On the phone with Jennifer, he mentioned having pain in his side, which she assumed was probably a muscle tear. Linda was planning to see Randy the next day when the phone rang. Ann Neuenschwander's husband had gone to see Randy that afternoon and found him barely breathing on the sofa.

At Davies Medical Center, Randy was immediately admitted to intensive care with one lung completely collapsed and the other partially collapsed. "What I later learned," Linda recalled, "was that his lungs were like Swiss cheese." His condition required immediate surgery, cutting through the ribs to reinflate and stitch his lungs back together. When Jennifer came to visit, his body looked like it had been bitten by a shark. "With a suppressed immune system to start with," she reflected, "that really was the beginning of the end."

The imperative for Randy's inner circle, his health, came sharply into focus as they scrambled to care for him. For that first week, with Barry still away, Linda largely found herself alone with him. Randy was frightened, she remembered, and also worried that the medications would affect his sobriety.

"He and I really talked about a lot of things," Linda remembered, "and he told me how much he appreciated me and what his aspirations were." Randy hoped this stage in life would be a jumping-off point, where he could go on to do whatever he wanted in the years ahead. He also had hopes of writing a syndicated column and becoming a "George Will of the Left." Despite their long friendship, Randy admitted taking Linda for granted but wanted to keep working together. He was also thinking about moving away from gay topics, mentioning a book idea involving Central America. "He was thinking beyond the scope of his first three books," Linda explained, "[to] doing a full-length treatment on a topic that wasn't related to gay issues."

The second priority was keeping the book on track and managing Randy's affairs. After eight hours a day in the hospital, Linda would go home to work another eight hours on his business matters. There was a cover piece for *Newsweek* that required fact-checking, which would alleviate some of the immediate financial pain. To do the edits, however, she needed to pry Randy's box of materials from his hands. Even in his weakened state, it seemed, he was clinging to the book as a lifeline.

"He was working on that, and I could see that that was keeping him going," Lisa Capaldini recalled. When she visited, Randy would perk up telling her about *Conduct*. At times, Capaldini wondered if he would pull through, but she could also tell that above all else, he wanted to keep fighting. Where other patients might say they were frightened or in pain, Randy would tell her, "I want to get out of here."

Through the first couple weeks, Michael Denneny had spoken with Randy by phone practically every day. "The book was supposed to go to press on January 1," Michael recalled, "and we were publishing in May [on] a very condensed schedule." When it was apparent that Randy wouldn't be leaving the hospital anytime soon, Michael swore his assistant to secrecy and booked a flight to San Francisco. "I knew [if] I was on the spot, I'd have total control of the situation," he explained. Arriving at the hospital, Michael waited five hours for Randy to wake up. After seeing his author's condition, he booked a hotel room and had Linda send over all of Randy's materials.

"They brought up typewriters and Xerox machines, and I had all the copy," Michael remembered, "and I spent three days going through everything." Examining the research, however, he realized they wouldn't be able to finish the book as Randy intended. "The last section was gonna be on the Gulf War," Michael explained, "and it was gonna be almost a reprise of this whole forty-year history." The final chapter would have to be cut, leaving Michael to sew together an ending.

Michael returned to the hospital and waited again for his author to regain consciousness. "I said, 'We can't do the Gulf War, but I think I can craft an ending from this various material in the last section. Do you give me permission to do it?'" From his bed, Randy answered, "Yeah." Seeing his weakened state, however, Michael decided to wait around. Three hours later, Randy woke again, and Michael repeated his earlier comments. After another two hours, when Michael brought it up a third time, Randy interrupted. "Are you trying to gaslight me? Didn't we have this discussion already?" Yes, Michael assured him, but he wanted to make sure Randy understood.

With the help of freelance editor Doris Ober, Michael kept working from his hotel room, turning the research into a conclusion that fit the earlier chapters. By day, he would sit with Randy and go through the materials, while at night he would write, then he'd come back the next day. "I wrote the last X number of pages of that book," Michael said, "and my challenge to anybody is to find the seam. Nobody has been able to find the seam where Randy stopped and I started, because I wrote it in, as much as I could, his voice."

The third priority concerned managing public relations. Randy had been hospitalized under an assumed name, and the staff had remained extraordinarily tight-lipped. Still, people had begun to notice. "I had told people he was in seclusion," Linda explained. "The publisher wants him to finish the book [and] had sent him off to a remote location without a phone and that the hardest thing about doing it was [that] we had to surgically remove the telephone receiver from his ear."

The longer he spent in the ICU, however, the more difficult it became to deflect attention. Needing a break, Michael called another of his gay authors, Steven Saylor, and invited him to dinner. For at least a couple hours, he was able talk about something other than Randy and the book, and Saylor never asked why he was in town. As they parted ways, however, Saylor said to Michael, "Tell Randy we're all hoping for him."

Linda recalled that it was literary agent Fred Hill who convinced Randy to make a public statement. At the *Chronicle*, Leah Garchik was surprised when the editors told her that Randy had specifically asked for her. Aside from their one fraught encounter back in 1983, the two had never been close. "I wasn't at his famous birthdays that everyone would tell me about, but I was floored that he trusted me with this." Leah was told his assumed name and sent to Davies, where she mentally prepared by putting on a sympathetic face. "And he scolded me for having that face on," she remembered. "He didn't want that sympathy; he was pretty matter of fact about it. And in fact, maybe that's why he had specified that it would be me, that he thought that I would have some distance from it."

The front-page story ran the following Tuesday and was quickly picked up by national news organizations. In the interview, Randy explained why he'd previously not gone public. "Every gay writer who tests positive ends up being an AIDS activist," he told her, "and I didn't want to end up being an activist. I wanted to keep on being a reporter." While he understood that people may be upset, Randy added, if he were someone else hearing about it, he'd simply say, "Hang in there. You're going to make it."

While he'd previously questioned whether it was even newsworthy, the public's response soon proved him wrong. From across the country, cards and letters poured in by the hundreds, from people of all backgrounds, straight and gay, strangers and friends. "The *Chronicle* stunned me today—I can't think straight!" wrote Selma Dritz. "I can only say 'May you live to 120 years, like Moses,' as we say to our nearest and dearest. He, too, was a voice crying in anger in the wilderness." Honoring Randy's wishes, Selma closed simply with, "Hang in there."

After seven weeks, Randy's release signified an end to the immediate crisis, but another, more prolonged ordeal was now at hand. His intimate conversations with Linda had ceased once Barry had returned. "For the first week, [Randy] was sick, but he wasn't sick in the sense that he was delirious," Linda observed. "After Barry got back, there was more evidence of that, I thought." As Randy's behaviors became more erratic, Linda began to suspect that someone was saying that she wanted him dead.

In the months ahead, a series of run-ins would further strain relationships within the inner circle. As holder of Randy's power of attorney, Linda had to make difficult decisions that would be communicated back to Randy in less than flattering terms. If it came down to liquidating Randy's assets, there would be hard choices to make about his properties, including Chez Rondey. "Barry just took everything out of context," she lamented, "because . . . all he heard from that conversation was, I wanted to take his home away."

"I kind of liked Barry at first, because he was young like me and he didn't fit in with all of Randy's older friends," Jennifer recounted. Their relationship turned sour, however, when he brought her some boxes of materials and started complaining about both Linda and Dash. "I think when he was at my apartment, he saw me as somebody his own age and he could complain, but he didn't understand that I was loyal to Linda, loyal to Dash, loyal to Randy, and I was not loyal to him," she recalled. "I think we could have been friends if Randy had not gotten sick. I think that put way too much on him."

In fairness, Linda acknowledged, Barry was caught in an impossible situation. "Now the thing Randy did that really pissed me off, the thing I tried to talk to Barry about was, 'Randy should not make you his caregiver,'" she explained. "'You are his husband. It is inappropriate for him to make you do these things.'" With money finally coming in again, Randy had the resources to hire an in-home nurse. However, Linda added, "This is where the penny-pinching comes in. Randy had this misplaced sense of when he should spend money and when he shouldn't."

Following Bill Clinton's inauguration, there would be no better time for *Conduct Unbecoming*'s release, as advocates and the national press were swarming to the issue. Surpassing Randy's previous books in length, detail, and sourcing, *Conduct* swept readers all the way from exotic, faraway countries to tiny American military towns, providing a vital tool for those pressing Clinton, and his Democratic majority, to make good on his promise. Like *Band*, it would become a go-to source in legal and legislative hearings. However, despite its timely release, *Conduct* never matched its predecessor's fame, selling fifty-two thousand first-edition copies—enough to call it a bestseller, but still falling short of the publisher's lofty expectations.

The difference, it seemed, was Randy. Although he tried to do media appearances, even welcoming interviewers into his homes, he was unable to mount a book tour or return to the lecture circuit. Consequently, for those who'd supported his earlier efforts, the recollection of *Conduct*'s release remained bittersweet. "It was the absence of my speaking to him that was so painful," lecture agent George Greenfield recalled, "because I knew what he was going through. And I didn't realize how sick he was until we all found out."

"One minute he is the old Randy Shilts, a blur of energy and issues and passion," wrote Jeffrey Schmaltz for the *New York Times*. "The next, he isn't Randy Shilts at all. He's just another gay man with AIDS, scared and tired, trading gossip about the newest drugs and monitoring the declining level of white blood cells that support his immune system."

When Cleve Jones came home from the most recent National March on Washington, he brought along a new boyfriend. "I met a boy in Richmond who was a big fan of Randy's," Cleve remembered, "and I said, 'Let's go up to the river, and I'll show you the redwood trees and just surprise him.'" Pulling into the driveway, they saw Dash and Randy's Jeep outside, but nobody answered the door. "So, I just walked in," he continued, "and there's Randy on oxygen. I hadn't seen him, and he was just skin and bones, and I was just heartbroken. I said, 'Why didn't you tell me?'" Cleve left the next day feeling dispirited. "So, I got up there, and it was Randy fucking dying in his little house," he lamented. "It was just so fucking sad."

Simultaneous to Randy's bad turn, his father's health had also been in steep decline. "My dad knew Randy was sick," Gary Shilts recalled, "because I remember just before he died, he said, 'Children are not supposed to die before their parents.'"

In early May, Russell "Bud" Shilts passed away from cancer. While Randy was in no condition to travel for the funeral, he did call his oldest brother with a surprising request. Gary had been ordained in the nondenominational Universal Life Church, making him a legally recognized officiant for weddings. "Randy called me up and wanted to have a wedding ceremony with Barry," he remembered.

Gary had been following news out of Hawaii, where the state Supreme Court had ordered a lower court to consider the question of same-sex marriage. "That sounds like a great idea," he told Randy, "but be careful, you might end up being married. Eventually gay marriage will become legal, and then you might actually end up married as well."

After a long pause, Randy responded, *"Married?"*

The hastily assembled commitment ceremony happened on May 31, 1993, with a small gathering of friends and family at Chez Rondey. Linda got a late start to the day, driving up with Dan Yoder. Although she suspected it had been rushed because of Randy's insecurities about dying alone, she still felt it was important to be there and brought along her camcorder. "Someday we'll make this movie, Randy," she told him as he rested, half-dressed, on the living room sofa. "Ten to fifteen minutes with all the Beatles music you want to hear."

As caterers circulated with hors d'oeuvres, Linda panned the room to show the massive Kodiak bear holding blue balloons. Out on the deck, Gary Shilts stood chatting with his sister-in-law, Dawn. "This is not just a ceremony, not just a ring," Gary told the assembled guests during the backyard ceremony. In front of him stood Randy in full tuxedo with a white corsage, hair neatly combed but lacking its distinguishing curls. In front of him stood Barry in white sport jacket and black dress pants. After exchanging vows and rings, the two men held a long embrace before they, in turn, were embraced by their loved ones.

It would be the last time Gary and Reed Shilts saw their brother alive. Privately, Randy shared with Gary his idea for another book. Because so many men he'd interviewed for *Conduct* had disclosed that their first sexual experiences were with priests, he wanted to investigate the cover-up of sexual misconduct in the Catholic church. The book, he told Gary, would be called *Cardinal Sin*.

Despite a slew of disagreements, which led Ron Bernstein to threaten to set fire to HBO's offices, *Band* remained on track for an early September premiere, while debates around gays in the military continued to swirl. When Bill Clinton announced his new policy, dubbed "Don't Ask, Don't Tell," Jennifer Finlay

Dan Yoder (left), Barry Barbieri, and Randy Shilts, May 1993 at Randy's Guerneville home. *Photo by Dawn Shilts, courtesy of the photographer*

Reed (left), Gary, and
Randy Shilts with Dash,
May 1993 at Randy's
Guerneville home.
Photo by Dawn Shilts,
courtesy of the photographer

threw a shoe at the television. "I could tell [Clinton] had read the book when he gave his speech," she said. "The language he used was Randy's language, and you could tell he was affected by the stories. I was so angry at the Clinton Administration, because I fully blamed them for the rapid decline of [Randy's] health." After all that, she fumed, "How can you come to *that* solution after reading *that* book?"

The gulf between Randy and his friends continued to widen as Barry kept them mostly at arm's length. Worried about the isolation, Jennifer suggested having an AA meeting at Chez Rondey. "They will bring you a meeting if you're sick," she explained. "They bring it to you. It's not normal, but in a situation like that, they absolutely would do something like that." Similarly, Linda pleaded for a small, scaled-back Shiltsmas to celebrate Randy's birthday. "I thought, it's his last one. He needs this. And people want to come and see him," she explained. It didn't have to be fancy, but it would let Randy see the people who loved him. Barry vetoed both ideas.

From one moment to the next, Randy could swing from coherent to completely in a fog. But, Linda noted, he always managed to be alert for media appearances, including lengthy interviews in the *Advocate, San Jose Mercury News West,* and *Rolling Stone.* To his dismay, however, each new story seemed to slant toward his least favorite topic. During a sit-down for KPIX, Hank Plante asked Randy how he thought his work would be viewed "twenty, thirty, forty years from now," only to learn that he'd upset his longtime friend, who'd interpreted it to mean, "How do you want to be remembered when you're gone?"

The last time Elaine Herscher saw Randy was at a local awards ceremony, where the emcee awkwardly observed how nice it was for him to be recognized, while he was still alive. The comment caused Elaine to nearly burst into tears. "As soon as it was over, Randy got up to leave," she remembered. "I jumped up and hugged him, and he said, 'I have to get out of here.'"

For *Band*'s September premiere, HBO arranged screenings in Washington, DC, Los Angeles, and San Francisco. However, Randy told Howard Bragman, his dependence on oxygen had made air travel impossible. For the L.A. premiere, Howard made a call to HBO, which arranged medical transportation from Guerneville to Hollywood. And at the Castro Theatre, Randy received a loud standing ovation from the packed house. A number of people, including Jennifer, would remember it as the last time they saw him alive.

In what was left of an exhausting year, Linda was doing her best to keep Randy's affairs on track, updating their weekly meeting agenda with "Getting Randy Better" at the top of every itinerary. Included were details of his funeral wishes (press conference and public service at City Hall, no "Amazing Grace," and "something political" to agitate for more AIDS funding) and how he wanted to be buried: two side-by side plots with a flat granite slab placed vertically over the grave, like a quilt panel.

The disputes with Barry had left Linda weary and ready to hand off most of the work, but she was determined to protect her friend's wishes. Randy had made several provisions in his will, including an endowment with the University of Oregon, a sizable donation to 18th Street Services, and a small trust to provide for his brother David. At the end of November, however, he made a startling change, removing Linda and Richard as coexecutors and

Actor Sir Ian McKellen and Randy Shilts at the Castro Theatre premiere of *And the Band Played On*, August 28, 1993. *Photo by Deanne Fitzmaurice for the San Francisco Chronicle / Polaris Images*

separating the literary estate, which would be overseen by Michael Denneny, from his nonliterary estate. In addition to becoming the primary heir, Barry would now assume the executorship for everything except Randy's papers. "Randy really crippled his estate by doing that," Linda commented. Although she was still supposed to receive a substantial sum, her larger concern was for holding the estate accountable. Linda insisted that she only wanted Randy's wishes honored, and it bothered her to see changes made at a time when his competency could fluctuate dramatically.

Shortly before the holidays, Linda was working with CBS to schedule a *60 Minutes* interview with Randy. There would be one more Christmas at Chez Rondey, but she opted to stay away. It would, however, be the last time Steve Newman saw Randy alive. "He was happy," Steve reflected. "I think he found happiness and was happy with Barry, with a sense of accomplishment, and he wanted to do more. He smiled and laughed and said goodbye."

The *60 Minutes* team came and went, with an airdate planned for later in 1994. In Portland, Anne Neuenschwander had arranged to come visit, making it to the airport before the weight of everything came crashing down. "I couldn't go," she tearfully recalled. "I just broke down in the airport. I kept wanting to talk to him, and I couldn't."

In late January, a letter appeared in the *Advocate*, penned by its most famous former reporter. In what was essentially his farewell to the community, Randy likened the current state of gay and lesbian civil rights to Black Americans in the 1920s, with growing recognition of injustices but still decades away from decisive legislation. "I hate to brag," he continued, "but I feel that my latest book . . . is the best thing I've ever done. I truly believe that in years to come it will be seen as being far more significant than *And the Band Played On*." To his knowledge, *Conduct* was the first book to bring gay, lesbian, and women's issues together for a general readership. Additionally, he promised, the forthcoming paperback edition would include the ending he'd originally hoped to write. "And while we're talking conclusions," Randy wrote, "hopefully, history will record that I was a hell of a nice guy and that the people who have criticized me are a bunch of fools and bimbos."

The last time Linda and Randy spoke was by phone. "I was just glad the last time I talked to him, he was lucid," she remembered. Linda cautioned that he likely wouldn't get all of what he wanted for his funeral, and that Barry wouldn't go along with everything.

Randy tried to reassure her, saying, "Oh, I think he'll be okay," to which she responded, "I hope so, but I doubt it."

Before they hung up, Linda told her oldest friend, "I love you."

Randy's final words to her were, "I love you too."

18 | DARK AND STORMY

THE CALL FROM BARRY came early on February 17, waking Linda to the news that Randy had passed away at home. For the moment, however, she had to focus on finishing corrections to the *Conduct Unbecoming* paperback edition. "I couldn't disclose to the world that Randy died until after I [did] all of the corrections," she remembered. "And so, I figured, I gotta get this out, get this to FedEx and out to the publisher before the shit hits the fan." Around six o'clock, Wes Haley called to ask, "What happened? I heard something happened to Randy."

Inquiries were already coming into the *Chronicle*, which Wes tried to stymie while Linda worked to get ahead of the story. When she called Gary Shilts, his first concern was about telling his daughters. Not long after, a CBS producer called him with some background questions for the *60 Minutes* piece. "Well, Randy died this morning," Gary told her.

"What time did he die?" the producer asked.

Gary wasn't sure.

"Okay, goodbye." She hung up.

Linda realized the national press had the story when the White House called her, looking for someone to offer condolences. They could try Barry, she curtly replied, but he likely wouldn't answer. "Save the president some time."

"That was just a bad day," Jennifer Finlay remembered. Amid winds and heavy rain, she'd gone to Randy's condo to wait for his oxygen tanks to be picked up. For Jennifer, the moment his death hit home was when she was sitting alone in the empty apartment. In Randy's bedroom, she spied a yellow heart catheter on the dresser and, without thinking, picked it up to throw it

225

away, finding that it was encrusted with dried blood. "I know personally that HIV is delicate," she reflected, "but I was terrified of it. I shouldn't have been, but I was so sad."

Per Randy's wishes, Elaine Herscher got a quote from Watergate reporter Carl Bernstein, which appeared in the *Chronicle*'s death announcement. "Randy Shilts was a great journalist," Bernstein told her. "Finally in our profession there is some first-rate journalism being done about gays and lesbians, and that is largely attributable to Randy Shilts's work."

More tributes soon arrived, with Congresswoman Lynn Woolsey, representing the district where Randy died, delivering brief accolades on the floor of the US House.

Linda was correct when she predicted that Randy wouldn't get everything he wanted. Only elected officials were allowed City Hall funerals, although its flags were ordered to half-mast. After putting out feelers, she heard from Rev. Cecil Williams at Glide Memorial Church, a progressive, inclusive congregation in the Tenderloin. "[Randy] was so involved in this community," Williams remembered. In 1987, he'd traveled to Côte d'Ivoire on the same trip with Randy. "And I would put it, he was a good man, a good person, a good human being." The public funeral at Glide was set for February 22, with Williams officiating.

In light of Randy's passing, CBS News opted to air his *60 Minutes* interview ahead of schedule, touching on highlights of his life from childhood to coming out, his early career, and AIDS. In Kalamazoo, Michigan, his sister in-law Dawn sat down to watch it with her conservative family, leading to an intense, almost painful conversation with her siblings about homosexuality. "We did this role play for about four hours," she remembered. "There were people in the room who thought we would never speak to each other again, but our relationship went deeper because of that conversation."

The prospects for political spectacle jumped to near certainty when Pastor Fred Phelps and the Westboro Baptist Church announced plans to picket Randy's funeral. Although Phelps had written Cecil Williams with an offer to meet and pray together, the chances for comity and friendship were doomed from the start, as the fringe group's news release included Randy's photograph with the caption FILTHY FACE OF FAG EVIL.

By late morning, when the hearse carrying Randy's casket arrived, the streets were already teeming with activists ready for a fight. "You could smell blood in the air," remarked Waiyde Palmer, who recalled seeing people young and old alike carrying bricks and bottles. "Even though we did not agree on anything . . . we still counted him as family and would defend him, and his life and death, against those who would destroy us to our last breath."

The San Francisco police did their part, Linda recalled, by tracking Phelps's rental car from the airport. As Phelps tried to navigate city streets, officers kept rerouting him, delaying his arrival until the service was underway. "We sat in the limo, and we watched the battle of sorts outside," remembered Wes Haley, who served as a pallbearer that day. To move the casket, they had to stand it vertically to fit in an elevator at the back of the church; with each bump, Wes swore he could hear Randy shouting, "*Bitch!!*"

Inside, a diverse assembly filled every pew and aisle of Glide's spacious sanctuary. "This is a celebration, brothers and sisters," Williams announced. Behind him stood members of the Glide Ensemble, splendidly robed and swaying with the music. "A celebration of Randy Shilts," Cecil continued. "A celebration of his life, yeah!" In the front row, Jennifer lost it when she saw Ann Neuenschwander break down in tears. Linda had invited David Perlman, Frank Robinson, labor leader Howard Wallace, Michael Denneny, Selma Dritz, Marcus Conant, Don Francis, Fred Hill, Sergeant Perry Watkins, and the National Lesbian and Gay Journalists Association's Leroy Aarons to deliver eulogies. Following a stirring rendition of "Lean on Me," the tributes began.

With an apology to Cecil Williams, Frank Robinson opened his remarks by addressing Phelps directly. "The reverend came to San Francisco to, quote, 'Shadow these people like some sort of ugly dog,' he told the congregation. "That's of course the kind of statement I would expect from a son of a bitch." More than a friend, Frank continued, Randy was one of his heroes. About Randy's detractors within the gay community, he added, "I sometimes wondered if they realized how much he loved it, how hard he fought to fight the injustices that had been done to it."

Speaker after speaker testified to Randy's character, his tenacity, and the power of his example. After Howard Wallace's remarks, Cecil Williams came forward to announce, "The Reverend Fred Phelps has come, and the Reverend Fred Phelps has *gone*." The sanctuary erupted with joyous music, as people leaped to their feet and cheered.

Next came Michael Denneny, calling Randy "one of the truly great journalists of our time." Randy had the courage to speak his mind, regardless of the consequences, Michael continued, and he rightly saw his job as "more than just doing PR for the gay community."

The tone grew sharper with Selma Dritz, her head barely poking over the lectern. Laying the blame squarely on political leaders, she said, "They blocked, and they prevented funding which would've permitted us to find much sooner an effective prevention, an effective treatment, an effective vaccine for the men, the women, and the *babies*—including Randy maybe—who might be alive today if not for their active opposition." Rapping the lectern with her fists, she concluded, "In Randy's name, *I say they have much to answer for.*"

When Perry Watkins stepped to the microphone, dressed impeccably in his dark blue army dress uniform, crisp white gloves, and black bowtie, he kept his remarks simple. "Randy allowed each of us to be proud of our diversity," he began. "His contributions will impact social evolution throughout eternity." Turning to the casket, Watkins donned his white hat, stood to attention, and offered the military salute, saying, "Well done, soldier."

Following a stirring homily by Cecil Williams, the service concluded with music from the Glide Ensemble as the sanctuary slowly emptied. Near the front, Steve Newman stood somberly watching. Serving as a pallbearer had been difficult enough, but the spectacle outside had driven him to a state of near rage. "We are sitting there visualizing what is going on outside," he recounted. "I was so fucking pissed off while I'm sitting there, but I am in a church, and I'm at Randy's funeral. It turned into despair, absolute despair."

After the burial in Guerneville Cemetery, Barry quietly pulled Steve aside; he wanted to tell someone the details of Randy's final moments. It had started in the middle of the night with a cough, Barry told him, which escalated into violent hacking. "[Randy] started coughing up blood, and the coughing got worse," Steve continued. "He basically coughed up all of his lung." When emergency responders arrived, their actions only made the situation worse. "The paramedics came and saw the bloody mess, and that he had HIV, and they didn't want to deal with it," Steve explained. Although they only needed to follow universal precautions, the EMTs refused to render assistance until given full-body protective wear, by which time it was too late.

Neither Linda nor Jennifer made the drive to Guerneville Cemetery. The next day, Linda was driving home when another motorist hit her car. "And I was just laughing about it," she remembered, "because it was just a good thing it hadn't happened the day before." For Jennifer, the entire ordeal had left her exhausted and deeply hurt. "Any time I saw SHILTS IN HELL, I wanted to kill [somebody]," she reflected.

After a day of nonstop crying, Jennifer took two of her girlfriends and started driving, ending up at the Marin Headlands. Leaping from the car, she screamed, grabbing and hurling the largest tree branch she could find before turning around and charging back at the rental car. Blinded by rage and grief, she threw herself across the hood, bashing her chin against the windshield.

"Randy would love yet again one of my many girlfriend misadventures," Jennifer wrote in her journal about that day. Feeling that she hadn't yet said a proper goodbye, she tried to put her feelings into words:

> *Thanks Randy, I will maintain your memory with the full honor that you taught me to have for myself. You gave me more chance to become myself than anything or person had ever. You were more than an employer, a mentor or a friend—you were one of the biggest loves of my life. I was always intimidated by you because you were smarter than me and famous, but you gave me the life I will have. You gave me something that is nearly impossible to see or understand—a future. You will always be a part of my future and I will do you proud. Thank you. I will always love you beyond words.*

The following week, more tributes came from San Francisco's gay papers, acknowledging not only Randy's controversies and combativeness but also his audacity and fearlessness. Still, the *BAR*'s editorial page couldn't resist one more dig: "Actually, we were surprised Phelps hated Shilts. We assumed the message Randy so frequently spread was close to Phelps's own positions—certainly, closer than it usually was to his many gay detractors."

Among those detractors were some who, like Phelps, seemed intent on enjoying a final victory lap at Randy's expense. "Ding dong, the witch is dead," declared *Diseased Pariah News*, a popular AIDS activist zine. "And now that Randy Shilts' bones lie rotting in the earth . . . we can let his poor soul rest." The publication had assailed Randy in previous issues, and now with his passing, there was no reason to hold anything back. Editor Beowulf Thorne did offer praise for *The Mayor of Castro Street*, but that was where it ended. Thorne launched into a lengthy recap of Randy's supposed sins: a lack of objectivity, his coverage of the bathhouses, and of course, Patient Zero.

However, in Thorne's opinion, Randy's greatest betrayal was the conceal-ment of his HIV diagnosis. "Randy Shilts, the great beacon of HIV elucidation, the man who made millions off of AIDS but never put any money back into HIV services or support, hid the fact that he was HIV positive himself," Thorne wrote. "Really Randy, your constituents didn't expect you to be perfect, but we certainly didn't expect you to be a traitor. Rest in peace, you hateful little shit."

In its brief lifetime, *Diseased Pariah News* would gain much-deserved praise for its irreverent takes on living with HIV, despite the disease's negative stigma. With respect to Randy, however, Thorne's tirade illustrated how a particular opinion, repeated often enough, can become accepted as unvarnished truth. Aside from Chez Rondey, Randy's money went largely to covering costs like his health care and paying the people who researched *Conduct Unbecoming*. What's more, Linda's record-keeping showed how he frequently donated to AIDS charity events around the country and consistently directed contribu-tions to 18th Street Services, including a carveout in his will. Finally, there is no evidence—physical or anecdotal—that the "hateful" Randy Shilts ever celebrated the death of any person with AIDS or that he kept an enemies list of the activists who'd criticized him.

In the aftermath, disputes around Randy's estate would harden into a pro-longed legal battle between Linda, supported by the Shilts family, and Barry. The lawsuit wouldn't be settled until 1999, after which Chez Rondey was placed on the market and sold. Knowing the property's history, its owners worked diligently to maintain it as Randy had, keeping a number of furniture pieces that had been left behind. More than twenty years after Randy's passing, his sofa still sat near the stone fireplace with his mounted deer head keeping watch, while outside stood Dash's still-unused doghouse. The famous Kodiak bear, however, was nowhere to be found.

19 | THE BAND PLAYED ON

IT WAS A WARM, windy September day in 1989 when Eric Marcus climbed the steps above Castro to reach the Saturn Street apartment of one of his heroes. Eric had embarked on his own ambitious project, collecting oral histories for his book *Making Gay History*. His interviewee that day was friendly, but Eric observed that his host could be almost as unruly as the good-natured golden retriever who kept intruding on their conversation. "Randy interrupted his [own] interruptions," Eric laughed, causing him to wonder if his host might have attention-deficit disorder.

It was Randy's willingness to share information, specifically FBI files he'd obtained through the Freedom of Information Act, that cemented Eric's appreciation for a man he considered a colleague, friend, and mentor. "The one thing that Randy asked of me when he gave me his FBI files was that I help other writers with their books when I had the opportunity," Eric later told an aspiring Shilts biographer. "So you can think of this simply as Randy helping you—almost directly."

In 1993 Clinton Fein was taking the summer off when he happened to pick up a copy of *Conduct Unbecoming*. "It was such an eye opener for me," he reflected. Coming from South Africa, his views of the American struggle for civil rights changed completely after reading it. Subsequently, Clinton contacted Michael Denneny and acquired the CD-ROM rights to *Conduct Unbecoming*, a move which Randy knew of and approved, even though the two never met. "We collected all of these images of all these people to show, in essence, that they were just like anyone else," he explained. As a result, *Conduct* would become a pioneering work of digital media, building on Randy's narrative by adding links to audiovisual content and the source documents he'd cited. The CD-ROM was picked up by *Wired* magazine's online shop, making it one of the first items sold through e-commerce.

Subsequently, Clinton became a political artist and dogged free speech activist, winning a historic Supreme Court case in 1997 establishing a precedent for protecting First Amendment rights in the digital era. "I can just say, what an incredible influence one man, that I never actually met, has been in my life just by reading a book he wrote, that was so brilliant," Clinton enthused. "I became an American citizen so that I wouldn't get into trouble and deported for doing *Conduct Unbecoming*, the CD-ROM. It triggered so many meaningful events in my life, this man, who I never met."

Whatever Randy may have felt about the practice of outing, activists' efforts to expose hypocrisy among antigay conservatives benefitted from his legacy with the publication of *I Had to Say Something*, a 2006 memoir by former escort Michael Jones. The book made national headlines detailing Jones's relationship with Colorado minister Ted Haggard, a charismatic leader in evangelical circles. Key to its success were two Shilts proteges: research assistant Jennifer Finlay and Jones's coauthor and close friend, Sam Gallegos. "I'm quite proud of that," Sam commented. "I'm very grateful to Randy and Linda. All these years later, I had the courage to do something like that."

For Jennifer, the years following Randy's death remained a painful subject. Despite her impressive work on *Conduct*, she found herself frozen out by San Francisco employers for having Randy's name on her resume. Even worse were the managers who'd invite her in for an interview, only to probe insensitively for gossip about a mentor she still grieved. After getting a master's degree in library science, Jennifer moved to rural North Carolina, working as the librarian in a small town with a checkered racial history, which she dutifully worked to uncover and digitally preserve. Although she would still call herself a San Franciscan, the trauma surrounding Randy's passing made it unlikely that Jennifer would ever return to the city.

After experiencing a number of financial setbacks over Randy's estate, Linda Alband eventually returned to Portland, using her considerable management skills to oversee operations for an Oregon nonprofit advocating for universal health care. More than anyone else, Linda worked to keep Randy's memory alive by staying connected to his friends and associates and assisting any researchers who contacted her. When visited by a writer with an interest in Randy's more intimate life story, she arranged a night out on the town with Ann Neuenschwander, sharing stories over drinks and a basket of fries (with ketchup, Randy's favorite) before taking in a show by the people who gave Randy his first big break in journalism: drag queens.

Since Randy's passing in 1994, the world has changed in more ways than he likely would have predicted. How he might have responded to the advent of new, lifesaving HIV medications, 9/11, and the digital age, especially social media and smartphones, remains an intriguing consideration. The trail he blazed for LGBTQ journalists ushered younger generations into the spotlight, from his one-time sparring partner Michelangelo Signorile to conservative, openly HIV-positive Andrew Sullivan. In the alternative press, columnist Dan Savage blazed his own trail, dispensing sex advice to straight and gay readers alike and breaking longstanding taboos around discussing human intimacy. And on television, journalists like Rachel Maddow and Anderson Cooper now speak openly of their same-sex spouses, bolstered by the Supreme Court's historic 2015 ruling on marriage equality.

"I did a live shot for Anderson, a live remote the night of the final Supreme Court victory," Cleve Jones recalled. "I reminded Anderson that every major gay and lesbian organizational leader had opposed Edie Windsor's effort. And then I said, 'This is a vindication for the grassroots that I feel myself to be part of, but really the credit for this victory goes to the American people, whose hearts and minds have changed.'" Afterward, Cleve thought to himself, *God-damn it! I wish Randy could've heard that, because he would've been so proud of me. He would've just said, "You nailed that."*

Beyond marriage equality, Randy likely would've had plenty to say about several major news stories, especially the rapid, deadly spread of a new global pandemic, COVID-19. And realistically, he likely would have wrestled with his own traumas, along with many long-term HIV survivors who are now more likely to die from natural aging than the virus that tore through their community.

In academic circles, scholarly appraisals of Randy's work began as far back as *The Mayor of Castro Street*, with the highest intensity targeting *Band* and the enduring Patient Zero story. While these appraisals merit serious discussion, arguably they, in turn, would have benefitted from a more in-depth understanding of the developmental milestones and influential relationships that shaped Randy's growth from childhood to the end of his life. Moreover,

Randy's experiences with addiction, recovery, and trauma merit much closer attention than they've received. Simply noting that he went clean and sober, as if it were a one-time event, renders any attempt to understand Randy's worldview, relationships, and motivations substantially incomplete.

Picturing an older, perhaps wiser, but certainly just as combative Randy Shilts in contemporary times can be tempting to imagine. But it's also tantalizing to recall Randy in what he might have termed the "before times," when a brash, curly-haired, shabbily dressed young reporter roamed the San Francisco streets, bars, and bathhouses, joining his contemporaries in an everlasting game of oversexed catch-and-release. On one night, he might have a debauched encounter and write it up as erotic fiction; on another, maybe he'd end up handcuffed naked to a parking meter. Blissfully unaware of how his life would unfold, that young man bubbled with extraordinary confidence. Yet, he also fretted about his appearance, lack of money, and lovability, pausing every so often to ask of his surroundings, "Is that all there is?"

In *The Mayor of Castro Street*, Randy suggested that Harvey Milk still lived "as a metaphor for the homosexual experience in America." The fact that Randy became one of LGBTQ culture's most influential and controversial chroniclers signifies how he was, for all his limitations, making history at the same time he was reporting it. Though Randy at that age might not have foreseen the cruel circumstances ahead, he certainly had big ideas in mind when he told his one-night stand, "I'm one of the most interesting people you'll ever meet." In the bigger picture of Randy Shilts's life, considering all the accomplishments and accolades, the criticism he provoked, and the untold numbers he inspired both in admiration and disdain, a comprehensive fact-check can only render one conclusion: true.

Randy Shilts autograph card.
Courtesy of Linda Alband

ST. MARTIN'S PRESS

ACKNOWLEDGMENTS

I AM GRATEFUL FIRST to my former partner, Jaxon Bonsack, as well as my mother, sisters, nephews, and niece for their support. Along the way, I had help and encouragement from many friends and associates, including Martha Bates, Richard Camacho, Holly Cullerton, Austin DeRaedt, Colleen Fisher, Amy Heinz, Susan Jarosak, Kim Kittleman, Diane Knust, Liz Lightfoot, Jay Manley, Vance Martin, Val Meyers, Megan Morrissey, Jean Quam, Jessica Schwake, Suzanne Shatila, Kareem Smith, Daniel Spadafore, Jackie and Jerry Timm, Jason Vivian, and Scott Westerman.

A number of my sources went out of their way to help, especially Linda Alband, Randy Alfred, and Jennifer Finlay. My thanks also to everyone who provided interviews: Donald Abrams, Terry Bean, Ron Bernstein, Larry Bush, Katy Butler, Grethe Cammermeyer, Lisa Capaldini, Walter Caplan, Amelia Craig Cramer, James Curran, Jon Davidson, Belva Davis, Tanya Domi, Clinton Fein, Douglas Foster, Don Francis, Sam Gallegos, Robert Gallo, Leah Garchik, Laurie Garrett, George Greenfield, Mary Guinan, Wes Haley, Elaine Herscher, Michael Housh, Cleve Jones, Sally Eck Jones, Stuart Jones, Howie Klein, Matthew Krieger, Anne Kronenberg, Ken Maley, Eric Marcus, David May, Duncan McDonald, Harriet Merrick, John Mitchell, Andrew Moss, Daniel Nicoletta, Steve Newman, Lori Olszewski, George Osterkamp, Waiyde Palmer, Hank Plante, Carolyn "Dusty" Pruitt, Carol Queen, Penny Rand, Steve Robin, Benjamin Schatz, Chris Schroeder, Randy Shandobil, Reed and Dawn Shilts, Mervyn Silverman, Susan Sward, Mike Thoele, Dana Van Gorder, Paul Volberding, Tim Westmoreland, Evelyn C. White, Bridget Wilson, Tim Wolfred, and Michael Wong. Sadly, seven of my sources have subsequently passed away: Howard Bragman, Michael Denneny, Roy Halvorsen, Ann Neuenschwander, David Perlman, Gary Shilts, and Cecil Williams.

My archival research included numerous collections, and I am grateful for the assistance of Tim Wilson at the San Francisco Public Library's James Hormel LGBTQIA+ Center; the GLBT Historical Society; New York Public Library; University of Oregon; University of California, San Francisco; University of Minnesota; and Aurora Public Library. Thanks also to my literary agent George Greenfield, as well as senior editor Jerome Pohlen, managing editor Devon Freeny, and their colleagues at Chicago Review Press.

Finally, thank you to Randy Martin Shilts. I wish you were alive to tell your own story, but I've done the best I could with the rich materials, relationships, and memories you left behind.

NOTES

PROLOGUE: A CHARACTER IN TWO SCENES

"How're you doing": David May, *A Nice Boy from A Good Family* (Las Vegas: Nazca Plains, 2009), 37. All actions and quotations in this section come from the chapter "Something Sensational to Read in the Train." May confirmed the story's accuracy during a telephone interview by the author on November 14, 2019.

"There's no such thing": "Montreal AIDS Conference Closing Ceremonies 1989" (videocassette), box 6, Linda Alband Collection of Randy Shilts Materials (collection no. 2003-09), courtesy of Gay, Lesbian, Bisexual, Transgender Historical Society, San Francisco. All visual details, unscripted comments by Shilts, and audience reactions in this section come from a viewing of the videotape on November 7, 2019.

His friend Cleve Jones: Cleve Jones, interview by the author, San Francisco, August 26, 2016.

"As a journalist": Randy Shilts, "1989 Speech to International Conference on AIDS," box 1, folder 38, Linda Alband Collection of Randy Shilts Materials. All quotations from Shilts's prepared remarks in this section come from this document.

1. THE GRADUATE

ritual would seldom vary: Randy Shilts, in *Wednesday's Children: Adult Survivors of Abuse Speak Out*, ed. Suzanne Somers (New York: Putnam, 1992), 163, box 2, file 139, Linda Alband Collection of Randy Shilts Materials.

"Whenever I smell": Gary Shilts, interview by the author, Aurora, IL, August 10, 2015. Unless otherwise noted, all quotes attributed to Gary Shilts in this chapter are taken from this interview.

"friendships usually develop": Gary Shilts to Randy Shilts, October 25, 1982, shared with the author on August 10, 2015.

"gift of gab": Senior Class of Galesburg High School, *Souvenir*, 1940, courtesy of Galesburg Charleston Memorial District Library, e-mailed by Reed Shilts to the author on July 18, 2015.

"win Russ": Comstock High School, *Owlette*, April 1941, courtesy of Galesburg Charleston Memorial District Library, e-mailed by Reed Shilts to the author on July 18, 2015.

cleaning became more haphazard: Linda Alband, personal conversation with the author, November 15, 2016.

struggled to make simple meals: Alband, personal conversation.

"My mother was given": Randy Shilts, in *Wednesday's Children*, 163.

"I felt my parents": Shilts, 163.

"I was constantly at odds": Gary Shilts to Randy Shilts, October 25, 1982.

"School became my escape": Randy Shilts, in *Wednesday's Children*, 163.

other children taunted him: Randy Shilts, short story fragment, February 23, 1971, box 2, file 10, Randy Shilts Papers, 1955–1994 (GLC 43), courtesy of James C. Hormel LGBTQIA Center, San Francisco Public Library, San Francisco.

"She said that only sissies": Shilts, short story fragment.

seriousness that struck Stuart Jones: Stuart Jones, interview by the author, Holland, MI, October 13, 2016. Unless otherwise noted, all quotes attributed to Stuart Jones in this chapter are taken from this interview.

God and Country medal: Photo from *Aurora Beacon-News*, December 9, 1965, box 1, file 6, Randy Shilts Papers.

"Nobody talked about that": Randy Shilts, in *Wednesday's Children*, 164.

The most accepting comment: Shilts, 164.

protective relationship with his younger brothers: Reed Shilts, interview by the author, Kalamazoo, MI, August 13, 2015. Unless otherwise noted, all quotes attributed to Reed Shilts in this chapter are taken from this interview.

Randy barely knew: Sally Eck Jones, interview by the author, Holland, MI, October 13, 2016. Unless otherwise noted, all quotes attributed to Sally Eck Jones in this chapter are taken from this interview.

Appraising the new wardrobe: Jones, interview.

card-carrying member: Randy Shilts, Students for Reagan membership card, December 5, 1967, box 2, file 12, Randy Shilts Papers.

he'd hand out leaflets: Reed Shilts, interview by the author.

began to attract attention: Ron Krueger, "He Eats, Thinks and Drinks Ideas: Randy Shilts and Young Americans for Freedom," *Aurora Beacon-News*, January 23, 1968, box 2, file 2, Linda Alband Collection of Randy Shilts Materials.

"study the philosophies": Krueger, "He Eats, Thinks and Drinks Ideas."

"Always be so broad-minded": Aurora West High School, *EOS*, 1968, box 1, file 1, Randy Shilts Papers.

a woman slapped him: Ruth Hallenstein to Kane County Draft Board, November 10, 1969, box 2, file 33, Randy Shilts Papers.

Reviewing the Beatles': Randy Shilts, "The Beatles: On the Revolution." *Red and Blue,* February 7, 1969, box 2, file 4, Randy Shilts Papers.

"Mama Bitch and Papa Bitch": Randy Shilts, journal entry, April 4, 1978, transcript of Randy Shilts personal journals by Jennifer M. Finlay, 1996, box 1, file 5, Randy Shilts Papers.

"I couldn't stand my parents": Shilts, journal entry.

The idea came to him: Randy Shilts, journal entry, December 25, 1979, transcript by Finlay, 1996, box 1, file 5, Randy Shilts Papers.

he hurried toward the gate: Randy Shilts, journal entry, January 15, 1972, box 2, file 31, Randy Shilts Papers.

"He never again": Randy Shilts, "Of Passing Dreams (and Stars)," January 15, 1970, box 2, file "Poetry," Randy Shilts Papers.

"Still," he recalled: Randy Shilts, journal entry, December 25, 1979.

2. KILLING THE LION

didn't take long for Linda Alband: Linda Alband, interview by the author, Portland, OR, November 16, 2015. Unless otherwise noted, all quotes attributed to Linda Alband in this chapter are taken from this interview.

she never forgot the first time: Ann Neuenschwander, interview by the author, Portland, OR, November 17, 2015. Unless otherwise noted, all quotes attributed to Ann Neuenschwander in this chapter are taken from this interview.

In fall 1970: Chris Schroeder, interview by the author, Portland, OR, November 13, 2016. Unless otherwise noted, all quotes attributed to Chris Schroeder in this chapter are taken from this interview.

"I was overwhelmed": Randy Shilts, journal entry, July 6, 1971, box 2, file 31, Randy Shilts Papers.

On the Fourth of July: Shilts, journal entry.

He'd written so much: Shilts, journal entry.

writing about an untimely death: Randy Shilts, "The Killing of a Lion," August 3, 1971, box 2, file 4, Randy Shilts Papers.

classes were growing tedious: Randy Shilts, journal entry, October 6, 1971, box 2, file 31, Randy Shilts Papers.

moved into a new apartment: Randy Shilts, journal entry, January 6, 1972, box 2, file 31, Randy Shilts Papers.

"sexual problems": Shilts, journal entry.

sleeping with one of his professors: Schroeder, interview by the author.

"really heavy": Randy Shilts, journal entry, March 11, 1972, box 2, file 31, Randy Shilts Papers.

Although the professor frustrated him: Randy Shilts, journal entry, March 17, 1972, box 2, file 31, Randy Shilts Papers.

"My deepest heterosexual": Randy Shilts, journal entry, March 11, 1972.

friend who'd reacted coolly: Randy Shilts, journal entry, March 12, 1972, box 2, file 31, Randy Shilts Papers.

Another friend: Randy Shilts, journal entry, March 27, 1972, box 2, file 31, Randy Shilts Papers.

He quickly tired: Randy Shilts, journal entry, March 22, 1972, box 2, file 31, Randy Shilts Papers.

Dreams of sex with men: Shilts, journal entry.

"I expected a mystical magic": Randy Shilts, journal entry, March 11, 1972.

"I've lost control of things": Randy Shilts, journal entry, March 22, 1972.

in the company of a "latent homosexual": Randy Shilts, journal entry, March 11, 1972.

"I am terrified of people": Shilts, journal entry.

"Sexual contacts have to be": Randy Shilts, journal entry, March 27, 1972.

On Easter weekend: Randy Shilts, journal entry, April 1, 1972, box 2, file 31, Randy Shilts Papers.

"I want to fall in love": Shilts, journal entry.

he was afraid of losing: Randy Shilts, journal entry, April 27, 1972, box 2, file 31, Randy Shilts Papers.

"Maybe the lion is dead": Randy Shilts, journal entry, March 22, 1972.

week had already been memorable: Randy Shilts, journal entry, May 20, 1972, box 2, file 31, Randy Shilts Papers.

"alienate[d] me from penises": Shilts, journal entry.

In front of his entire class: Shilts, journal entry.

"Sexually, the repressions and fears": Randy Shilts, journal entry, June 2, 1972, box 2, file 31, Randy Shilts Papers.

"Most of my friends know": Shilts, journal entry.

truth took on a few embellishments: Randy Shilts, interview by Eric Marcus, San Francisco, September 12, 1989, Making Gay History, https://makinggayhistory .com/podcast/randy-shilts/.

letter from Bud: Russell "Bud" Shilts to Randy Shilts, June 22, 1972, box 2, file "Corresp., Draft Articles, Etc.," Randy Shilts Papers.

"Now you are a man": Russell "Bud" Shilts to Randy Shilts, circa August 1972, box 2, file "Corresp., Draft Articles, Etc.," Randy Shilts Papers.

Randy waited to share: Gary Shilts, interview by the author.

"My work is done": Shilts, interview.

"I have to slow down": Randy Shilts, journal entry, June 2, 1972.

"I walk down the street": Randy Shilts, journal entry, circa August 1972, box 2, file 31, Randy Shilts Papers.

"the people that make the sex": Randy Shilts, journal entry, June 2, 1972.

"Love myself": Shilts, journal entry.

3. COME OUT FOR SHILTS!

Eugene Gay People's Alliance: "Creating Change: Forty Years of LGBTQ Activism at the University of Oregon," University of Oregon Libraries, accessed April 6, 2022, https://blogs.uoregon.edu/creatingchange/2016/03/21/creating-change-forty-years -of-lgbtq-activism-at-the-university-of-oregon/.

"It wasn't a large organization": Terry Bean, telephone interview by the author, July 28, 2016. Unless otherwise noted, all quotes attributed to Terry Bean in this chapter are taken from this interview.

"We had rap sessions": Randy Shilts, interview by Marcus.

"It's sort of how our problems": Shilts, interview.

"When I went to Eugene": Randy Shilts, journal entry, June 12, 1973, box 2, file 31, Randy Shilts Papers.

"gain the respect": Shilts, journal entry.

quickly rose to leadership: "GPA Elects New Leader," *Oregon Daily Emerald*, February 1, 1973, box 11, file "Advocate," Randy Shilts Papers.

students were getting fed up: Torrie McAllister, "Senate Future May Be Up for Vote," *Oregon Daily Emerald*, February 13, 1973.

"One day in my": Randy Shilts, journal entry, June 12, 1973.

"My exposure as a gay Senator": Randy Shilts, letter to the editor, *Oregon Daily Emerald*, February 19, 1973.

Randy managed to win: Torrie McAllister, "Senate Abolishment Bill Passes by Large Majority," *Oregon Daily Emerald*, February 23, 1973.

placed his name on the ballot: Ken Mays, "Fee Committee Begins Budget Hearings Tonight," *Oregon Daily Emerald*, March 28, 1973.

"I was very powerful": Randy Shilts, interview by Marcus.

"With all this money": "Shilts: 'Incredible Programs We Could Do,'" *Oregon Daily Emerald*, March 30, 1973.

No COMPROMISE: Randy Shilts and Gloria Gonzalez, *Shilts and Gonzalez* (campaign pamphlet), 1973, box 2, file 9, Randy Shilts Papers.

their platform promised: Randy Shilts and Gloria Gonzalez, *Come Out for Shilts* (campaign pamphlet), 1973, box 2, file 9, Randy Shilts Papers; Associated Students of the University of Oregon, *ASUO Voters' Guide—Winter 1973*, box 2, file 9, Randy Shilts Papers.

a distant third: "Leo-Barnett and Marshall-Fitzpatrick Ticket for ASUO," *Oregon Daily Emerald*, May 2, 1973.

In its proposed budget: Art Bushnell, "Leo Vetoes IFC Recommendations: Eliminates Day Care Funding, Proposes Increase for AD," *Oregon Daily Emerald*, June 1, 1973.

The move drew a veto: "Budget Battles Between IFC and Leo Continue," *Oregon Daily Emerald*, June 20, 1973.

two leaders battled for weeks: James Russell, "Leo Criticizes AD Budget Cut: Calls IFC Irresponsible," *Oregon Daily Emerald*, July 16, 1973; James Russell, "Budget Causes Controversy," *Oregon Daily Emerald*, July 18, 1973.

Clark sided with Leo: Darrell Murray, "Commentary: Spiro Would Be Proud; AD Rhetoric Is No Substitute for the Facts," *Oregon Daily Emerald*, October 8, 1973; Bushnell, "Leo Vetoes IFC Recommendations."

Merrick first came to Eugene: Harriet Merrick, interview by the author, Eugene, OR, November 10, 2016. Unless otherwise noted, all quotes attributed to Harriet Merrick in this chapter are taken from this interview.

Thanks to Randy's budgeting: Randy Shilts, interview by Marcus.

"gay-straight sock hop": "Gay Peoples Alliance Sponsors Sock Hop," *Oregon Daily Emerald*, October 2, 1973.

To the sound of '60s: "The Gay Sock-Hop," *Oregon Daily Emerald*, October 9, 1973.

"There were three guys": Randy Shilts, interview by Marcus.

"The importance of the gay-straight hop": "Gay Sock-Hop," *Oregon Daily Emerald*.

"You have to be": Randy Shilts, interview by Marcus.

skirmishes with Greg Leo: Marianne Rinaldo, "ASUO Committee Upholds IFC," *Oregon Daily Emerald*, October 11, 1973; Marianne Rinaldo, "Leo-Barnett Recall Rejected 3 to 1," *Oregon Daily Emerald*, December 5, 1973.

In early 1974: Randy Shilts, journal entry, January 9, 1978, transcript by Finlay, box 1, file 5, Randy Shilts Papers.

he approached Carol: Carol Queen, interview by the author, San Francisco, August 25, 2017.

"While I try to be": Randy Shilts, journal entry, October 26, 1971, box 2, file 7, Randy Shilts Papers.

"We used to have": Bill Cagle, conversation with the author, San Francisco, August 26, 2016.

"I couldn't write": Randy Shilts, interview by Marcus.

"Your presentation must be": Willis Winter, comments to Randy Shilts, "They've Lost Their Father . . . Now What Will They See?," circa 1973, box 2, file 22, Randy Shilts Papers.

"Floating": Randy Shilts, "A Return to Babel: The Unanswered and the Unanswerable," circa 1973, box 2, file 22, Randy Shilts Papers.

writing extensively on gay-related topics: Randy Shilts, "Homophobia: A Case Study," September 27, 1973, box 2, file 22, Randy Shilts Papers; Randy Shilts, "Mass Media and Gay Liberation," circa 1973, box 2, file 22, Randy Shilts Papers.

joined the paper as managing editor: Masthead, *Oregon Daily Emerald*, May 9, 1974.

4. PRETTY BOY

Around a hot July bonfire: Randy Shilts, "The Summer of '74," box 2, file 18, Linda Alband Collection of Randy Shilts Materials. All events and most quotes in this section are attributed to the same primary source.

"a pompous, conceited": Shilts, "Summer of '74."

"I'll never forget": Shilts, "Summer of '74."

Randy would later recall: Randy Shilts, unpublished essay, circa 1979, box 19, folder "Summer Vacation '79," Randy Shilts Papers.

"This is a growth industry": Shilts, unpublished essay.

"happily engaged in every": Shilts, unpublished essay.

"Skip," a rough "he-man": Shilts, unpublished essay. In the unpublished essay, Randy used pseudonyms instead of real names.

"Remember," he growled: Shilts, unpublished essay.

His coworker Skip: Shilts, unpublished essay.

prepared for his autumn move: Randy Shilts, "The Summer of '74."

"I wanted this summer to be": Shilts, "Summer of '74."

"a small society of outcasts": Randy Shilts, unpublished essay, circa 1979.

"toads" and "worst cases": Shilts, unpublished essay.

5. THEY'D RATHER HAVE AN ALCOHOLIC

"In walks this fairly": Duncan McDonald, interview by the author, Eugene, OR, November 11, 2016.

"I was introduced": John Mitchell, interview by the author, Eugene, OR, November 11, 2016.

"It's kind of like": Drex Heikes, quoted in "The Message Is in the Media: Randy Shilts," *Northwest Gay Review*, December 1974–January 1975, box 2, folder 2, Linda Alband Collection of Randy Shilts Materials.

On weekends, they'd all: Mitchell, interview by the author.

"I wasn't sure": Mike Thoele, interview by the author, Junction City, OR, November 9, 2016.

Creative interviewing emphasizes: Ken Metzler, "Tips for Interviewing," University of Oregon, accessed April 8, 2022, https://darkwing.uoregon.edu/~sponder/j641 /Interview.htm.

"It just bristled": Thoele, interview by the author.

Randy landed interviews: Randy Shilts, "The Trembling Brunette Belle Whispered Yes," *Oregon Daily Emerald*, November 22, 1974.

"The whole thing is a show": Shilts, "Trembling Brunette Belle."

faculty submitted his piece: "Shilts Places in Hearst Contest," *Oregon Daily Emerald*, January 7, 1975.

"No matter how qualified": Randy Shilts, quoted in "Message Is in the Media," *Northwest Gay Review*.

"I figured . . . all you have to do": Randy Shilts, interview by Marcus.

In February a reworked version: Randy Shilts, "Fantasy Kingdoms of Rhinestone & Royalty," *Emerald Empire: Sunday Magazine of the Eugene Register-Guard*, February 9, 1975, box 23, folder 8, Randy Shilts Papers.

followed it up with an investigative piece: Randy Shilts, "Secret Identity Troubles Homosexuals," *Willamette Valley Observer*, February 1975, box 23, folder 8, Randy Shilts Papers.

The award letter: Randolph A. Hearst to Randy Shilts, March 17, 1975, box 11, folder 9, Randy Shilts Papers.

coveted invitation soon arrived: Amy Fink to Randy Shilts, April 21, 1975, box 11, folder 9, Randy Shilts Papers.

Randy arrived in San Francisco: Randy Shilts to Nathan Blumberg, July 21, 1975, box 11, folder 9, Randy Shilts Papers. Events from the Hearst competition are reconstructed from Shilts's correspondence with Blumberg. The Hearst Foundation was solicited for information; however, staff ceased communicating with the author in January 2017.

"And the lead of one of my stories": Randy Shilts, interview by Marcus.

"It was so devastating": Shilts, interview.

The university's president: Robert D. Clark to Randy Shilts, May 22, 1975, box 11, folder 9, Randy Shilts Papers.

"I was outraged": Roy Halvorsen, interview by the author, Eugene, OR, November 11, 2016.

The School of Journalism's dean: John Crawford to Ira Walsh, May 30, 1975, box 11, folder 9, Randy Shilts Papers.

"If we upgraded the score": Ira Walsh to John Crawford, June 2, 1975, box 11, folder 9, Randy Shilts Papers.

"It is conceivable" Randy Shilts to Blumberg.

"They said they made": Randy Shilts, interview by Marcus.

"I like these streets": Randy Shilts, journal entry, circa July 1975, box 24, folder 3, Randy Shilts Papers.

"Once their cars break down": Shilts, journal entry.

"After graduating from college": Shilts, journal entry.

"Here's the scoop": Randy Shilts to Ann Neuenschwander and Chris Schroeder, August 28, 1975, shared with the author on November 17, 2015.

Gregory-Lewis had invited Randy: Sasha Gregory-Lewis to Randy Shilts, May 7, 1975, box 11, folder 5, Randy Shilts Papers.

"Sorry to hear about": Sasha Gregory-Lewis to Randy Shilts, June 27, 1975, box 11, folder 5, Randy Shilts Papers.

Randy's Advocate debut: Randy Shilts, "What's Happening with Gay Studies U.S.A.?" *Advocate*, June 18, 1975, courtesy of Jean-Nickolaus Tretter Collection in Gay, Lesbian, Bisexual and Transgender Studies at the University of Minnesota.

"Randy Shilts is an up and coming": Shilts, "What's Happening."

"We'll overlook the fact": "Outrageous," June 3, 1975, *Advocate*, box 2, file 17, Linda Alband Collection of Randy Shilts Materials.

The paper would pay him: Gregory-Lewis to Randy Shilts, June 27, 1975.

encouraged him to focus on national stories: Randy Shilts to Sasha Gregory-Lewis, August 8, 1975, box 11, folder 5, Randy Shilts Papers; Randy Shilts to Sasha Gregory-Lewis, September 8, 1975, box 11, folder 5, Randy Shilts Papers.

Randy caught word of probate proceedings: Randy Shilts, "Ruling Due in Parents Test Case," *Advocate*, September 24, 1975, courtesy of Jean-Nickolaus Tretter Collection.

"The impartial administration of justice": Randy Shilts, "Foster Homes for Gay Children—Justice or Prejudice?" *Advocate*, December 17, 1975, courtesy of Jean-Nickolaus Tretter Collection.

Desperate for cash: Randy Shilts to Charles L. Gould, September 16, 1975, box 11, folder 9, Randy Shilts Papers; Roy Halvorsen to Randy Shilts, October 10, 1975, box 11, folder 9, Randy Shilts Papers.

"I wish merely to communicate": Roy Halvorsen to Ira Walsh, November 26, 1975, box 11, folder 9, Randy Shilts Papers.

In the end, everyone stuck: Halvorsen, interview by the author.

"Sooner or later I better sit down": Randy Shilts, journal entry, November 30, 1975, Moscow, ID, box 11, folder 36, Randy Shilts Papers.

"I seem to be nobody": Randy Shilts, journal entry, December 2, 1975, Moscow, ID, box 11, folder 36, Randy Shilts Papers.

"To be sure, I never": Randy Shilts, journal entry, November 30, 1975.

he'd write up and phone in his stories: Randy Shilts to Sasha Gregory-Lewis, November 17, 1975, box 11, folder 5, Randy Shilts Papers.

After an October fling: Randy Shilts, journal entry, November 30, 1975; Randy Shilts to Sasha Gregory-Lewis, October 27, 1975, box 11, folder 5, Randy Shilts Papers.

Gregory-Lewis sent back: Sasha Gregory-Lewis to Randy Shilts, October 31, 1975, box 11, folder 5, Randy Shilts Papers.

"How inadequate I feel": Randy Shilts, journal entry, November 30, 1975.

"A major thing which": Shilts, journal entry.

profiled gay activist Gib Preston: Randy Shilts, "You Can't Keep Anything Quiet," *Advocate*, February 11, 1976, courtesy of Jean-Nickolaus Tretter Collection.

open road took him to Vancouver: "Homophobia Backfired When Stonewall Went House-Hunting," *Advocate*, November 5, 1975, courtesy of Jean-Nickolaus Tretter Collection.

"I could relate": Randy Shilts, journal entry, December 14, 1975, Seattle, WA, box 11, folder 36, Randy Shilts Papers.

"A key focus of the center": Shilts, journal entry.

"A part of me says": Shilts, journal entry.

only story he had left to cover: Randy Shilts to Sasha Gregory-Lewis, November 17, 1975.

"We had terrific sex together": Randy Shilts, journal entry, December 14, 1975.

"How could anybody not like you?": Shilts, journal entry.

Thinking back on their lovemaking: Shilts, journal entry.

"Don't try to opt": Shilts, journal entry.

"I'm brimming with ideas": Randy Shilts to Sasha Gregory-Lewis, December 16, 1975, box 11, folder 5, Randy Shilts Papers.

6. THE MISFIT OF CASTRO STREET

"Does he know what it is": Randy Shilts, journal entry, January 3, 1976, Half Moon Bay, CA, box 11, folder 3, Randy Shilts Papers.

her first and most frequent visitor: Alband, interview by the author. Unless otherwise noted, all quotes attributed to Alband in this chapter are taken from this interview.

"I was a deejay": Howie Klein, telephone interview by the author, January 28, 2020. Unless otherwise noted, all quotes attributed to Howie Klein in this chapter are taken from this interview.

"The Advocate is no place": Randy Shilts, journal entry, January 9, 1976, box 26, Reporter's Notebooks, Randy Shilts Papers.

His vision for that next level: Shilts, journal entry.

OK, Shilts: Shilts, journal entry.

suggesting that addiction could be endemic: Randy Shilts, "Alcoholism: A Look in Depth at How a National Menace Is Affecting the Gay Community," *Advocate*, February 25, 1976, courtesy of Jean-Nickolaus Tretter Collection.

"Out of sight, removed": Shilts, "Alcoholism."

Randy's most extensive writing: Randy Shilts to Robert McQueen and Sasha Gregory-Lewis, January 19, 1976, box 12, box 6, Randy Shilts Papers.

At his suggestion: Shilts to McQueen and Gregory-Lewis.

labeled alcoholism "an insidious disease": "An Insidious Disease: Alcoholism," *Advocate*, February 25, 1976, courtesy of Jean-Nickolaus Tretter Collection.

"Permanents are the biggest thing": Randy Shilts, "Curls for the Curly: A Permanent Injunction," *Advocate*, March 24, 1976, courtesy of Jean-Nickolaus Tretter Collection.

In the same Tax Day issue: Randy Shilts, "April Fool! When the Tax Dollar Is Divvied Up This Year, Gay People Will Again Get Less, Though We Paid More," *Advocate*, April 7, 1976, courtesy of Jean-Nickolaus Tretter Collection; Randy Shilts, "Strictly Between the Lines," *Advocate*, April 7, 1976, courtesy of Jean-Nickolaus Tretter Collection.

"Homosexuality doesn't sell": Shilts, "Strictly Between the Lines."

"Gay V.D. workers": Randy Shilts, "V.D. and Other Sexually Transmitted Diseases in the Gay Community," *Advocate*, April 21, 1976, courtesy of Jean-Nickolaus Tretter Collection.

"Mr. Shilts obviously did": W.T. [pseud.], letter to the editor, *Advocate*, March 10, 1976, courtesy of Jean-Nickolaus Tretter Collection.

"Mr. Shilts, God Bless!": Michael Austin, letter to the editor, *Advocate*, March 24, 1976, courtesy of Jean-Nickolaus Tretter Collection.

critics also put in a word: Russell Hunter, letter to the editor, *Advocate*, March 24, 1976, courtesy of Jean-Nickolaus Tretter Collection.

In midspring: Randy Shilts to Ann Neuenschwander, April 5, 1976, shared with the author on November 17, 2015; Randy Shilts to Ann Neuenschwander, February 10, 1976, shared with the author on November 17, 2015.

"I've got quite a bit": Randy Shilts to Ann Neuenschwander, May 15, 1976, shared with the author on November 17, 2015.

"I've realized how much": Shilts to Neuenschwander.

"We're to see each other again": Randy Shilts, journal entry, May 21, 1976, transcript by Finlay, box 1, file 5, Randy Shilts Papers.

Why couldn't that be him?: Shilts, journal entry.

"Would if my love": Shilts, journal entry.

"So I've chased": Shilts, journal entry.

"My head is filled": Shilts, journal entry.

"Oh, son": Walter Caplan, interview by the author, San Francisco, March 12, 2016. Unless otherwise noted, all quotes attributed to Walter Caplan in this chapter are taken from this interview.

Randy noted an impressive flurry: Randy Shilts, "A Most Conventional Convention," *Advocate*, August 11, 1976, courtesy of Jean-Nickolaus Tretter Collection.

"Gay rights have yet to emerge": Shilts, "Most Conventional Convention."

"The dark moods didn't make": Randy Shilts, "The Decade's Best-Kept Secret: Hepatitis Doesn't Come from Needles," *Advocate*, January 12, 1977, courtesy of Jean-Nickolaus Tretter Collection.

"People at work are getting worried": Randy Shilts to Ann Neuenschwander, August 7, 1976, shared with the author on November 17, 2015.

"I've been so god damn miserably": Randy Shilts to Ann Neuenschwander, August 14, 1976, shared with the author on November 17, 2015.

"I think it's because": Shilts to Neuenschwander.

"My doctor thinks": Randy Shilts to Ann Neuenschwander, August 18, 1976, shared with the author on November 17, 2015.

He fully returned to work: Randy Shilts to Ann Neuenschwander, circa December 1976, shared with the author on November 17, 2015.

"There is a greater possibility": Randy Shilts, "Decade's Best-Kept Secret."

Randy would cite her again: Randy Shilts, "A New Plague on Our House," *Advocate*, April 20, 1977, courtesy of Jean-Nickolaus Tretter Collection.

"Cute little devil": Randy Shilts, journal entry, December 31, 1977, transcript by Finlay, box 1, file 5, Randy Shilts Papers.

"He said he had to get something": Shilts, journal entry.

7. THE FOREST FOR THE TREES

"This probably will be": Randy Shilts to Ann Neuenschwander, January 24, 1977, shared with the author on November 17, 2015.

he'd gone to Oklahoma: "Community '77: Surprises in the Sooner State," *Advocate*, February 23, 1977, courtesy of Jean-Nickolaus Tretter Collection.

"I saw him standing": Randy Shilts to Ann Neuenschwander, January 24, 1977.

Diminutive and soft-spoken: Shilts to Neuenschwander.

"The main reason he's coming here": Shilts to Neuenschwander.

"Danny isn't like me": Randy Shilts to Ann Neuenschwander, February 3, 1977, shared with the author on November 17, 2015.

They marked Dan's arrival: Shilts to Neuenschwander; Randy Shilts to Ann Neuenschwander, May 26, 1977, shared with the author on November 17, 2015.

"I thought that might be a feather": George Osterkamp, interview by the author, San Francisco, August 25, 2017. Unless otherwise noted, all quotes attributed to George Osterkamp in this chapter are taken from this interview.

threw a multitude of ideas: Randy Shilts, memo to George Osterkamp, January 31, 1977, box 14, folder 3, Randy Shilts Papers.

"My whole world is trembling": Randy Shilts to Ann Neuenschwander, February 3, 1977.

"When you're looking at the late '70s": Laurie Garrett, interview by the author, New York, NY, June 23, 2017. Unless otherwise noted, all quotes attributed to Laurie Garrett in this chapter are taken from this interview.

appearing on Bay Area airwaves: Randy Shilts, "Lesbian Mother Child Custody Case," KQED News, March 8, 1977, Bay Area Television Archive at San Francisco State University, https://diva.sfsu.edu/collections/sfbatv/bundles/189769; Randy Shilts, "Gay Teachers in San Francisco," KQED News, May 24, 1977, Bay Area Television Archive at San Francisco State University, https://diva.sfsu.edu/collections/sfbatv /bundles/189772; *The Untold Tales of Armistead Maupin*, directed by Jennifer M. Kroot (The Film Collaborative, 2017), 1:31.

"The thing that pissed him off": Ken Maley, interview by the author, San Francisco, August 24, 2017. Unless otherwise noted, all quotes attributed to Ken Maley in this chapter are taken from this interview.

a chillier reception from the Advocate: Randy Shilts to Sasha Gregory-Lewis, April 13, 1977, box 14, folder 17, Randy Shilts Papers.

In addition to spending work time: Randy Shilts to Ann Neuenschwander, February 3, 1977.

When he flew to Miami: Randy Shilts, journal entry, December 31, 1977, transcript by Finlay, box 1, file 5, Randy Shilts Papers.

they'd reneged on their promise: Randy Shilts to Ann Neuenschwander, May 26, 1977.

assembled another array of sources: Randy Shilts, "Gay Youth: The Lonely Young," *Advocate*, June 1, 1977, courtesy of Jean-Nickolaus Tretter Collection.

"Ours is a culture": J. Thornhill, letter to the editor, *Advocate*, July 13, 1977, courtesy of Jean-Nickolaus Tretter Collection.

gays laid the blame: Randy Shilts, "Death in San Francisco," *Advocate*, August 10, 1977, courtesy of Jean-Nickolaus Tretter Collection.

"People were very, very angry": Randy Alfred, interview by Randy Shilts, in "Gay Militancy," KQED News, June 21, 1977, Bay Area Television Archive at San Francisco State University, https://diva.sfsu.edu/collections/sfbatv/bundles/189495.

Maley acting as his informal agent: Randy Shilts, journal entry, December 31, 1977.

Ken appreciatively snapped his picture: Ken Maley, photograph of Randy Shilts, September 2, 1977, box 31, Ken Maley Papers, 1967–2015 (GLC 174), courtesy of James C. Hormel LGBTQIA Center, San Francisco Public Library, San Francisco.

"Randy Shilts was a camera store customer": Dan Nicoletta, telephone interview by the author, July 21, 2020. Unless otherwise noted, all quotes attributed to Dan Nicoletta in this chapter are taken from this interview.

"There was a whole cadre": Cleve Jones, interview by the author. Unless otherwise noted, all quotes attributed to Cleve Jones in this chapter are taken from this interview.

"Randy was like a young punk kid": Anne Kronenberg, telephone interview by the author, September 9, 2016. Unless otherwise noted, all quotes attributed to Anne Kronenberg in this chapter are taken from this interview.

an even-handed profile: Randy Shilts, "Candidates: They're Off and Running, but . . . Will a Gay Candidate Win?" *Advocate*, November 30, 1977, courtesy of Jean-Nickolaus Tretter Collection.

Randy and camera crew joined: Randy Shilts, journal entry, January 9, 1978, transcript by Finlay, box 1, file 5, Randy Shilts Papers.

pretty big hints to his parents: Randy Shilts, interview by Marcus.

"It's fine with me": Randy Shilts, journal entry, January 24, 1978, transcript by Finlay, box 1, file 5, Randy Shilts Papers.

Youngest son David's condition: Gary Shilts, interview by the author.

"I just couldn't think": Randy Shilts, journal entry, January 24, 1978.

he confessed to Daniel: Randy Shilts, journal entry, April 4, 1978, transcript by Finlay, box 1, file 5, Randy Shilts Papers.

Whenever Belva Davis heard: Belva Davis, interview by the author, San Francisco, March 16, 2016. Unless otherwise noted, all quotes attributed to Belva Davis in this chapter are taken from this interview.

"In fact, it is those skills": Randy Shilts, journal entry, April 19, 1978, transcript by Finlay, box 1, file 5, Randy Shilts Papers.

"If these guys find out": Randy Shilts, "Locked Up with the Jailhouse Queens," *San Francisco Chronicle*, April 7, 1978.

attended the inaugural session: Randy Shilts, "Go EST Young Man," *New West*, June 19, 1978, box 2, folder 75, Linda Alband Collection of Randy Shilts Materials.

"I can't stand when people dislike me": Randy Shilts, journal entry, June 9, 1978, transcript by Finlay, box 1, file 5, Randy Shilts Papers.

"The adrenaline gets zooming": Randy Shilts, journal entry, June 24, 1978, transcript by Finlay, box 1, file 5, Randy Shilts Papers.

Randy canvassed the crowd: Randy Shilts, "Gay Freedom Parade, 1978," KQED News, June 26, 1978, Bay Area Television Archive at San Francisco State University, https://diva.sfsu.edu/collections/sfbatv/bundles/189493.

"It might be easy to miss": Shilts, "Gay Freedom Parade."

the two had already struck up a rapport: Randy Shilts, "A Gay Journalist's Friendship with Briggs," *San Francisco Chronicle*, October 31, 1978, box 2, folder 74, Linda Alband Collection of Randy Shilts Materials.

Randy took the story of Prop 6: Randy Shilts, "Move Over, Anita: 'In Politics, Anything Is Fair,'" *Village Voice*, October 16, 1978.

"The bottom choice": Shilts, "Move Over, Anita."

"I never took his protestations": Randy Shilts, "Gay Journalist's Friendship."

"Sure. Randy and I": Shilts, "Gay Journalist's Friendship."

Belva recalled the fierce dressing down: Davis, interview by the author.

"on behalf of all of us": Harvey Milk to Randy Shilts, October 16, 1978, box 9, file "Fan Mail," Randy Shilts Papers.

"Private V Public Briggs": Randy Shilts, "Gay Journalist's Friendship."

defeat for Prop 6: The Times of Harvey Milk, directed by Rob Epstein (TC Films International, 1984), 1:30.

a mocking typewritten "interview": Arthur Evans [The Red Queen, pseud.], "The Human Side of Hitler," circa 1978, box 5, file "Ephemera—Individuals," International Gay Information Center Collection, Manuscripts and Archives Division, New York Public Library.

8. SHADOW OF A DREAM

"Good evening": A Closer Look, KQED San Francisco, November 28, 1978, viewed by the author on February 5, 2018, in the home of Belva Davis.

Davis would remember: Belva Davis, comments to the author, San Francisco, February 5, 2018.

"I was having dinner with Chuck": Michael Denneny, interview by the author, New York, NY, June 23, 2017. Unless otherwise noted, all quotes attributed to Michael Denneny in this chapter are taken from this interview.

"miserable": Randy Shilts, journal entry, December 25, 1979, transcript by Finlay, box 1, file 5, Randy Shilts Papers.

mother-in-law Norma had greeted: Dawn Shilts, interview by the author, Kalamazoo, MI, August 13, 2015.

The actors involved: Randy Shilts, "The Life and Death of Harvey Milk," Christopher Street, March 1979, box 17, file 24, Randy Shilts Papers.

"'All the forces in the world'": Shilts, "Life and Death of Harvey Milk."

alliances would not be forged: Shilts, "Life and Death of Harvey Milk."

"Let the bullets that rip": Shilts, "Life and Death of Harvey Milk."

"It was a really great story": Harry Britt to Randy Shilts, March 17, 1979, box 29, file 5, Randy Shilts Papers.

"I feel some responsibility": David Goodstein to Charles Ortleb, March 14, 1979, box 29, file 4, Randy Shilts Papers.

"If Mr. Goodstein has difficulty": Randy Shilts, letter to the editor, Christopher Street, May 1979, courtesy of Jean-Nickolaus Tretter Collection.

"Out of the bars": Katy Butler, "A Bloody Protest at City Hall: Verdict Angers Gays," San Francisco Chronicle, May 22, 1979.

"Undirected anger": Randy Shilts, notepad labeled "Riots," May 21, 1979, box 26, Randy Shilts Papers.

"More than glass got shattered": Randy Shilts, "White Night Riot Aftermath I," KQED News, May 22, 1979, Bay Area Television Archive at San Francisco State University, https://diva.sfsu.edu/bundles/189781.

"In the gay community": Randy Shilts, "White Night Riot Aftermath II," KQED News, May 22, 1979, Bay Area Television Archive at San Francisco State University, https://diva.sfsu.edu/bundles/189782.

"In the past": Randy Shilts, "White Night Riot Aftermath III," KQED News, May 22, 1979, Bay Area Television Archive at San Francisco State University, https://diva.sfsu.edu/bundles/189783.

"I had two people inside me fighting": Shilts, "White Night Riot Aftermath III."

PIGS START VIOLENCE: Shilts, "White Night Riot Aftermath III."

At Oakland's independent station: Randy Shilts, interview by Marcus.

"The station was kind of dropping off": Randy Shandobil, interview by the author, Oakland, CA, August 24, 2016.

"Oh, I heard you got handcuffed": Cleve Jones, interview by the author. Unless otherwise noted, all quotes attributed to Cleve Jones in this chapter are taken from this interview.

In addition to television: Randy Shilts, interview by Randy Alfred, *The Gay Life*, KSAN radio, May 10, 1980, courtesy of Gay, Lesbian, Bisexual, Transgender Historical Society, https://www.archive.org/download/TheGayLife/glbths_1991-24_2_053_sc.mp3; Randy Shilts, résumé, circa 1980, box 3, file 4, Randy Shilts Papers.

CBS News came to him: Randy Shilts, "Cleve Jones Rising," *Chirstopher Street*, November/December 1980, box 23, files 2–3, Randy Shilts Papers.

"Buttfucking and blowjobs": Randy Shilts, interview by Dan Turner, "*B.A.R.* Interviews Writer Randy Shilts on Harvey Milk," *Bay Area Reporter*, November 20, 1980, box 29, file 5, Randy Shilts Papers.

his own feature on Cleve: Randy Shilts, "Cleve Jones Rising."

Randy even considered fashioning: Randy Shilts, "City Hall '79," box 2, folder 26, Linda Alband Collection of Randy Shilts Materials.

Randy drafted a retrospective: Randy Shilts, "From Homophile to LAMGs," circa 1979, box 19, file 25, Randy Shilts Papers.

"Here is where": Shilts, "Homophile."

"The gay phenomenon represented": Shilts, "Homophile."

"Unless pressured by": Shilts, "Homophile."

organizing "nostalgic" marches: Shilts, "Homophile."

"The nation's gay neighborhoods" Shilts, "Homophile."

"During the '70s": Shilts, "Homophile."

the *"gayttoization" of the Castro*: Shilts, "Homophile."

"In essence, we've lost the shame": Shilts, "Homophile."

"Within a few years": Shilts, "Homophile."

"Shilts sauntered into the office": Randy Shilts to Michael Denneny, circa 1981, box 29, file 1, Randy Shilts Papers.

research and writing finally commenced: Patricia Holt, "PW Interviews: Randy Shilts," *Publishers Weekly*, March 19, 1982, box 31, file "Publicity/Reviews," Randy Shilts Papers.

drove to Belva Davis's house: Davis, interview by the author.

KQED announced the cancellation: Randy Shilts, interview by Marcus.

"By then I had been on TV": Shilts, interview.

"I think if you tell people": Randy Shilts, interview by Turner.

"where each of the characters": Shilts, interview.

whom he'd recently pilloried: Randy Shilts, "Who Is David Goodstein?" *Blueboy*, June, 1980, box 2, file 93, Linda Alband Collection of Randy Shilts Materials.

"From my perspective": Nicoletta, telephone interview by the author.

"As I described my vantage": Michael Wong, journal, October 1980, shared with the author on August 20, 2017.

Although he'd previously interviewed: Randy Shilts to Robert Milk, October 31, 1980, box 29, file 1, Randy Shilts Papers.

"This book does not represent": Shilts to Milk.

led Sipple to become estranged: Jad Abumrad and Robert Krulwich, "Oliver Sipple," *Radiolab* (podcast), produced by Latif Nasser, WNYC, September 22, 2017, https://www.wnycstudios.org/podcasts/radiolab/articles/oliver-sipple.

Denneny received Randy's second installment: Randy Shilts to Denneny, circa 1981.

manuscript was probably littered: Shilts to Denneny.

"No long narration": Shilts to Denneny.

"I, of course, had read": Steve Newman, interview by the author, Sarasota, FL, January 5, 2016. Unless otherwise noted, all quotes attributed to Steve Newman in this chapter are taken from this interview.

9. THE BEST OF TIMES (THE WORST OF TIMES)

snapped a photo of his lover: Steve Newman, photograph of Randy Shilts, n.d., shown to the author on January 4, 2016.

"I thought I saw": Randy Shilts to Steve Newman, April 5, 1981, shown to the author on January 4, 2016.

"I love you": Randy Shilts, note to Steve Newman, n.d., shown to the author on January 4, 2016.

"I picked it up": Newman, interview by the author. Unless otherwise noted, all quotes attributed to Newman in this chapter are taken from this interview.

Steve snapped a picture: Steve Newman, photograph of Randy Shilts, n.d., shown to the author on January 4, 2016.

gave way to healthier choices: Randy Shilts, journal entry, January 2, 1982, box 1, file 5, Randy Shilts Papers.

"I need you so much": Randy Shilts to Steve Newman, May 13, 1981, shown to the author on January 4, 2016.

"Randy and I both knew": Randy Alfred, interview by the author, San Francisco, March 11, 2016. Unless otherwise noted, all quotes attributed to Randy Alfred in this chapter are taken from this interview.

"All along": Randy Shilts to Steve Newman, August 16, 1981, shown to the author on January 4, 2016.

"Everybody was great": Randy Shilts, interview by Marcus.

"There were a bunch": Katy Butler, telephone interview by the author, November 8, 2019.

"I would say": Susan Sward, interview by the author, San Francisco, March 14, 2016.

Randy's initial reporting: Randy Shilts, "Report on Ending Public Drunkenness," *San Francisco Chronicle*, August 20, 1981.

Gay-related features: Ransdell Pierson, "Uptight on Gay News," *Columbia Journalism Review*, March/April 1982, box 21, file "'82 Clippings," Randy Shilts Papers.

Randy bumped into Anne Kronenberg: Kronenberg, telephone interview by the author.

first raised concerns: M. S. Gottlieb et al., "Pneumocystis Pneumonia—Los Angeles," *Morbidity and Mortality Weekly Report* 30, no. 21 (June 5, 1981): https://www.cdc.gov/mmwr/preview/mmwrhtml/june_5.htm.

Perlman quickly followed up: "A Pneumonia That Strikes Gay Males," *San Francisco Chronicle*, June 6, 1981.

New York Times entered the fray: Lawrence K. Altman, "Rare Cancer Seen in 41 Homosexuals," *New York Times*, July 3, 1981, https://www.nytimes.com/1981/07/03/us/rare-cancer-seen-in-41-homosexuals.html.

first in-depth human-interest story: Randy Shilts, "A Gentle Look at an Autistic Brother," *San Francisco Chronicle*, January 19, 1982.

"This is The Gay Life": Randy Shilts, interview by Randy Alfred, *The Gay Life*, KSAN radio, February 28, 1982, courtesy of Gay, Lesbian, Bisexual, Transgender Historical Society, https://www.archive.org/download/TheGayLife2/glbths_1991-24_2_123_sc.mp3.

"To Randy—My colleague": Randy Shilts, autograph to Randy Alfred, San Francisco, February 25, 1982, shared with the author on February 5, 2018.

the *"selling"* of Harvey's legend: Allen White, "Harvey Milk Marketed in a Different Castro," *Bay Area Reporter*, February 25, 1982.

"We ran out of space": Larry Bush, telephone interview by the author, July 21, 2020.

"Randy Shilts has written": Randy Alfred, "Milk Bio Flawed," *Sentinel*, March 4, 1982.

Alfred had some say: Alfred, interview by the author.

"[Alfred] wanted to be": San Francisco Beat (dial-in radio news service), March 12–13, 1982, recording shared with the author by Randy Alfred on March 21, 2016.

"If it hadn't been in Shilts's": San Francisco Beat, March 12–13, 1982.

"The jealous types": Randy Shilts to Michael Denneny, February 28, 1982, box 1, folder 2, Linda Alband Collection of Randy Shilts Materials.

Jim Gordon wrote to Randy: Jim Gordon to Randy Shilts, March 2, 1982 [misdated 1978], box 13, folder 28, Harvey Milk Papers—Scott Smith Collection (GLC 35), courtesy of James C. Hormel LGBTQIA Center, San Francisco Public Library, San Francisco.

The Mayor of Castro Street performed: Keith Kahla, e-mail to the author, July 13, 2017.

attempts to jump-start a film project: Leah Garchik, Personals, *San Francisco Chronicle*, March 12, 1991.

activists demanded that any biopic: Randy Shilts and Scott Smith, "Please, Let's Make This Movie," February 20, 1992, box 1, folder 7, Linda Alband Collection of Randy Shilts Materials.

"Why do they keep wanting": Cleve Jones, interview by the author.

"Thank you for your interest": Randy Shilts, note to Steve Newman, n.d., shown to the author on January 4, 2016.

Randy Alfred had been generating: Bobbi Campbell, interview by Randy Alfred, *The Gay Life*, KSAN radio, January 10, 1982, courtesy of Gay, Lesbian, Bisexual, Transgender Historical Society, https://www.archive.org/download/TheGayLife2/glbths_1991-24_2_118_sc.mp3.

managed to secure a lengthy interview: Marcus Conant and Paul Volberding, interview by Randy Alfred, *The Gay Life*, KSAN radio, January 10, 1982.

Shilts's arrival on the GRID beat: Randy Shilts, "The Strange, Deadly Diseases That Strike Gay Men," *San Francisco Chronicle*, May 13, 1982.

able to focus almost exclusively: Steve Newman, e-mail to the author, October 24, 2018.

"I must admit the weatherman": Randy Shilts to *San Francisco Chronicle* newsroom, July 26, 1982, box 3, folder 3, Linda Alband Collection of Randy Shilts Materials.

the story of a young man: Paul Lorch, "KS Diagnosis, Takes Life," *Bay Area Reporter*, December 23, 1982, https://archive.org/download/BAR_19821223/BAR_19821223.pdf.

10. 1983

"It was like being": Andrew Moss, interview by the author, San Francisco, March 14, 2016. Unless otherwise noted, all quotes attributed to Andrew Moss in this chapter are taken from this interview.

"I thought it was real important": Randy Shilts, interview by Marcus.

leaking it to the press: Randy Shilts, *And the Band Played On: Politics, People, and the AIDS Epidemic* (New York: St. Martin's, 1987), 255.

Randy agreed to leave out: Randy Shilts, interview by Marcus.

"Worst crisis ever": Bill Kraus, Harvey Milk Democratic Club speech notes, March 22, 1983, box 34, file 4, Randy Shilts Papers.

The next day, Randy's story: Randy Shilts, "Study of S.F. Neighborhoods: Startling Finding on 'Gay Disease,'" *San Francisco Chronicle*, March 23, 1983.

International Lesbian and Gay Freedom Day: Peter Collier and David Horowitz, "Whitewash," *California*, July 1983, box 71, Laurie Garrett Papers, MSS 2013-03, Archives and Special Collections, University of California, San Francisco.

"These questions are simply": Randy Shilts, story draft, March 24, 1983, box 21, file 7, Randy Shilts Papers.

"Gary Walsh and I": Randy Shilts, "Traitors or Heroes? Notes from the Plague," *New York Native*, July 16–29, 1984, box 4, file "Misc.," Randy Shilts Papers.

"I would say that Gary": Matthew Krieger, telephone interview by the author, December 11, 2018.

"The pain would grip me": Randy Shilts, "Traitors or Heroes?"

"He's living it": Butler, telephone interview by the author.

"I mean, he was locked": David Perlman, interview by the author, San Francisco, March 17, 2016.

"up the noise level": Paul Lorch, "Gay Men Dying: Shifting Gears, Part I," *Bay Area Reporter*, March 17, 1983.

even Randy initially applauded: Randy Shilts, letter to the editor, *Bay Area Reporter*, March 31, 1983.

"sewer system into a playpen": Paul Lorch, "Gay Men Dying: Shifting Gears, Part II," *Bay Area Reporter*, March 24, 1983.

would lead to the "warehousing": Paul Lorch, "Gay Men Dying: Shifting Gears, Part III," *Bay Area Reporter*, March 31, 1983.

"I was trying to get": Mervyn Silverman, interview by the author, El Cerrito, CA, March 16, 2016. Unless otherwise noted, all quotes attributed to Mervyn Silverman in this chapter are taken from this interview.

"How do we pursue": Randy Shilts, interview by Marcus.

"Mayor Dianne Feinstein's administration": Randy Shilts, "The Politics of AIDS," *San Francisco Chronicle*, June 11, 1983.

Toklas leaders vehemently objected: Randy Stallings et al., letter to the editor, *Bay Area Reporter*, June 2, 1983.

"In eight years as a journalist": Collier and Horowitz, "Whitewash."

"I just told them": Randy Shilts, interview by Marcus.

"There was a lot of stress": Newman, interview by the author. Unless otherwise noted, all quotes attributed to Newman in this chapter are taken from this interview.

For him, some wine: Randy Shilts [Martin S., pseud.], "Young, Gifted, and Hooked," *San Francisco Focus*, January 1986, box 2, folder 111, Linda Alband Collection of Randy Shilts Materials.

fodder for Randy to later accuse: Randy Shilts to Steve Newman, n.d., shown to the author on January 4, 2016.

"I didn't disapprove": Mark Thompson, *Advocate Days & Other Stories* (Bar Harbor, ME: Queer Mojo, 2009), 46.

"the kinkiest garage sale": Randy Shilts, "A Gay Bathhouse Closes Its Doors in S.F.," *San Francisco Chronicle*, July 11, 1983.

bothered by Randy's lack: Thompson, *Advocate Days*, 47.

scribble out an obituary: Randy Shilts, draft obituary of Norma Shilts, box 23, file "Misc.," Randy Shilts Papers.

"From my California perspective": Randy Shilts, "Burying the Dream in Blue-Collar Michigan," *San Francisco Chronicle*, August 15, 1983.

All week long, Reed wondered: Reed Shilts, interview by the author.

Pulling a joint: Gary Shilts, interview by the author.

"the Chronicle's most famous token": Gary Schweikhart, "The Real AIDS Victims," *Sentinel*, July 21, 1983.

"Why," he noted: Randy Alfred, "Fact & Fiction," *Sentinel*, July 21, 1983.

"I just thought it was an issue": Randy Shilts, interview by Marcus.

"I would see him all the time": Garrett, interview by the author.

"People who are politically committed": Randy Shilts, interview by Marcus.

"I don't get any better": Shilts, interview.

"AIDS is not politics": Randy Shilts, "A Mother's Torment," *San Francisco Chronicle*, October 7, 1983.

another dispiriting bombshell: Randy Shilts, "Florida's Theory on AIDS 'Dumping,'" *San Francisco Chronicle*, October 11, 1983.

story attracted national attention: Randy Shilts, "AIDS Patient from Florida Dies at S.F. General Hospital," *San Francisco Chronicle*, October 21, 1983.

Dianne Feinstein, herself: Shilts, "AIDS Patient from Florida Dies."

Gainesville officials had defended: "The MacDonald Case," *San Francisco Chronicle*, October 21, 1983.

"It is sad that a young man": Randy Shilts, "AIDS Patient from Florida Dies."

funding commitment already surpassed: Dianne Feinstein, e-mail to the author via Justin Kramer, April 28, 2022.

collected an honorable mention: "The *Chronicle* Wins Awards in Press Club Competition," *San Francisco Chronicle*, November 5, 1983.

"What's the hardest part": Randy Shilts, "'The Establishment Lurches into Action," This World: Special AIDS Report, *San Francisco Chronicle*, January 15, 1984.

The disease had been no laughing matter: Randy Shilts, *And the Band Played On*, 382.

"Maybe we should have seen it coming": Randy Shilts, social impact story draft, November 13, 1983, box 21, folder 7, Randy Shilts Papers.

patronage at the bathhouses: Randy Shilts, "Some AIDS Patients Still Going to the Baths," *San Francisco Chronicle*, November 15, 1983.

"I had health people saying": Randy Shilts, interview by Marcus.

Randy once confided: Gary Shilts, interview by the author.

"Every time I've had risky sex": Paul Reed, "Looking for Mr. Safesex, Part II—What Is There After Sleaze . . . ?" *Bay Area Reporter*, November 3, 1983.

some men were organizing private parties: Randy Shilts, "'Of Course, Nobody Had Planned on This,'" This World: Special AIDS Report, *San Francisco Chronicle*, January 15, 1984.

called a meeting to make decisions: Leah Garchik, interview by the author, San Francisco, March 17, 2016.

"By 1983," he later wrote: Randy Shilts, *And the Band Played On*, 209.

11. GAY TRAITORS

The strains of "Let It Be": Randy Shilts, *And the Band Played On*, 427.

"It's not beautiful": Randy Shilts, "Traitors or Heroes?"

Randy personally penned: Randy Shilts, "Psychologist Gary Walsh Dies," *San Francisco Chronicle*, February 22, 1984.

"Octavia Hayes" related: Octavia Hayes, "Plot to Shame Shilts," *Sentinel*, March 15, 1984.

parole of Dan White brought protesters: Randy Shilts, "No Repeat of 'White Night' Expected," *San Francisco Chronicle*, January 5, 1984.

"important and needed": Allen White to William German, January 22, 1984, box 9, file "Fan Mail '84," Randy Shilts Papers.

Randy again questioned the effectiveness: Randy Shilts, "AIDS Expert Says Bathhouses Should Close," *San Francisco Chronicle*, February 3, 1984.

In a study by local therapist: Shilts, "AIDS Expert."

"I was good friends with Bill Kraus": Bush, telephone interview by the author.

"We discovered that the bathhouse owners": Michael Housh, interview by the author, San Francisco, August 24, 2016.

an "attack to close down": Paul Lorch, "Valentine's Red Herring," *Bay Area Reporter*, February 9, 1984.

"That was horrible": Neuenschwander, interview by the author.

one final bender: Ken Kelley, "The Interview / Randy Shilts," *San Francisco Focus*, June 1989, box 25, file "SF Focus Interview w/R.S. 1989," Randy Shilts Papers.

on February 23, 1984: Randy Shilts, journal entry, March 22, 1984, transcript by Finlay, box 1, file 5, Randy Shilts Papers.

"It's like I became wrapped up": Randy Shilts, interview by Marcus.

"Shits party!": Newman, interview by the author. Unless otherwise noted, all quotes attributed to Newman in this chapter are taken from this interview.

"I think [Steve and I]": Randy Shilts, journal entry, March 22, 1984.

a mildly campy account: Randy Shilts, "Sheriff Recruits in a Leather Bar," *San Francisco Chronicle*, March 12, 1984.

"Randy Shilts is a perfect example": "Shilts—Gay Uncle Tom," *California Voice*, March 15–21, 1984, box "Periodicals California Voice Vol. 5 (1983) to Vol. 6 (1984)," courtesy of Gay, Lesbian, Bisexual, Transgender Historical Society.

calling him a "sweetheart faggot": Anonymous to Randy Shilts, December 19, 1984, box 9, file "Fan Mail '84," Randy Shilts Papers.

"You are a traitor": A Pig in Paradise [pseud.] to Randy Shilts, March 14, 1984, box 9, file "Fan Mail '84," Randy Shilts Papers.

Responding to the Sentinel's: Randy Shilts, unsent letter to Octavia Hayes, March 18, 1984, box 9, file "Fan Mail '84," Randy Shilts Papers.

he did agree to sit down: Gary Schweikhart, "Shilts Responds to Critics," *Sentinel*, March 29, 1984.

petition drive: Randy Shilts, "Gay Campaign to Ban Sex in Bathhouses," *San Francisco Chronicle*, March 28, 1984.

hastily composed a letter: Randy Shilts, "S.F. Planning to Close Gay Baths," *San Francisco Chronicle*, March 30, 1984.

final tally of signatures: George Mendenhall, "Bathhouse Closing Decided, Delayed, Debunked," *Bay Area Reporter*, April 5, 1984.

"And I remember a couple times": Silverman, interview by the author. Unless otherwise noted, all quotes attributed to Silverman in this chapter are taken from this interview.

The resulting theatrics: Randy Shilts, *And the Band Played On*, 442; Alfred, interview by the author.

faced a virulent backlash: Mendenhall, "Bathhouse Closing Decided, Delayed, Debunked."

signers had nearly "killed off": Paul Lorch, "Killing the Movement," *Bay Area Reporter*, April 5, 1984.

director announced that the bathhouses: Evelyn Hsu, "S.F. Orders Ban on Sex in Bathhouses," *San Francisco Chronicle*, April 10, 1984.

"The last two weeks' general debate": Randy Alfred, "Private Rights & Public Health," *Sentinel*, April 12, 1984.

monthslong argument over delays: Randy Shilts, "Silverman Hit for Delay on Gay Bath Rules," *San Francisco Chronicle*, May 25, 1984.

denounced Randy Shilts as "homophobic": Ron Baker, "Is J.O. OK in S.F.?" *New York Native*, May 7–20, 1984, courtesy of Jean-Nickolaus Tretter Collection.

"Traitors or Heroes?": Randy Shilts, "Traitors or Heroes?"

The original "AIDS poster boy": Randy Shilts, obituary of Bobbi Campbell, *San Francisco Chronicle*, August 16, 1984.

"simplistic reductionism": Bobbi Campbell, letter to the editor, *New York Native*, September 10–23, 1984, courtesy of Jean-Nickolaus Tretter Collection.

clash over bathhouse regulations: Maitland Zane and Susan Sward, "Judge Reopens Bathhouses," *San Francisco Chronicle*, November 29, 1984.

glimpse of Randy in the background: Randy Shilts, interview by Marcus.

12. THE BIG BOOK

Robinson was imagining: Frank Robinson, *Not So Good a Gay Man: A Memoir* (New York: Tor, 2017), 277.

Robinson had even calculated: Linda Alband, text message to the author, August 10, 2019.

Robinson quickly changed: Robinson, *Not So Good a Gay Man*, 277.

Randy's working idea: Gary Shilts, interview by the author.

"I think it was just the next step": Newman, interview by the author. Unless otherwise noted, all quotes attributed to Newman in this chapter are taken from this interview.

"The story of the AIDS": Randy Shilts, "Assignment: AIDS," This World, *San Francisco Chronicle*, December 9, 1984, 8.

"It's unusual for reporters": James Curran, telephone interview by the author, June 17, 2020. Unless otherwise noted, all quotes attributed to James Curran in this chapter are taken from this interview.

"It was the only story": Randy Shilts, "Assignment: AIDS."

race to solve the mystery: Randy Shilts, "The Intercontinental Laboratory War," This World, *San Francisco Chronicle*, December 9, 1984, 12.

journalists would begin to scrutinize: Randy Shilts, *And the Band Played On*, 528–529.

news of AIDS diagnoses among men: Randy Shilts, "Working Prostitute Waits for Test—a 'Monster' Dilemma on AIDS," *San Francisco Chronicle*, January 5, 1985.

Initial plans to limit it: Randy Shilts, "AIDS Test to Be Widely Available," *San Francisco Chronicle*, January 31, 1985.

attributed to blood transfusions: Randy Shilts, "AIDS and Blood Transfusions," *San Francisco Chronicle*, February 28, 1985.

new debate was raging: Randy Shilts, "FDA Going Ahead with Tests for AIDS Despite Protests," *San Francisco Chronicle*, February 1, 1985.

"It would kill me to find out": Randy Shilts, "Most, but Not All, Gays Want the Test," *San Francisco Chronicle*, June 7, 1985.

"Our major thing was to break": Denneny, interview by the author. Unless otherwise noted, all quotes attributed to Denneny in this chapter are taken from this interview.

"weave the warp": Randy Shilts, proposal for *And the Band Played On*, box 36, folder 1, Randy Shilts Papers.

bolstered by a Mother Jones story: David Talbot and Larry Bush, "At Risk," *Mother Jones*, April 1985, box 71, Laurie Garrett Papers.

When Randy broached the idea: Thomas Ainsworth, first e-mail to the author, July 8, 2020.

Ainsworth's office was used to: Thomas Ainsworth, second e-mail to the author, July 8, 2020.

attacks against Randy in the gay press: Brian Jones, "Safe Sex?" *Bay Area Reporter*, March 21, 1985.

gay bashing in the city was surging: Randy Shilts, "Anti-Gay Gang Beats Rider on Castro Bus," *San Francisco Chronicle*, June 10, 1985.

"Nobody knew exactly": Randy Shilts, "BLS 6/27/85. Experiences of a Gay Journalist. Randy Shilts" (videotaped remarks), June 27, 1985, box 148, Randy Shilts Papers.

was giving him hope: Randy Shilts, *And the Band Played On*, 568–569.

more cause for optimism: Randy Shilts, "'We're a Great Team,' Say Returned S.F. Hostages," *San Francisco Chronicle*, July 8, 1985.

In the New York Times: Associated Press, "Rock Hudson Is Ill With Liver Cancer," *New York Times*, July 24, 1985.

responded with a lengthy profile: Randy Shilts, "AIDS Victims Seeking Help at Paris Clinic," *San Francisco Chronicle*, July 24, 1985.

Hudson's representatives publicly confirmed: Associated Press, "Hudson Has AIDS, Spokesman Says," *New York Times*, July 26, 1985.

reached out to his friends: Perry Lang and Randy Shilts, "Why Rock Hudson Kept Quiet About Being Gay," *San Francisco Chronicle*, July 25, 1985.

"So, I have this image": Cleve Jones, interview by the author.

"*It should not have taken*": Randy Shilts, "The Story in the Closet," *San Francisco Chronicle*, August 3, 1985.

"*I also want to point out to you*": Michael Denneny, telephone call with the author, August 5, 2020.

"*Newsman Randy Shilts has signed*": Herb Caen, "Gamut from Ho to Hum," *San Francisco Chronicle*, September 10, 1985.

"*The Pepsi generation*": Randy Shilts [Martin S., pseud.], "Young, Gifted, and Hooked."

All that history: Randy Shilts, journal entry, April 6, 1984, transcript by Finlay, box 1, file 5, Randy Shilts Papers.

13. THAT NEBULOUS COMMODITY

"*If you tell me to stand*": Wes Haley, interview by the author, San Lorenzo, CA, March 15, 2016. Unless otherwise noted, all quotes attributed to Wes Haley in this chapter are taken from this interview.

"*With me being the only Black woman*": Evelyn C. White, telephone interview by the author, November 22, 2016.

"*He just exuded*": Elaine Herscher, interview by the author, Berkeley, CA, November 3, 2019.

he still wrote to its reporter: Mike Hippler to Randy Shilts, March 7, 1984, box 9, file "Fan Mail," Randy Shilts Papers.

advised him to get good stories: Hank Plante, telephone interview by the author, April 15, 2020.

519 interviews: Randy Shilts, *And the Band Played On*, 607–613.

didn't think he'd been infected: Matthew Krieger, conversation with the author, San Francisco, November 5, 2019.

"*To have a coherent narrative*": Denneny, interview by the author. Unless otherwise noted, all quotes attributed to Denneny in this chapter are taken from this interview.

"*Our first AIDS patients*": Paul Volberding, interview by the author, San Francisco, March 21, 2016.

"*Government is not the solution*": Ronald Reagan, inaugural address, January 20, 1981, Ronald Reagan Presidential Foundation & Institute, https://www.reaganfoundation.org/ronald-reagan/reagan-quotes-speeches/inaugural-address-2/.

"*CDC was just ready*": Donald Francis, interview by the author, South San Francisco, CA, March 11, 2016.

"*scientific competition*": Talbot and Bush, "At Risk."

"*full of himself*": Garrett, interview by the author. Unless otherwise noted, all quotes attributed to Garrett in this chapter are taken from this interview.

Gallo continued to defend: Robert Gallo, telephone interview by the author, December 7, 2017. Unless otherwise noted, all quotes attributed to Robert Gallo in this chapter are taken from this interview.

1984 press conference: Robert Gallo, "Press Conference: Secretary Margaret Heckler," Hubert H. Humphrey Building, Washington, DC, April 23, 1984, Jon Cohen AIDS Research Collection at the University of Michigan, https://quod.lib.umich.edu/c/cohenaids/5571095.0488.004?rgn=main;view=fulltext.

Randy listed a single interview: Randy Shilts, "AIDS Vaccine, Treatments in Sight, Researcher Says," *San Francisco Chronicle*, April 21, 1986.

"Bill was a very interesting person": Housh, interview by the author.

"[It] is clear that virtually all": Randy Shilts, *And the Band Played On*, 187.

experienced a painful backlash: Shilts, 305.

Adding to his frustrations: Shilts, 224–225.

"He called me": Donald Abrams, telephone interview by the author, July 1, 2020.

"in a sort of soft-spoken": Timothy Westmoreland, telephone interview by the author, June 4, 2020.

"one-horse department": Selma Dritz, interview by Randy Shilts, San Francisco, n.d., box 33, folder 19, Randy Shilts Papers.

In an early CDC study: David M. Auerbach et al., "Cluster of Cases of the Acquired Immune Deficiency Syndrome," *American Journal of Medicine* 76 (March 1984): 487–492.

Randy interviewed Dr. Linda Laubenstein: Randy Shilts, *And the Band Played On*, 55.

"I'm going to nag you": Randy Shilts to Selma Dritz, February 26, 1986, box 1, folder 4, Selma Dritz Papers, 1983–1998 (MSS.2009.04), Archives and Special Collections, University of California, San Francisco.

spoke with Dr. William Darrow: William Darrow, interview by Randy Shilts, n.d., box 33, folder 18, Randy Shilts Papers.

The two were already acquainted: Mary Guinan, e-mail to the author, August 7, 2021.

In addition to his attractiveness: Randy Shilts, Patient Zero notes, box 34, folder 23, Randy Shilts Papers.

"Sex was a way": Shilts, Patient Zero notes.

strategizing how to bring Gaetan: "30 30 AIDS Vancouver: 1983—the Forum," AIDS Vancouver, accessed May 13, 2022, https://www.youtube.com/watch?v=f5wJXYxNu88.

"I think Randy was fascinated": Mary Guinan, e-mail to the author, August 10, 2021.

"Gaetan was the perfect": Silverman, interview by the author.

"Whether Gaetan Dugas actually was": Randy Shilts, *And the Band Played On*, 439.

investigators interviewed sex partners: Darrow, interview by Randy Shilts.

"After a long hiatus": Selma Dritz to Randy Shilts, February 12, 1987, box 9, file "No Answer, 1986–1988," Randy Shilts Papers.

"[It's] been a year and a half": David M. Lowe, "Randy Shilts: A Decade of Controversial Credibility," *Sentinel*, circa 1987, box 1, folder 11, Randy Shilts Papers.

AIDS stories expanded to include: Randy Shilts, "Koop Urges Reagan to Take the Lead in 'War' on AIDS," *San Francisco Chronicle*, March 5, 1987.

"We were on our way up to Diamond Heights": Neuenschwander, interview by the author.

14. NO PRIZE FOR MODESTY

"The National March on Washington": Randy Shilts, "Hundreds of Thousands March—for Gay Rights in Washington—Reagan Policy on AIDS Protested," *San Francisco Chronicle*, October 12, 1987.

"He almost got killed": Davis, interview by the author.

"The hoofbeats of the coming Apocalypse": Randy Shilts, "Fear of Epidemic in the Mud Huts," *San Francisco Chronicle*, October 5, 1987.

"Randy was a master": Douglas Foster, telephone interview by the author, July 23, 2020.

"When we went in": Denneny, interview by the author.

St. Martin's went ahead: "The Man Who Gave Us AIDS," *New York Post*, October 6, 1987, box 1, folder 11, Randy Shilts Papers.

"playing a key role": Associated Press, "Canadian Said to Have Had Key Role in Spread of AIDS," *New York Times*, October 7, 1987.

"[Gaetan is] in no way representative": Craig Wilson, "The Chronicler of AIDS; Randy Shilts, Tracking the Epidemic," *USA Today*, October 12, 1987.

published the Patient Zero plotline: Randy Shilts, "Patient Zero: The Man Who Brought the AIDS Epidemic to California," *California*, October, 1987, box 2, folder 9, Selma Dritz Papers.

"cheap publicity stunt": Wilson, "Chronicler of AIDS."

"the most thorough, comprehensive": "Editorial: *And the Band Played On*," *Sentinel*, October 2, 1987.

"a watershed in the course": Paul Reed, "Shilts' Book Shows Politicization of AIDS," *Bay Area Reporter*, October 8, 1987.

"not an objective work": Charles Ortleb, "Randy Shilts's Agenda," *New York Native*, October 19, 1987, courtesy of Jean-Nickolaus Tretter Collection.

"The gay community is getting a bad rap": Ed Sikov, Media Watch, *New York Native*, October 26, 1987, courtesy of Jean-Nickolaus Tretter Collection.

he pointed out that Randy: Ed Sikov, Media Watch, *New York Native*, November 9, 1987, courtesy of Jean-Nickolaus Tretter Collection.

"Randy was not pure": Benjamin Schatz, telephone interview by the author, February 9, 2022. Unless otherwise noted, all quotes attributed to Benjamin Schatz in this chapter are taken from this interview.

"I never saw what Randy was doing": Bush, telephone interview by the author.

"to the unusual mobility": William Hines, "Scrambling for Power over the Bodies of AIDS Victims," *Chicago Sun-Times*, October 4, 1987, box 1, folder 11, Randy Shilts Papers.

"ALL THEY GOTTA DO": Anonymous to Randy Shilts, n.d., box 1, folder 11, Randy Shilts Papers.

"Homosexuals debate": Robert Reinhold, "AIDS Book Brings Fame to a Gay San Franciscan," *New York Times*, October 31, 1987.

reached the New York Times bestsellers list: Best Sellers, *New York Times*, November 15, 1987.

NBC miniseries: Louis Chunovic, "TV, Film Rights to AIDS Study Sold; Miniseries Planned," *Hollywood Reporter*, November 6, 1987, box 1, folder 3, Linda Alband Collection of Randy Shilts Materials.

"a horrible combination": "Patient Zero," hosted by Harry Reasoner, *60 Minutes*, CBS, November 15, 1987.

"I believe in moral absolutes": Charlotte Bercaw, "Shilts Gets Grip on His Being, Then Worldwide Epidemic," *Aurora Beacon-News*, November 15, 1987.

"I always felt there was": George Greenfield, interview by the author, New York, NY, June 25, 2017. Unless otherwise noted, all quotes attributed to George Greenfield in this chapter are taken from this interview.

"I'm pleased with you": Selma Dritz to Randy Shilts, September 30, 1987, box 9, file "Correspondence, Sept. 1987," Randy Shilts Papers.

"Your book is a beautiful book": Mary Guinan to Randy Shilts, October 28, 1987, box 9, file "Correspondence, October 1987," Randy Shilts Papers.

"I think the method": Curran, telephone interview by the author.

"a good book": Moss, interview by the author.

"Mr. Shilts, to give him credit": Andrew Moss, letter to the editor, *New York Review of Books*, December 8, 1988, https://www.nybooks.com/articles/1988/12/08/aids-without-end-2/.

"I said, 'I have no concern'": Gallo, telephone interview by the author.

John Crewdson's book on Gallo: John Crewdson, *Science Fictions: A Scientific Mystery, a Massive Cover-Up, and the Dark Legacy of Robert Gallo* (New York: Little, Brown, 2002), 587–588.

"I think [Randy] confuses": Westmoreland, telephone interview by the author.

"It is a book that I want to like": Sandra Panem, "A Drama and Questions," *Science* 239 (February 26, 1988), box 3, folder 23, Randy Shilts Papers.

"He was nervous": Garrett, interview by the author.

Randy had tried to emphasize: Randy Shilts to Lawrence Mass, September 29, 1987, Lawrence Mass Papers, 1958–2008 (MssCol 1893), Manuscripts and Archives Division, New York Public Library.

Symptoms of AIDS-related post-traumatic stress: David Fawcett, "AIDS Survivor Syndrome: It's Real," The Body, February 27, 2018, https://www.thebody.com /article/aids-survivor-syndrome-its-real.

"Nobody should be telling me": William W. Darrow, "In Memoriam: Randy M. Shilts, 1952–1994," *Journal of Sex Research* 31, no. 3 (1994): 249.

"The only people who have": Kelley, "Interview / Randy Shilts."

"the friends of Bill W.": Randy Shilts, *And the Band Played On*, xii.

he promised that all proceeds: *Once in a Generation Comes a Book That Can Change the World* (pamphlet), box 1, folder 11, Randy Shilts Papers.

substantial commercial success: Kahla, e-mail to the author.

Esquire included Randy: "Man Power: Randy Shilts," *Esquire*, June 1, 1988, https:// classic.esquire.com/article/1988/06/01/randy-shilts.

Band came close to winning: National Book Critics Circle Award, 1987 Winners & Finalists, accessed February 2, 2024, https://www.bookcritics.org/past-awards/1987/.

more than seven hundred thousand Americans: "The HIV/AIDS Epidemic in the United States: The Basics," Kaiser Family Foundation, June 7, 2021, https://www.kff.org /hivaids/fact-sheet/the-hivaids-epidemic-in-the-united-states-the-basics/.

Randy himself would applaud: Randy Shilts, interview by Marcus.

15. GHOST STORIES

Agnos declared it Randy Shilts Day: Housh, interview by the author.

"Scared the fucking shit out of me": Haley, interview by the author.

"Dash was his baby": Alband, interview by the author.

"It was pretty hard": Newman, interview by the author.

On a family visit: Gary Shilts, interview by the author.

"We have never been ashamed": Ruth Pollack Coughlin, "America Responds to Deadly Tune of 'Band,'" *Detroit News*, October 16, 1988, box 2, folder 111, Linda Alband Collection of Randy Shilts Materials.

"Here I was chastising": Coughlin, "America Responds."

piece detailing the disproportionate impact: Randy Shilts, "Black Response Lags Behind Epidemic," *San Francisco Chronicle*, March 27, 1989.

"That's the only time": Greenfield, interview by the author.

"The bitter irony is": Randy Shilts, "Talking AIDS to Death," *Esquire*, March 1989, box 1, folder 40, Linda Alband Collection of Randy Shilts Materials.

"I finally had to say to him": Perlman, interview by the author.

"There were many in the organizing committee": Garrett, interview by the author.

closing remarks to an estimated: "Speedup in Research Urged by AIDS Writer," *San Francisco Chronicle*, June 10, 1989.

"Some [of their] actions": Randy Shilts, "Politics Confused with Therapy," *San Francisco Chronicle*, June 26, 1989.

"[civil] disobedience is bound": Shilts, "Politics Confused."

"Does it stop the dying?": Randy Shilts, "Wrestling with AIDS," KQED News, December 14, 1989, https://diva.sfsu.edu/collections/sfbatv/bundles/190109.

"combative and limited": Waiyde Palmer, telephone interview by the author, February 4, 2022.

Randy saw the usefulness: Randy Shilts, "The Era of Bad Feelings," *Mother Jones*, November, 1989, box 1, folder 39, Linda Alband Collection of Randy Shilts Materials.

he panned the activists: Randy Shilts, "AIDS Protests at Churches," *San Francisco Chronicle*, December 18, 1989.

the pseudonym, "Zero, P.": Elena Smith [Sutro Library staff], e-mail to Jennifer Finlay, January 10, 2022, shared with the author on January 10, 2022.

it was another starring moment: "Randy Shilts," *San Francisco Chronicle*, February 18, 1994.

"Read the logical conclusion": Randy Shilts, "Lessons," in *The Quake of '89, as Seen by the News Staff of the San Francisco Chronicle* (San Francisco: Chronicle Books, 1989), 109–111.

more than fourteen thousand deaths: "A Brief Timeline of AIDS," Fighting AIDS Continuously Together (FACT), accessed September 24, 2018, http://www.factlv .org/timeline.htm.

fatalities from the Loma Prieta earthquake: Jason E. Eberhart-Phillips et al., "Profile of Mortality from the 1989 Loma Prieta Earthquake Using Coroner and Medical Examiner Reports," *Disasters* 18, no. 2 (June 1994): https://doi .org/10.1111/j.1467-7717.1994.tb00298.x.

"I said, 'You're looking like'": Herscher, interview by the author.

treatment for an unpublished novel: Randy Shilts, "Ghosts" (unpublished manuscript), box 1, folder 25, Linda Alband Collection of Randy Shilts Materials.

"Though they were dressed with remarkable similarity": Shilts, "Ghosts."

Randy shared the story: Michael Denneny to Randy Shilts, December 19, 1989, box 88, file "Ghosts," Randy Shilts Papers.

he announced a sabbatical: John Stanley, "A Look at Ethical Challenges of Epidemic," *San Francisco Chronicle*, December 17, 1989.

"I think his time in L.A.": Ron Bernstein, telephone interview by the author, February 25, 2022.

16. THE FAMILY

The walk-up at Fifteenth and Market: Jennifer Finlay, interview by the author, Hertford, NC, January 11, 2020. Unless otherwise noted, all quotes attributed to Jennifer Finlay in this chapter are taken from this interview.

"You're Randy Shilts": Howard Bragman, telephone interview by the author, February 10, 2022. Unless otherwise noted, all quotes attributed to Howard Bragman in this chapter are taken from this interview.

"He made a very strong case": Denneny, interview by the author.

"There is a country where citizens": Randy Shilts, proposal for *Conduct Unbecoming*, box 43, file "Final Draft Proposal," Randy Shilts Papers.

"People in the military were outside": Alband, interview by the author. Unless otherwise noted, all quotes attributed to Alband in this chapter are taken from this interview.

case of army colonel Edward Modesto: Randy Shilts, "Army Colonel Could Be Jailed on Gay-Related Charges," *San Francisco Chronicle*, October 18, 1990.

Caen broke the news: Herb Caen, This Old Town, *San Francisco Chronicle*, November 1, 1990.

"incompatible with military service": Randy Shilts, proposal for *Conduct Unbecoming*.

issued a "stop-loss" order: Randy Shilts, "Military May Defer Discharge of Gays / Pentagon Has 'Operational Needs' in Gulf," *San Francisco Chronicle*, January 11, 1991.

All three men would feature: Randy Shilts, *Conduct Unbecoming: Gays & Lesbians in the U.S. Military* (New York: St. Martin's, 1993).

One of those ads caught the attention: Steve Robin, telephone interview by the author, February 5, 2022.

"I think that any impact-litigation firm": Amelia Craig Cramer, telephone interview by the author, July 24, 2020.

"Gay-lib-type folks": Carolyn "Dusty" Pruitt, telephone interview by the author, August 3, 2020.

In San Diego, activist Bridget Wilson: Bridget Wilson, Zoom interview by the author, December 11, 2020.

"I was a young kid": Sam Gallegos, telephone interview by the author, March 9, 2020.

he had every document photocopied: Finlay, interview by the author.

"It was a horrible environment": Penny Rand, telephone interview by the author, July 30, 2020.

"I still think I would do it": Tanya Domi, Zoom interview by the author, December 31, 2020.

"I did not want to leave": Grethe Cammermeyer, telephone interview by the author, March 4, 2020.

"Talking to Randy": Jon Davidson, telephone interview by the author, July 27, 2020.

an internal army memo: Randy Shilts, "Pentagon Memo Urged Reversing Ban on Gays in Military / Army Says the Officer's Opinion Is His Own," *San Francisco Chronicle*, June 25, 1991.

"a dirty business": Randy Shilts, "Outing: Pro and Con / The Outing of Gays Is Unwarranted and Hurtful," *San Francisco Chronicle*, August 8, 1991.

Randy's depiction of the core issue: Michelangelo Signorile, *Queer in America: Sex, the Media, and the Closets of Power* (New York: Doubleday, 1993), 151.

"In the past, the only time": Randy Shilts, "Johnson Disclosure Renews the Focus on AIDS Epidemic," *San Francisco Chronicle*, November 8, 1991.

the media's obsession: Randy Shilts, "Good AIDS, Bad AIDS," *New York Times*, December 10, 1991.

17. FOOLS AND BIMBOS

"Dash, go get Linda": Linda Alband, "Dash's Birthday Party 6/7/92" (videocassette), tape 1, June 7, 1992, videocassette, tape 1, box 6, Linda Alband Collection of Randy Shilts Materials.

"My life, I feel": Randy Shilts to Howard Bragman, May 20, 1992, box 3, folder 5, Linda Alband Collection of Randy Shilts Materials.

Howard, to his recollection: Bragman, telephone interview by the author. Unless otherwise noted, all quotes attributed to Bragman in this chapter are taken from this interview.

HBO Pictures had picked up: Liz Smith, "Schumacher to Direct 'Band Played On,'" *San Francisco Chronicle*, May 22, 1991; Jesse Hamlin, Something Else, *San Francisco Chronicle*, October 1, 1991.

struggles to turn The Mayor of Castro Street: Edward Guthmann, Something Else, *San Francisco Chronicle*, March 5, 1992.

"Those people in Outrage": Edward Guthmann, Something Else, *San Francisco Chronicle*, March 12, 1992.

acknowledged the need for radical activism: Laurie Udesky, "Randy Shilts: 'For Me, Coming Out Was Very Political,'" *Progressive*, May 1991, box 2, folder 131, Linda Alband Collection of Randy Shilts Materials.

"lavender fascists": John Weir, "Inside Story: Reading," *Out*, August–September 1993, Linda Alband Collection of Randy Shilts Materials, https://calisphere.org /item/8e61603b-7cd5-4a6a-9b35-fb0757d2f54d/.

cemented some activists' feelings: Signorile, *Queer in America*, 152.

"He was one of the speakers": Cammermeyer, telephone interview by the author.

"They said Randy would say": Gary Shilts, interview by the author. Unless otherwise noted, all quotes attributed to Gary Shilts in this chapter are taken from this interview.

"I blame AZT": Finlay, interview by the author. Unless otherwise noted, all quotes attributed to Finlay in this chapter are taken from this interview.

helped him draft a will: Randy Shilts, last will and testament, February 21, 1992, box 3, folder 31, Linda Alband Collection of Randy Shilts Materials.

"I met him as someone": Lisa Capaldini, interview by the author, San Francisco, August 28, 2017. Unless otherwise noted, all quotes attributed to Lisa Capaldini in this chapter are taken from this interview.

Linda's efforts at polite tolerance: Alband, interview by the author. Unless otherwise noted, all quotes attributed to Alband in this chapter are taken from this interview.

At that year's Shiltsmas party: Linda Alband, "Randy's Birthday Party 8/92" (videocassette), tape 1, August 8, 1992, box 6, Linda Alband Collection of Randy Shilts Materials.

HBO signaled a renewed effort: Jesse Hamlin, Something Else, *San Francisco Chronicle*, August 11, 1992.

"What was shocking": Francis, interview by the author.

Leishman, who'd written: Steven Epstein, *Impure Science: AIDS, Activism, and the Politics of Knowledge* (Berkeley: University of California Press, 1996), http://ark.cdlib.org /ark:/13030/ft1s20045x/.

"I'm almost 98 percent positive": Philip J. Hilts, "Heating Blood Criticized as Treatment of AIDS," *New York Times*, September 5, 1990.

"The book was supposed to go": Denneny, interview by the author. Unless otherwise noted, all quotes attributed to Denneny in this chapter are taken from this interview.

Leah Garchik was surprised: Leah Garchik, interview by the author, San Francisco, March 16, 2016.

"Every gay writer": Leah Garchik, "Reporter, Author Randy Shilts Reveals That He Has AIDS," *San Francisco Chronicle*, February 16, 1993.

"The Chronicle stunned me today": Selma Dritz to Randy Shilts, February 16, 1993, box 7, unmarked folder, Randy Shilts Papers.

fifty-two thousand first-edition copies: Kahla, e-mail to the author.

"It was the absence": Greenfield, interview by the author.

"One minute he is the old Randy": Jeffrey Schmaltz, "At Home with Randy Shilts; Writing Against Time, Valiantly," *New York Times*, April 22, 1993.

"I met a boy in Richmond": Cleve Jones, interview by the author.

"Someday we'll make this movie": Linda Alband, "Randy's Wedding 5/31/93" (videocassette) May 31, 1993, box 6, Linda Alband Collection of Randy Shilts Materials.

a slew of disagreements: Bernstein, telephone interview by the author.

"twenty, thirty, forty years": Plante, telephone interview by the author.

The last time Elaine: Herscher, interview by the author.

loud standing ovation: Lori Olszewski and David Tuller, "Writer Randy Shilts Dies at 42—Pioneer Coverage of AIDS," *San Francisco Chronicle*, February 18, 1994.

details of his funeral wishes: Linda Alband, "Randy Shilts: On Going Considerations," November 29, 1993, box 4, folder 21, Linda Alband Collection of Randy Shilts Materials.

Randy had made several provisions: Randy Shilts, last will and testament, February 21, 1992.

he made a startling change: Randy Shilts, last will and testament, November 11, 1993, box 3, folder 32, Linda Alband Collection of Randy Shilts Materials.

"He was happy": Newman, interview by the author. Unless otherwise noted, all quotes attributed to Newman in this chapter are taken from this interview.

"I couldn't go": Neuenschwander, interview by the author.

"I hate to brag": Randy Shilts, letter to the editor, *Advocate*, January 25, 1994, Linda Alband Collection of Randy Shilts Materials, https://calisphere.org/item/052b2d0c -6036-4457-a0aa-789e8a6a1c23/.

18. DARK AND STORMY

"I couldn't disclose to the world": Alband, interview by the author. Unless otherwise noted, all quotes attributed to Alband in this chapter are taken from this interview.

"Well, Randy died": Gary Shilts, interview by the author. Unless otherwise noted, all quotes attributed to Gary Shilts in this chapter are taken from this interview.

"That was just a bad day": Finlay, interview by the author. Unless otherwise noted, all quotes attributed to Finlay in this chapter are taken from this interview.

"Randy Shilts was a great journalist": Olszewski and Tuller, "Writer Randy Shilts Dies at 42."

Congresswoman Lynn Woolsey: 140 Cong. Rec. H2265 (daily ed. February 22, 1994), https://www.congress.gov/bound-congressional-record/1994/02/22/house-section.

"[Randy] was so involved": Cecil Williams, telephone interview by the author, March 22, 2016.

"We did this role play": Dawn Shilts, interview by the author.

Westboro Baptist Church announced plans: Fred Phelps to Cecil Williams, February 21, 1994, box 3, folder 19, Linda Alband Collection of Randy Shilts Materials.

Although Phelps had written: Dennis McMillan, "Shilts Protest Short-Lived," *Sentinel*, February 23, 1994, box 3, folder 22, Linda Alband Collection of Randy Shilts Materials.

"You could smell blood": Palmer, telephone interview by the author.

"We sat in the limo": Haley, interview by the author.

"This is a celebration": Linda Alband, "Celebration of the Life of Randy Shilts, Glide Memorial United Methodist Church" (videocassette), February 22, 1994, shared with the author by Jennifer Finlay.

"We are sitting there": Newman, interview by the author.

"Randy would love yet again": Jennifer Finlay, journal, February 22, 1994, shared with the author on January 7, 2020.

"Thanks Randy": Finlay, journal.

"Actually, we were surprised": "Altar Egos," *Bay Area Reporter*, February 24, 1994.

"Ding dong, the witch is dead": Beowulf Thorne, "Eating Our Own," *Diseased Pariah News* 9 (1994): http://s3-us-west-2.amazonaws.com/ucldc-nuxeo-ref-media /a7ab4d42-2cd6-4245-be31-49c74ad95bc0.

19. THE BAND PLAYED ON

"Randy interrupted": Eric Marcus, interview by the author, New York, NY, June 26, 2017.

"The one thing that Randy asked": Eric Marcus, e-mail to the author, July 20, 2016.

"It was such an eye opener": Clinton Fein, Zoom interview by the author, December 12, 2020.

"I'm quite proud of that": Gallegos, telephone interview by the author.

For Jennifer, the years following: Finlay, interview by the author.

Alband eventually returned to Portland: Alband, interview by the author.

"I did a live shot": Cleve Jones, interview by the author.

Milk still lived "as a metaphor": Randy Shilts, *The Mayor of Castro Street*, (New York: St. Martin's, 1982), 348.

INDEX

Page numbers in italics indicate photographs